CiTY·SMaRT™
GUIDEBOOK

Memphis

Second Edition

by Linda Romine

John Muir Publications
Santa Fe, New Mexico

John Muir Publications, P.O. Box 613, Santa Fe, New Mexico 87504

Printed in the United States of America.
Second edition. First printing September 1999

ISBN: 1-56261-504-1
ISSN: 1092-9045

Editors: Peg Goldstein, Chris Hayhurst
Graphics Editor: Bunny Wong
Production: Janine Lehmann
Design: Janine Lehmann
Cover Design: Suzanne Rush
Maps: Julie Felton
Typesetter: Kathy Sparkes—White Hart Design
Printer: Publishers Press
Front cover: ©Mike Booher/Transparencies Inc.—Downtown MATA
Back cover: ©Andre Jenny/Unicorn Stock Photos—Sun Studio

Distributed to the book trade by
Publishers Group West
Berkeley, California

CONTENTS

MAP CONTENTS

Restaurants, hotels, museums, and other facilities marked by the
♿ symbol are wheelchair accessible.

See Memphis the CiTY·SMaRT™ Way

The Guide for Memphis Natives, New Residents, and Visitors

In *City•Smart Guidebook: Memphis,* local author Linda Romine tells it like it is. Residents will learn things they never knew about their city, new residents will get an insider's view of their new hometown, and visitors will be guided to the very best Memphis has to offer—whether they're on a weekend getaway or staying a week or more.

Opinionated Recommendations Save You Time and Money

From shopping to nightlife to museums, the author is opinionated about what she likes and dislikes. You'll learn the great and the not-so-great things about Memphis's sights, restaurants, and accommodations. So you can decide what's worth your time and what's not; which hotel is worth the splurge and which is the best choice for budget travelers.

Easy-to-Use Format Makes Planning Your Trip a Cinch

City•Smart Guidebook: Memphis is user-friendly—you'll quickly find exactly what you're looking for. Chapters are organized by travelers' interests or needs, from Where to Stay and Where to Eat, to Sights and Attractions, Kids' Stuff, Sports and Recreation, and even Day Trips from Memphis.

Includes Maps and Quick Location-Finding Features

Every listing in this book is accompanied by a geographic zone designation (see the next page for zone details) that helps you immediately find each location. Staying on Poplar Avenue and wondering about nearby sights and restaurants? Look for the East Memphis label in the listings and you'll know that that great statue or café is not far away. Or maybe you're looking for the Pyramid. Along with its address, you'll see a Downtown label, so you'll know just where to find it.

All That and Fun to Read, Too!

Every City•Smart chapter includes fun-to-read city trivia, tips (to learn how to cook Tennessee Turnip Greens, see page 79), and illuminating sidebars (read about the International Conference on Elvis Presley on page 110). And well-known local residents provide their personal "Top Ten" lists, guiding readers to the city's best shopping spots, night spots, and more.

MEMPHIS ZONES

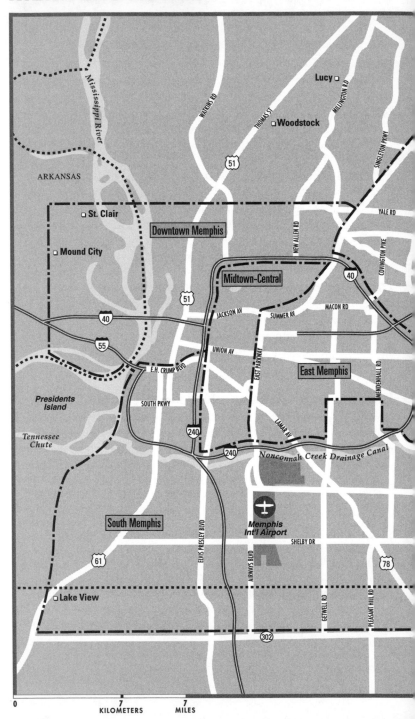

MEMPHIS ZONES

Downtown Memphis
Bounded by I-240 on the east, E. H. Crump Boulevard on the south, the Mississippi River on the west, and Frayser Boulevard on the north.

Midtown/Central
Bounded by I-40 on the north, East Parkway on the east, and I-240 on the south and west. Includes the Medical Center, the Cooper-Young District, Overton Square, and Summer Avenue inside the I-240 loop.

East Memphis
Bounded by East Parkway on the west, Jackson Avenue and I-40 on the north, and I-240 on the east and south. Includes the University of Memphis, the Poplar/I-240 area, and the Poplar Avenue corridor.

Bartlett, Cordova, Germantown
Bounded by I-40 and Austin Peay on the west and Highway 385 on the south. Includes the eastern suburbs.

South Memphis
Bounded by I-240 and Highway 385 on the north, Highway 309 on the east, Highway 302 on the south, and the Mississippi River on the west. Includes the airport, Whitehaven, Shelby County, the Mall of Memphis, and Hickory Hill.

1

WELCOME TO MEMPHIS

Barbecue and the blues, Graceland and Grisham, Sun Records, and sunsets over the Mississippi River. Long revered as the home of the blues and the birthplace of rock 'n' roll, Memphis's musical heritage dates to just after the turn of the century, when a black Beale Street band leader named W. C. Handy first trumpeted "The Memphis Blues." A few decades later, a white truck driver named Elvis Presley would walk into Sun Studio, cut a modest birthday record for his mama, and emerge as the world's first rock 'n' roll superstar. Today, nearing 25 years since his death, Elvis's Memphis mansion, Graceland, attracts larger crowds of tourists than any other home in the United States other than the White House. In recent years, the legal thrillers of best-selling author John Grisham have again cast Memphis in the international spotlight. With such fictional works and subsequent film adaptations as *The Firm*, *The Client*, and *The Rainmaker*, Grisham, a former Memphis-area attorney, writes with endearing familiarity about the people and places of the South. Even with his phenomenal publishing success, Grisham has attempted to remain true to his roots, coming back to Memphis for periodic book signings and the occasional self-deprecating speech to members of the downtown Rotary Club.

Scratch below the surface of these immediate Memphis stereotypes, however, and you'll discover that there's much more to this vibrant Southern city than meets the eye or ear. World-class art exhibitions, global cotton brokerage firms, Fortune 500 companies, a thriving transportation/distribution hub, and a multibillion-dollar healthcare industry are enterprises that make Memphis unique.

Sometimes referred to as the "Bluff City" because of its perch overlooking the majestic Mississippi River, Memphis was named for the

TIP

Foreign currency–exchange offices are located at the Memphis International Airport (901/922-8000), at First Tennessee Bank's downtown branch (901/523-4425), and at National Bank of Commerce's downtown branch (901/523-3434).

ancient Egyptian capital situated along another famous river, the Nile. It was in homage to this regal namesake that the city, in 1991, erected its gleaming, 32-story steel Pyramid arena along the riverbanks.

Having been steeped in the lineage of pharaohs, it seems appropriate that Memphis has also become a modern-day American city with other ties to royalty. For instance, among the well-known "kings" often associated with Memphis are blues greats such as B. B. King; the late Albert King and his adopted grandson, blues guitarist Little Jimmy King; and the King of Rock himself, Elvis. Even the King of Pop, Michael Jackson, has firmly established his place in the Memphis music lexicon, no matter how fleetingly, by virtue of his brief but extraordinarily public marriage to Elvis and Priscilla's daughter, Lisa Marie Presley.

On a much more serious note, the contributions of martyred civil rights activist Rev. Martin Luther King Jr. are more powerful than those of any who came before or after him. Dr. King's impact on the identity and future of Memphis cannot be overstated. This passionate clergyman and human rights advocate had come to Memphis to assist in a black sanitation workers' strike when he was assassinated on April 4, 1968, on the balcony of the Lorraine Motel. Today the site of that tragedy has been transformed into the uplifting National Civil Rights Museum, where Dr. King's legacies of love, tolerance, and nonviolence are being taught and nurtured for future generations.

With a population of 1 million and a land area of 295 square miles, the Memphis metropolitan area is the largest in the state. Of Tennessee, that is. Because the flat Delta landscape bears less in common with the mountainous regions to the east than with the cotton fields of the Magnolia State, Memphis is often jokingly referred to as the capital of Mississippi.

In actuality, Memphis is centrally located between St. Louis to the north and New Orleans to the south, Atlanta to the southeast and Dallas to the southwest. The Memphis area that encompasses eastern Arkansas, northern Mississippi, and western Tennessee is often referred to as the Mid-South.

Memphis residents are a hardy breed. Memphis has survived the Civil War, devastating yellow-fever epidemics, and bitter racial turmoil, only to

Memphis Convention and Visitors Bureau

Sun Studio

emerge at the end of the twentieth century stronger and even more united than ever before.

A Brief History of Memphis

The Early Days

The Chickasaw Indians were among the first recorded groups of people to inhabit the area of present-day Memphis. Spanish explorer Hernando de Soto and the conquistadors are believed to be the first white men to explore the area, when their expedition led them to the muddy riverbanks in 1541.

Over the next few centuries, other European explorers, monarchs, and Native Americans all vied for ownership of this land that provided fertile ground for farming, dense forests for hunting, and river waters for the harvesting of oysters. LaSalle claimed the Mississippi River Valley for France in 1682, and by 1739 French explorers had built Fort Assumption on the site. Subsequently, King Louis XVI gave all of France's Louisiana possessions to

TRIVIA

John Luther "Casey" Jones goes down in Tennessee history as a bona fide hero. In 1900 the Jackson, Tennessee–born railroader, on a routine trip from Memphis to New Orleans, lost his life trying to save the "Old 382" train before it crashed into another train in southern Mississippi. Jones saved the lives of all the train's passengers.

Spain. In 1795 Fort Saint Ferdinand of the Bluffs was erected in honor of Spanish King Ferdinand VII.

Early American settlers also elbowed their way into the territory. After Tennessee was admitted to the Union and the Spaniards had been driven out, the Chickasaw Indians ceded western Tennessee to the United States in 1818. Three Tennessee landowners—John Overton, James Winchester, and future president Andrew Jackson—established the town of Memphis the following year. While Memphis was named for the magnificent Egyptian capital in modern-day Africa, Shelby County was named for the Revolutionary War hero and first governor of Kentucky, Isaac Shelby.

Officially incorporated in 1826, Memphis was a promising young city that capitalized on its natural port facilities along the Mississippi River. Cotton and other goods could be shipped up and down the waterway, and Memphis was on the pulse of a growing transportation system.

City leaders developed the downtown area with a variety of ambitious construction projects. In 1842 work was begun on the Gayoso House, which would become the city's first luxury hotel. Other significant factors affecting Memphis's growth in the mid-nineteenth century were the building of a naval shipyard in 1845 and the 1850 merger between the separate communities of Memphis and South Memphis.

Another merger of sorts occurred in 1857, when completion of the Memphis–Charleston Railroad linked the Mississippi River to the Atlantic Ocean. With water and rail routes established, the seeds were even more firmly planted for one of the country's emerging transportation and distribution hubs. With the addition of air travel and over-the-road trucking a century later, Memphis would earn the universal distinction as "America's distribution center."

Memphis also traded in another commodity, however—that of slaves. Over the years thousands of imported African families were splintered as black men, women, and children were auctioned off to the highest bidders, the wealthy owners of Delta cotton plantations chief among them.

As was true in other U.S. communities, the ravages of the Civil War were felt in Memphis. In 1862 the Union defeated Confederate naval forces in the Battle of Memphis. (Local residents are said to have stood

TRIVIA

In 1866 a collision between two horse-drawn carriages sparked days of bitter racial violence in Memphis. The black driver in the crash was arrested, while the white driver was not. A group of black Civil War veterans tried to step in and prevent the arrest, thereby inciting white mobs to go on a deadly rampage through a black community. Churches and schools were burned, and about 50 people were killed.

Elvis Trivia

- *Elvis sold more than a billion records worldwide—more than any other artist in recorded history.*
- *In the United States alone, Elvis had 18 number-one records, 40 Top 10s, and 114 Top-40 singles.*
- *Elvis starred in 31 films, including* Jailhouse Rock *and* King Creole. *Two of his best-selling soundtracks came from* GI Blues *and* Blue Hawaii.
- *Elvis's 1973 TV special,* Elvis—Aloha from Hawaii, via Satellite, *was seen in 40 countries by as many as 1.5 billion people. The show was viewed in more American homes than was man's first walk on the moon.*
- *Elvis received 14 Grammy nominations and won three for gospel recordings. He also received a Lifetime Achievement Award in 1971, at the age of 36.*
- *Attracting more than 700,000 visitors annually, Graceland is second only to the White House among the most-visited homes in the United States.*
- *There are more than five hundred active Elvis fan clubs world-wide—more than for any other celebrity.*
- *First issued by the U.S. Postal Service in 1993, the Elvis stamp is the top-selling commemorative postage stamp of all time.*
- ***Source: Graceland***

on the riverbank, now known as Confederate Park, to watch the swift but fatal fight.) Federal troops occupied the town and established Memphis as a Union headquarters. They set up a supply depot, a black refugee center, and a prisoner-of-war camp.

With the end of the Civil War in 1865, the Memphis Freedmen's Bureau began providing banking, education, and other services for blacks. However, as early as 1825 Frances Wright had organized the utopian community of Nashoba, for the self-emancipation of slaves, near present-day Germantown. In 1864 public schooling of blacks officially began.

Reconstruction was stymied in Memphis in the 1870s, when a series of yellow-fever epidemics claimed more than 8,000 lives. Many of those

MEMPHIS TIMELINE

1541 Spanish explorer Hernando de Soto views the Mississippi River and encounters Indians living on the fourth Chickasaw bluff near modern-day Memphis.

1762 King Louis XVI gives France's Louisiana possessions to Spain.

1796 Tennessee is admitted to the Union.

1819 James Winchester, John Overton, and Andrew Jackson form Shelby County and found the city of Memphis.

1826 Memphis is incorporated.

1828 The first yellow-fever epidemic kills 150 people.

1840 The *Memphis Appeal* begins publication.

1842 Construction begins on Gayoso House, the city's first luxury hotel.

1857 The Memphis–Charleston Railroad is completed; it links the Mississippi River to the Atlantic Ocean.

1862 The Union defeats Confederate naval forces in the Battle of Memphis; federal troops occupy the town.

1864 Public schooling of blacks begins.

1865 The Civil War ends.

1870s Yellow-fever epidemics claim more than 8,000 lives, reducing the Memphis population by half.

1879 Memphis is forced to surrender its city charter.

1893 The city charter is restored; black millionaire Robert Church Sr. buys the first city bond.

1909 W. C. Handy writes "Memphis Blues" as a campaign song for E. H. Crump, who is elected mayor; "Boss" Crump will dominate local politics for the next 45 years.

1916 Clarence Saunders opens Piggly Wiggly, the nation's first self-service market.

1935 Tennessee Williams writes his first play, *Cairo! Shanghai! Bombay!,* during visits to his grandparents' home in Memphis.

1940 B. B. King performs for the first time on Beale Street.

1948 WDIA becomes the nation's first radio station to adopt an all-black format.

1952 Sun Records releases Jackie Brenston's "Rocket 88." Kemmons Wilson opens the nation's first Holiday Inn.

1954 Elvis Presley records his first hit for Sun Records and rises to international stardom.

Stax Records is formed, launching hits by Booker T. and the MGs, Otis Redding, Wilson Pickett, and Sam & Dave.	**1960**
St. Jude Children's Research Hospital opens.	**1962**
Ardent Studios, which today remains Memphis's most active and visible recording studio, is founded.	**1966**
The Rev. Martin Luther King Jr. is assassinated.	**1968**
Al Green's "Tired of Being Alone" and "Let's Stay Together" become the first of more than a dozen Top 10 singles to be released by the Hi Records label.	**1971**
Federal Express Corp. is established.	**1972**
Furry Lewis opens for the Rolling Stones.	**1975**
Elvis Presley dies at Graceland.	**1977**
Memphis native Benjamin L. Hooks is elected executive director of the NAACP.	**1979**
Memphis Business Journal begins publication.	**1979**
Graceland opens to tourists.	**1982**
A redeveloped Beale Street opens with nightclubs and restaurants.	**1983**
"Ramesses the Great" exhibition launches the Wonders Series.	**1987**
Memphis elects Dr. W. W. Herenton as its first African American mayor; the National Civil Rights Museum opens at the site of the Lorraine Motel; the $65 million Pyramid arena opens downtown; B. B. King's namesake nightclub opens on Beale Street.	**1991**
The Firm becomes the first in a series of big-budget films to be shot in Memphis.	**1992**
Dr. Peter C. Doherty, Ph.D., of St. Jude Children's Research Hospital's immunology department, is awarded the Nobel Prize for Medicine.	**1996**
Elvis Presley's Memphis, a restaurant and live-music club sanctioned by the operators of Graceland, opens on Beale Street; the Nashville-based Gibson Guitars Corp. breaks ground on a guitar manufacturing plant and theme café.	**1997**
Memphis enjoys a $1.4 billion boom in expansion and renovation projects; the Memphis Redbirds, the city's new baseball team, play their first season.	**1998**
Construction of the Memphis Redbirds' $68.5 million downtown stadium, AutoZone Park, nears completion.	**1999**

who didn't perish fled the town in fear of contracting the deadly disease, cutting Memphis's population in half and leaving the city bankrupt.

In hindsight it seems ironic that most of the victims of the epidemic were white (most African Americans at that time were believed to be immune to the malaria-like sickness), a fact that left the city's many black residents to care for the sick and the dying, police the streets, and attempt to keep the city alive.

In 1879 the city was forced to surrender its charter. And with the segregation and civil rights struggles of the 1950s and 1960s still more than three-quarters of a century away, it was a black man, Robert Church Sr., a former slave and the South's first black millionaire, who was the only person with the means and the optimism to invest in the city's future. Church bought the first bond that would help Memphis reestablish its city charter and thus ensure its survival into the twentieth century.

Twentieth-Century Memphis

If there is a common theme running through the past hundred years in Memphis, it is audible in American popular music. Beginning with Handy's blues and continuing through the area's jazz bands of the 1930s and '40s, to the explosion of rock 'n' roll at Sun in the 1950s, and soul and rhythm and blues at Stax and Hi Records in the '60s and '70s, Memphis has witnessed or given birth to the most significant musical developments of the twentieth century.

The city's most famous historic district is Beale Street, where trumpeter Handy first penned a new form of music known as the blues. The year was 1909, and Handy was commissioned by the white mayoral candidate, E. H. "Boss" Crump, to write a song that would help get Crump elected. The spirited, bluesy chorus that Handy would later publish as "The Memphis Blues" did the trick. Crump would dominate local politics for the next 45 years.

Music was also influential on another important front. In 1948 WDIA became the nation's first radio station to adopt an all-black format. The station's white owners made the bold move and, in trying to attract a black audience, hired the first black DJ, Nat D. Williams. WDIA, which helped launch the careers of such stars as B. B. King and Rufus Thomas, remains on the airwaves today. In 1950, not far from WDIA, Sam Phillips was trying to cash in on black music by recording rural blues artists at his Sun Studio. It was there in the narrow, brown-brick building that still stands at 706 Union Avenue that a black vocalist by the name of Jackie Brenston recorded the hit single "Rocket 88," widely regarded as the first true rock 'n' roll song. It laid the groundwork for what was to follow.

What followed was Elvis. And elsewhere around town, all kinds of unimaginable, cross-cultural collisions were resulting in an exciting array of new art forms. In 1960 Stax Records was formed, creating an outlet for such chart-toppers as Booker T. and the MGs, Otis Redding, Wilson Pickett, Isaac Hayes, and Sam & Dave.

Around the corner from Stax, in the same South Memphis neighborhood, another studio, Hi Records, recorded songs by a soul singer from Forrest City, Arkansas. Al Green's "Tired of Being Alone" and "Let's Stay Together," produced by Willie Mitchell, became the first of more than a dozen Top 10 singles to be released by Hi Records.

Against this stimulating musical accompaniment, and against the turbulent backdrop of the civil rights movement, Memphis was changing. As in other urban areas during the 1970s, "white flight" saw many of Memphis's middle-class white residents abandon cities for the distant suburbs. Blight hit hard in Memphis—many buildings were razed, while others were left to decay. Renewal would be slow in coming.

In 1974 a bill passed by the state legislature and approved by county voters set into place the current form of government—a city mayor, county mayor, and board of commissioners. Today Shelby County, led by Mayor Jim Rout, has a modern urban government on equal footing with the city. Shelby County encompasses 784 square miles and more than 860,000 people.

Urban renewal began in earnest in the early 1980s, when the renovated Peabody Hotel reopened to the public, along with a revamped Beale Street. Also during this time, Elvis Presley's mansion, Graceland, opened to tourists.

The city's tourism efforts were further boosted by a new initiative developed under the tenure of Memphis City Mayor Richard Hackett. A major

Memphis Climate

	Average Daily High (°F)	Average Daily Low (°F)
January	48.5	30.9
February	53.5	34.8
March	63.2	43.0
April	73.3	52.4
May	81.0	61.2
June	89.3	68.9
July	92.3	72.9
August	90.8	71.1
September	83.9	64.5
October	74.3	51.9
November	62.3	42.7
December	52.5	34.8

Source: U.S. Department of Commerce, National Oceanic and Atmospheric Administration

art exhibition on the Egyptian figure Ramesses the Great drew hundreds of thousands of visitors to Memphis in 1987. The project was such a success that it launched the entity known as Wonders: The Memphis International Cultural Series. Over the next decade the series would present six critically acclaimed international art exhibitions in Memphis, attracting millions of visitors and millions of dollars.

The 1990s marked an exciting period in Memphis's growth. In 1991 the city elected its first African American mayor, former City Schools Superintendent Dr. W. W. Herenton. That same year the National Civil Rights Museum opened at the site of the Lorraine Motel where Dr. King had been shot nearly 25 years earlier, the $65 million Pyramid sports and entertainment arena opened downtown, and B. B. King's namesake nightclub opened as the premier address on Beale Street.

Hollywood also came to town, beginning in 1992, when director Sydney Pollack and an all-star cast led by Tom Cruise spent months in Memphis to film the screen adaptation of Grisham's first best-selling novel, *The Firm*. A series of high-profile, big-budget films followed, including *The Client*, *A Family Thing*, *The People vs. Larry Flynt*, and *The Rainmaker*.

Memphis Today
While it may lack the rhinestone dazzle of Nashville, Tennessee's capital to the east, Memphis today is a city that takes pride in its past accomplishments while continuing to nurture its distinctly casual, laid-back approach to living. Many Memphis boosters believe that this naive indifference or calculated aloofness has been both a deterrent and a blessing to the city—prohibiting progressive ideas at one end of the spectrum, while allowing the kind of free-form distillation of ideas that can lead to the most profound inspiration at the other. The attitude is most apparent in the music, the eclectic pollination of country and blues, hillbilly and rock, gospel and soul. But this independent spirit has nurtured many other ideas as well.

The People of Memphis

Memphis is the nation's 18th largest city, and its population of 610,000 is nearly 55 percent African American. Most of the remaining residents are

TRIVIA

Since its founding in 1972, Federal Express has invested more than $400 million in Its Memphis facility. FedEx handles an average of 3.1 million packages daily, with overnight deliveries to 201 countries worldwide.

Cotton snakes on Front Street

white, although growing numbers of Hispanic (.07 percent) and Asian (.08 percent) immigrants have begun moving into the city. Extending beyond the city limits to encompass the entire metropolitan area, the demographics shift, with the latest survey showing a population that is 57 percent white, 41.8 percent black, 1 percent Asian/Pacific Islander, and 0.8 percent Hispanic.

And while it's true that Memphis boasts its share of millionaires, mansions, and Fortune 500 companies, the city also bears the burden of run-down housing projects and areas consumed by crime. Like other major U.S. cities, Memphis also struggles with such daunting social issues as homelessness, poverty, and gangs. Crime is perhaps the major concern among local residents. Despite the genuine friendliness of its people and the laid-back atmosphere that make much of Memphis so endearing, crime statistics confirm that violence against locals and tourists alike has become a sad fact of life. While some Memphis neighborhoods are unsafe at any time of day or night, no area of the city seems immune to the seemingly random acts of crime that routinely make headlines. Therefore, visitors would be well advised to use equal parts of caution and common sense when touring the city.

Weather

Memphis has four distinct seasons, including relatively brief though often icy winters and hot, humid, and muggy summers. Typically, the first buds on the trees appear by early March and, by April or May, the city is abloom with pink and white azaleas, iris (Tennessee's state flower), and blossoming dogwood and redbud trees. Autumn provides extended,

Indian-summer days followed by cooler, crisp temperatures and late-fall foliage that doesn't fire up in color until early November. Precipitation averages about 57 inches per year, and the average temperature is 62 degrees Fahrenheit. Summer temperatures hover around 81 degrees, while winters average a low of 36 degrees.

Dressing in Memphis

Don't be alarmed! Those fire-engine red pullover sweaters that seem to be worn by half the downtown lunch crowd on any given weekday identify these working professionals as employees of AutoZone—a major Memphis-based company that recently relocated their world headquarters to Front Street.

Elsewhere, however (and even on special dress-down days at Auto-Zone), casual dress is accepted almost everywhere in Memphis. Of course there are special occasions when residents put on the ritz. The annual Church of God in Christ (COGIC) convention each November is one of them. Thousands of conventioneers, known within their denomination as "saints," wash the downtown city streets and sidewalks in a sea of stylish hats, bejeweled dresses, and fine suits.

Among locals, everything from denim to sequins can be seen at performing arts events such as the opera and ballet. And only one or two of the city's most elite restaurants require jackets, and none require ties. In the sweltering Memphis summers, cool, lightweight cottons are a must, while raincoats and umbrellas are necessary in the spring and late fall.

Winters, overall, are warmer than in northern cities, but bear in mind that the weather in Memphis can become very cold. Ice storms make driving and walking on city sidewalks and streets treacherous. Pack a warm coat and weather-resistant boots, especially if visiting in January or February.

Beale Street

Memphis Convention and Visitors Bureau

When to Visit

Memphis boasts lengthy springs and autumns, when temperatures are blissfully mild and Mother Nature is at her most glorious. Beginning in April, residents and tourists gear up for the monthlong Memphis in May International Festival, a citywide series of outdoor concerts, art exhibitions, and other special activities such as the famed Memphis in May World Championship Barbecue Cooking Contest.

Elvis fans flock to the King's home and final resting place at Graceland every August to take part in a nine-day marathon of memorials and other tributes. Audubon Park is the setting for the Pink Palace Museum's outdoor arts-and-crafts festival each October. The annual New Year's Eve bash on Beale Street is becoming an increasingly popular attraction for out-of-towners and local residents alike. However, the city's many blues clubs, museums, galleries, and other cultural organizations offer a wide range of events and performances to entertain visitors all year.

Calendar of Events

JANUARY
Dr. Martin Luther King Jr.'s Birthday; Elvis Presley Birthday Celebration at Graceland; O'Landa Draper's Associates Gospel Music Lovers' Workshop (various locations)

FEBRUARY
African American History Month (various locations); Beale Street Zydeco Festival, Beale Street Historic District; Kroger St. Jude International Indoor Tennis Championship, Racquet Club

MARCH
Emerald Isle Shenanigans, Magevney House Irish celebration; Festival of Flowers, Memphis Botanic Garden

APRIL
Africa in April Cultural Awareness Festival; Crossroads Music Showcase; Earth Day, Overton Park

MAY
Crawfish Festival; Memphis in May International Festival; W. C. Handy Blues Awards

JUNE
Culture in the Courtyard, National Civil Rights Museum; Germantown Charity Horse Show, Germantown Horse Show Arena; Native American Powwow, Shelby Farms Show Place Arena

JULY
FedEx St. Jude Golf Classic, Tournament Players Club at Southwind, PGA Tour; Memphis Music and Heritage Festival

A Playwright Is Born

Tennessee Williams got more than a nickname from Memphis. Born in Clarksdale, Mississippi, Tom Williams visited his grandparents in 1935. They lived at 1917 Snowden Avenue, in a house that still stands near the Southwestern (now Rhodes) College campus. Although not a student, Williams received permission from the college president to use the campus library, where he is thought to have first encountered the writings of Anton Chekhov and other literary influences. Williams wrote his first play, Cairo! Shanghai! Bombay!, *in Memphis and attended its premiere performance on July 12, 1935, at Rose Arbor on 1780 Glenview. Later in life, after he had adopted the nickname Tennessee and penned such American stage classics as* A Streetcar Named Desire. *Williams recalled that early Memphis production: "The laughter . . . enchanted me," the great playwright said. "Then and there the theater and I found each other, for better and for worse."*

AUGUST
Institute for the Living South's Elvis Presley International Conference (locations vary); Elvis Tribute Week, Graceland; Memphis Blues Festival

SEPTEMBER
Black Family Reunion Celebration, Overton Park; Cooper–Young Festival, Cooper–Young Historic District; Germantown Festival; Goat Days International Family Festival, Millington; Freedom Conference and Banquet, National Civil Rights Museum; Kids-Only Garage Sale, Children's Museum; Labor Day Music Festival, Beale Street; Mid-South Fair; Native American Days at Chucalissa; Southern Heritage Classic, Liberty Bowl Memorial Stadium

OCTOBER
Cordova Arts and Crafts Festival; Pink Palace Crafts Fair, Audubon Park; Pumpkin Patch, Children's Museum; Zoo Boo, Memphis Zoo

NOVEMBER
Christmas lights display, Graceland; Church of God in Christ Holy

Convocation, Memphis Convention Center; Enchanted Forest, Agricenter International

DECEMBER
Beale Street New Year's Eve Bash; Kwaanza celebrations (various locations); Liberty Bowl Football Classic, Liberty Bowl Memorial Stadium; Liberty Bowl Rodeo, Shelby Farms Show Place Arena; Memphis Christmas Parade

Business and Economy

Memphis is a city of entrepreneurs, a handful of whom are known the world over for the lasting contributions they have made to various businesses and industries. For instance, in 1916 Clarence Saunders opened his first Piggly Wiggly, the nation's first self-service market. Years later, in 1952, Kemmons Wilson opened the nation's first Holiday Inn in Memphis. Fred Smith launched his small business in Memphis back in the late 1970s. It goes without saying that his was truly a fly-by-night success: Smith is founder of FedEx, the world's largest package-delivery company.

Many analysts agree that Memphis's unique, diversified economy has helped save it from the severe economic ups and downs of the past 20 years. When recessions have hit hard in other parts of the country, Memphis, with its economic base grounded in such varied industries as agribusiness, high technology, transportation and distribution, and healthcare, has weathered the unstable periods with relative strength and resilience. The city has more than a thousand manufacturing plants alone. And small-business owners are the economic backbone of the community.

Just as it did in the nineteenth century, cotton continues to play an important role in Memphis. Cotton brokerage houses such as Dunavant Enterprises, the largest cotton merchandising firm in the world, rank among the city's top 100 private companies. The area's top three cotton firms pull in a combined estimated total of more than $3 billion in annual gross revenues. In addition to the National Cotton Council, Memphis is also home to the National Hardwood Lumber Association.

Then there's the Elvis factor: Everybody knows how much Memphis loves the King, but he just keeps looking better and better. Memphis-based Elvis Presley Enterprises, Inc.,

St. Jude Children's Research Hospital

Memphis Convention and Visitors Bureau

Recommended Reading

Careless Love: The Unmaking of Elvis Presley, *by Peter Guralnick (Little, Brown & Co.)*
The sequel to Guralnick's groundbreaking biography of Memphis's most famous son picks up where Last Train to Memphis *(see next page) left off. He traces the King's career heights as well as his sad decline in this thoughtful, evenhanded work.*

Deep Blues, *by Robert Palmer (Viking Penguin)*
The late musicologist and critic for The New York Times *and* Rolling Stone *evokes a strong sense of time and place in this classic book, which includes the author's interviews with Muddy Waters and other blues musicians of the Mississippi Delta.*

The Firm, *by John Grisham (Doubleday)*
This fictional legal thriller put modern-day Memphis on the literary map. The breakthrough bestseller by the former local criminal defense attorney was one of the first in a long line of novels that are often set in and around Memphis and Mississippi.

Good Rockin' Tonight, *by Colin Escott and Martin Hawkins (St. Martin)*
This book, taking its title from an early Elvis Presley hit, traces the origins and 1950s heyday of Sam Phillips' Sun Studio and independent record label that launched the King.

Images of America: Memphis, *by John Dougan (Arcadia Publishing)*
Archival black-and-white photographs documenting the history of Memphis are grouped by categories such as architecture, early nineteenth-century floods, community life, business, and sports in this highly readable softcover book by a local librarian.

It Came from Memphis, *by Robert Gordon (Faber and Faber)*
Memphis music critic and filmmaker Robert Gordon takes a broad look at the fascinating characters and collective cultural idiosyncrasies that make Memphis unique, from the ailing blues legend Furry Lewis to druggy hangouts such as Beatnik Manor.

Last Train to Memphis: The Rise of Elvis Presley, *by Peter Guralnick (Little, Brown & Co.)*
The prolific, Boston-based musicologist has written perhaps the definitive early biography of Elvis. Among Guralnick's other seminal works on American popular music is Sweet Soul Music *(Harper & Row), which is especially rich in Memphis cultural history.*

Memphis Afternoons, *by James Conaway (Houghton Mifflin)*
Conaway, a former Washington Post *journalist and author of several successful books of fiction and nonfiction, remembers the Memphis of his youth in this poignant coming-of-age novel set in the 1950s.*

Metropolis of the American Nile: Memphis and Shelby County, An Illustrated History, *by John E. Harkins (Windsor Publications)*
This detailed, comprehensive history of Memphis and Shelby County is one of the best sources for information on the area's past. It's packed with interesting photographs and trivia.

Mine Eyes Have Seen: Dr. Martin Luther King Jr.'s Final Journey, *by D'Army Bailey (Guild Bindery Press)*
A respected Memphis judge, actor, and cofounder of the National Civil Rights Museum, Bailey remembers the slain martyr Dr. King in this moving memoir.

Nothin' But the Blues: The Music and the Musicians, *by Lawrence Cohn (Abbeville Press)*
This encyclopedic resource features detailed histories and discographies of blues singers, as well as analyses and essays.

Rhythm Oil, *by Stanley Booth (Pantheon)*
A longtime insider writes about Memphis musicians—known and unknown—in this entertaining book.

Wheelin' on Beale, *by Louis Cantor (St. Martin)*
A white, former WDIA disc jockey recalls how the Memphis radio station made the transition to America's first all-black format in 1948.

TIP

The Tennessee State Welcome Center, 119 N. Riverside Dr., is open 24 hours a day, seven days a week.

which operates Graceland and the entire Presley estate, has estimated annual revenues of $250 million—and climbing.

Another important Memphis business presence is Ducks Unlimited, Inc., which recently relocated its headquarters from the Chicago suburbs to a 100,000-square-foot complex at the Agricenter International, a $7 million complex housing the Wetlands and Waterfowl Conservation Association's administrative and support operations. The organization employs about 200 people.

Since the 1970s the city has actively nurtured its identification as "America's Distribution Center." From its perch on the Mississippi River, Memphis is one of the country's largest inland ports. Its international airport is the busiest air cargo port in the world. As a distribution hub, Memphis companies have the ability to transport goods over roadways and railways overnight to more than 150 metropolitan markets, or about 65 percent of the U.S. population. Employing about two hundred people locally, Northwest Airlines operates its southern hub at Memphis International Airport, where it has nearly one hundred scheduled daily departures and flights to 62 cities. Through a joint operating agreement with KLM Airlines, on June 27, 1995, Northwest began twice-weekly, nonstop Memphis-to-Amsterdam flights. This new service, the city's only nonstop transatlantic offering, is seeing more than 4,000 originating passengers leave Memphis International on a monthly basis. In the summer of 1996 Northwest and KLM began offering daily flights to Amsterdam.

Other major passenger airlines operating at Memphis International Airport are American, Delta, United, and USAir. These five airlines board an average of 240,000 passengers monthly. Five regional commuter airlines board another 50,000 passengers each month.

Health care has become an extremely important economic force in Memphis. About one in nine jobs in Shelby County is related to the local health-care industry. The city's major medical institutions are currently involved in capital improvements totaling more than $200 million. Memphis has 18 hospitals and is home to such leading institutions as St. Jude Children's Research Hospital and LeBonheur Children's Medical Center. Baptist Memorial Hospital, the nation's largest private hospital, is also located in Memphis, as is the National Organ Transplant Fund, Inc. In 1991 Dr. William Novick, M.D., helped launch the International Children's Heart Foundation, which provides lifesaving cardiac care to children in underdeveloped nations. The Memphis-based organization moved into its new headquarters—a restored mansion in Victorian Village that was purchased and donated by local charitable groups—in 1998.

Memphis is a city of millionaires. More than one hundred of the private companies operating in Memphis each generate gross revenues exceeding $20 million annually—the top 26 bring in $100 million or more. The one hundred largest private companies together employ 26,000 people and have collective revenues of more than $10 billion.

Retail sales for the Memphis MSA are around $10 billion annually—double what they were as recently as 1982—and are increasing at a rate of almost $1 billion per year. A half-dozen enclosed regional malls dot the city. The latest mall to open in the eastern suburbs is Wolfchase Galleria, near Germantown Parkway and U.S. Highway 64.

Per-capita income for residents in the Memphis MSA grew 21 percent between 1990 and 1994, a rate 34 percent higher than the U.S. urban average, according to statistics compiled by the U.S. Bureau of Economic Research at the University of Memphis. Unemployment in the city is around 4 percent.

Money magazine has ranked Memphis 12th out of the one hundred largest U.S. metro areas in terms of the property tax burden, with number one being the lowest. Tennessee ranks fifth out of 50 states in terms of total tax burden. Tennessee residents pay no state income taxes, but the city sales tax is 8.25 percent.

Downtown Construction

A flurry of new construction has resulted in shimmering new skyscrapers and contemporary mansions overlooking the bluffs at the southern edge of downtown. Peabody Place, an ongoing downtown project, is the largest urban redevelopment program underway in the United States today. Nashville-based Gibson Guitar Corp. is opening an $11.2 million, 750,000-square-foot guitar-manufacturing plant and café near Beale Street, and will premiere a Smithsonian-curated exhibition on Memphis music. Two new museums—the Fire Museum and a Chinese art gallery—opened downtown

TRIVIA

The history of the downtown Lincoln American Tower, 60 N. Main, dates to 1924. The skyscraper once housed the offices of Lloyd T. Binford, a film censor who, like other moral arbiters of the day, banned Ingrid Bergman films here after the Swedish-American actress had an affair and child with Italian filmmaker Roberto Rossellini. Binford is also remembered for censoring the films of comedian Charlie Chaplin.

Only in Memphis

by Jeff Nesin, president of the Memphis College of Art

Many extraordinary aesthetic experiences are possible in more than one place on the planet. Here are a few favorites that are possible only in and around Memphis.

MEMPHIS MUSIC (AIRWAVES DIVISION)

- ***All Blues Saturday*** (WDIA AM 1070): It's like the '70s never happened.

- ***Cap'n Pete's Blues Cruise*** (WEVL AM 89.9, Friday, 9 p.m.): It's like the '60s never happened.

- ***Randy on the Radio*** (WEVL FM 89.9): *Soul Patrol* (Friday, 2–4 p.m.) and *Tie-dyed Music* (Monday, 4–6 p.m.): Since some of us know that the '60s and '70s did, in fact, happen, Randy Haspel brings you that era's most profound (and pleasurable) musical legacy.

- **The Place 2B** (1035 E. Brooks Rd., Memphis, 901/396-6739): Mighty soul veteran Ollie Nightingale plays here every Sunday night. It's *the* place to finish a Sunday begun at Rev. Al Green's church.

SIMULTANEOUS NOURISHMENT OF THE BODY AND SPIRIT

- **Payne's Barbecue** (1762 Lamar, Memphis, 901/272-1523): It's like McDonald's never happened. Even the coleslaw is astonishing!

- **Tom's B-B-Q & Deli** (4087 Getwell, Memphis, 901/365-6690): Any place that's justly proud of their "World Famous Rib Tips" is my kind of place.

- **Gus's World Famous Hot & Spicy Chicken** (Hwy. 70, Mason, 901/294-2028): Amos Milburn must have had Gus's in mind. It's the mother ship of chicken shacks!

- **Earl's Hot Biscuits** (2005 I-55, West Memphis, Ark., 501/735-5380): It's like health food never happened. A great place for breakfast anytime.

in 1998, and new hotels are being added almost daily, it seems. The Memphis Cook Convention Center is slated for an $80-million renovation on the North end of Main Street, while at the South end, Memphis's historic Central Station train depot is also undergoing a $23.3 million facelift. The new Memphis Redbirds baseball team's $68.5 million downtown stadium, AutoZone Park, is nearing completion, as is the $22 million renovation of the adjacent eight-story William R. Moore building and parking garage, at Third and Monroe, which will be called Toyota Center. Also on the way: a new 23-screen downtown movie theater and separate IMAX theater. All in all, downtown Memphis is in the midst of a $1.4 billion revitalization. But there's still a way to go. Officials estimate that even when all projects currently on the books are completed, we'll be only half finished with all that needs to be done.

Cost of Living

According to a recent national cost-of-living index, Memphis rates favorably with other U.S. cities. Composite scores, based on costs of groceries, housing, utilities, transportation, and health care, place Memphis at about 5 percent below the country's average, ranking the city as a less expensive place to live than comparable metropolitan areas such as Dallas, Atlanta, St. Louis, and both Raleigh and Charlotte, North Carolina. The prices below give an idea of the median price for desirable goods and services:

Five-mile taxi ride	$7
Hotel double room	$75
Average dinner	$10–$15
Movie admission	$6.50
Daily newspaper	$.50

Housing

From ritzy mansions and condos overlooking the Mississippi River to restored historic properties in midtown and sprawling family homes in the eastern suburbs, Memphis offers every kind of housing. The median sales price for homes in the Memphis area is around $90,000.

Schools

Public schools are separated into two systems: Memphis City, with 106,000 students in 157 schools; and Shelby County, whose 42,000 students attend 39 schools. In addition, the area's 70 private schools educate nearly 10 percent of the student population in Memphis. Four-year colleges in the city include Christian Brothers University, Rhodes College, Memphis College of Art, the University of Memphis, and LeMoyne-Owen College, one of the nation's oldest private and historically black colleges. The school's history dates back to the Union capture of the city in 1862, when American missionaries began teaching the thousands of freed slaves who sought better lives in Memphis.

Libraries

The Memphis metro area has several outstanding branches. The main library, the Memphis/Shelby County Public Library and Information Center at 1850 Peabody, is old and in serious need of repair—in fact, it's scheduled for a relocation and major expansion within the next few years.

The nicest library in the Memphis area is in Germantown, at 1925 Exeter. The brand-new facility—done in soothing whites, with blonde wood and floor-to-ceiling windows that let in lots of natural light—is located next to a beautiful, wooded park with picnic tables, gazebo, nearby tennis courts, and hiking trails. There's even a post office conveniently located across the street. Free computers are available for browsing the Internet, or for word-processing tasks. The library has a good selection of videos and CDs (especially strong in the jazz category), as well as all of the books, periodicals, and other reference materials you'd expect to find at any library. There are also executive meeting rooms, a delightful children's area with regularly scheduled story-times for preschoolers, and helpful librarians. The branch is open daily except Sundays.

Memphis's newest library branch opened in March 1999 at 7200 East Shelby Drive, at Germantown Road. The 30,000-square-foot facility was built for the 90,000 residents in southeast Shelby County. This site is convenient to the hotels along the Nonconnah (Bill Morris) Parkway corridor.

For more information on any branch, call the Friends of the Library at 901/725-8895, or visit their Internet address, www.memphislibrary.lib.tn.us. Other convenient library branches are at the following locations: Bartlett, 6382 Stage Rd., 901/386-8968; Cordova, 1017 Sanga Rd., 901/754-8443; Cossitt, 33 S. Front St., 901/526-1712; Poplar/White Station, 5094 Poplar Ave., 901/682-1616.

Memphis Convention and Visitors Bureau

2

GETTING AROUND MEMPHIS

The metropolitan Memphis area consists primarily of Shelby County, although the city's geographical location places it within commuting distance of West Memphis, Arkansas, across the Mississippi River directly to the west of downtown; and to the suburbs of Southaven and Horn Lake, located about a 20-minute drive to the south in the rapidly growing area of DeSoto County, Mississippi.

Memphis's Layout

Panoramic views of Memphis, with its angular architectural skyline sprouting from atop a bluff above the muddy Mississippi River, can be quite dramatic as seen when approaching the city from the two interstates. From Little Rock, Arkansas, a 90-minute drive to the west, I-55 curls through Memphis before connecting with Mississippi to the south. From Nashville, about a four-hour drive to the northeast, I-40 leads west into Memphis, spans the Mississippi River bridge into West Memphis, Arkansas, then veers north toward St. Louis.

Memphis is also served by State Highways 51, 61, 64, 70, 72, 78, and 79. The most celebrated of these—historic Highway 61—has changed completely from the cotton-lined, dusty dirt road that once led thousands of poor Delta sharecroppers from the Old South of Mississippi toward northern cities such as Memphis and Chicago. In recent years the vast, flat cotton fields that once blanketed this rural area have begun to be gobbled up by glittering casinos, paved lots, and luxury hotel complexes. After a series of fatal car accidents involving motorists driving the narrow,

Top Five Off-the-beaten-path Sites "In the Footsteps of Elvis"

1. *Lauderdale Courts*, *255 N. Lauderdale: This housing project is where Elvis and his parents lived from 1949 to 1953. When the decaying building was scheduled for demolition in 1996, public outcry prevented the loss of this historic landmark. It's now slated for an adaptive reuse project, so that future generations can see where the little boy lived before becoming King and moving to Graceland.*

2. *Humes Jr. High School*, *659 Humes: Formerly Humes High School, this is where Elvis is said to have caught the showbiz bug by performing in talent shows. He graduated from the school on June 3, 1953.*

3. *1034 Audubon Drive: This three-bedroom East Memphis ranch house, recently the focus of a Home and Garden Television network special, is where Elvis lived from 1956 to 1957, before he moved to Graceland. Elvis is said to have paid $40,000 for the house. It's now being restored as a tourist attraction by a local couple who vow to keep the decor as it was when its most famous resident called it his castle.*

4. *Playhouse on the Square*, *51 S. Cooper St.: Today you can catch the latest Broadway drama or Rodgers and Hammerstein musical at this venue, home to the city's only professional theater company. But in its former life, this was the Memphian, a movie theater Elvis and his gang used to rent for late-night viewings.*

5. *Baptist Memorial Hospital*, *899 Madison Ave.: The medical complex that fronts Union Avenue near the I-240 expressway is where Elvis was pronounced dead on August 16, 1977. On a lighter note, his daughter, Lisa Marie, was born there on February 1, 1968.*

paved two-lane road between the casinos and Memphis, the highway was widened, and other improvements were made.

While downtown Memphis is designed in a general grid pattern, beyond these few square city blocks the metropolitan area fans out primarily in one direction—eastward. For the first-time visitor, and even for longtime

The Main Street Trolley

Memphians, the city's street names can be maddeningly confusing. Major avenues and thoroughfares frequently change names with little or no warning. For instance, Bellevue in Midtown becomes Elvis Presley Boulevard just south of the city; Ridgeway, which intersects the congested Poplar Avenue–I-240 corridor in East Memphis, inexplicably becomes Hickory Hill a mile or so to the south—yet it's known as Shady Grove to the north. (Meanwhile, there's another Ridgeway just southeast of the previously mentioned Ridgeway.) The best course of action is to get a good, detailed city map and, if possible, call ahead for verbal directions when driving to a specific destination.

Public Transportation

The Main Street Trolley travels along Main Street between Auction Avenue to the north and Calhoun Street to the south. The one-way fare is 50¢ (25¢ during weekday lunch hour). Certain trolleys also make a circular loop down Main Street and all along the scenic Mississippi River front, although these are not scheduled as frequently. You may have to wait on a few trolleys before one arrives that will take you the entire circuit. Look for the sign on the front of the trolley that indicates it makes the river loop, or ask the driver. For more information call 901/722-7100.

City Buses
Although most white-collar professionals and many residents do not rely on bus transportation, Memphis Area Transit Authority buses do cover the

Brother can you spare a dime? Or at least couple of quarters for the trolley? In the spring of 1999 ticket vending machines were installed along the Main Street Trolley line. Riders may purchase one-way, daylong, or discounted tickets. The best part of the deal: These machines make change.

Memphis in the Movies

- ***A Family Thing***—Richard Pearce *(Leap of Faith)* directed Robert Duvall and James Earl Jones in this heartwarming 1995 racial drama. The movie was shot in downtown Memphis and surrounding rural areas, as well as in Chicago.

- ***The Client***—Another Grisham adaptation, this 1994 suspense film was directed by Joel Schumacher and starred Susan Sarandon (Academy Award Best Actress nominee), Tommy Lee Jones, Brad Renfro, and Mary Louise Parker.

- ***The Firm***—Directed by Sydney Pollack and starring Tom Cruise, Jeanne Tripplehorn, Gene Hackman, Holly Hunter (Academy Award Best Supporting Actress nominee), and Gary Busey, this 1993 film was based on John Grisham's first best-selling legal thriller.

- ***Great Balls of Fire***—Dennis Quaid, Winona Ryder, and Alec Baldwin costarred in this 1989 dramatization of the life of Sun Studio rockabilly star Jerry Lee Lewis.

- ***Memphis***—Pulitzer Prize–winning writer Larry McMurtry and Memphis native Cybill Shepherd cowrote this 1992 made-for-cable movie set in Memphis in the 1950s. Shepherd also starred in the film, which was based on the novel *September, September* by Memphis resident and Civil War historian Shelby Foote.

- ***Memphis Belle***—Directed by Michael Caton-Jones, and starring Matthew Modine, Eric Stoltz, Tate Donovan, D. B. Sweeney, and Harry Connick Jr., the 1990 film is a fictional reenactment of the legendary B-17's bombing mission over Germany during World War II.

- ***Mystery Train***—Directed by Jim Jarmusch, this quirky, low-budget 1989 film features three vignettes about Japanese tourists and others staying at a rundown Memphis hotel. The film stars Steve Buscemi and Joe Strummer, among others.

- *The People vs. Larry Flynt*—Director Milos Forman scored a major Hollywood comeback with this 1996 film starring Woody Harrelson and Courtney Love. Although Flynt's true story was set in Kentucky, Ohio, and Los Angeles, this Oliver Stone–produced film was shot almost entirely in downtown Memphis.

- *The Rainmaker*—Directed by five-time Academy Award winner Francis Ford Coppola, the film adaptation of best-selling author John Grisham's 1995 novel stars Matt Damon, Claire Danes, Danny DeVito, Jon Voight, and Mary Kay Place.

- *Silence of the Lambs*—That's the Shelby County courthouse in downtown Memphis featured in exterior shots in director Jonathan Demme's 1991 thriller starring Oscar winners Jodie Foster and Anthony Hopkins.

Also Worth a Look . . .

- *All Day and All Night*—This award-winning documentary by Memphis music critic Robert Gordon (*It Came From Memphis*) tells the stories of Beale Street musicians in their own words.

- *The Gospel According to Al Green*—Filmmaker Robert Mugge produced this documentary about the Hi Records soul star and Pentecostal preacher who still ministers Sunday mornings in Memphis.

- *Paradise Lost: The West Memphis Childhood Murders*—Though far from an enticement to tourists, this acclaimed 1996 documentary details the true story of three young boys who were brutally tortured and murdered in a wooded area near their homes in West Memphis, Arkansas.

- *U2: Rattle and Hum*—The Irish rock group's 1989 rockumentary includes scenes filmed at Graceland, overlooking the Mississippi River, and at the recording of "Angel of Harlem" (with the Memphis Horns) at Sun Studio.

city and immediate suburbs. Blue and white signs indicate bus stops. The exact fare of $1.10 is required, and transfers are 10¢. Trolley II service, at the rate of 35¢ each way, shuttles riders between downtown and the Medical Center. MATA's "showboat buses," designed to resemble riverboats on wheels, connect a select number of area attractions, restaurants, hotels, and shops. For more information, and to inquire about unlimited summer tourist bus passes, call 901/722-7100. For schedule information call 901/274-MATA.

Taxis

The two major taxi companies serving Memphis are Yellow Cab (901/577-7777) and City Wide Cab (901/324-4202). Fare is $2.90 for the first mile, and $1.40 for every additional mile, with each additional passenger costing an extra 50¢. The 20-minute ride from the airport to downtown hotels costs an average of about $17, while the trip to East Memphis hotels takes about the same length of time and costs approximately $16.

Airport Express

Shuttle service between the airport (Concourse B) and most hotels in the Memphis area operates daily from 7 in the morning until 11 at night at a cost of $8 one way or $15 round-trip. For more information call 901/922-8238.

TOP
TEN
TOP
TEN
TOP
TEN
TOP
TEN
TOP
TEN
TOP
TEN
TOP
TEN
TOP
TEN
TOP
TEN
TOP
TEN
TOP
TEN
TOP

Top Ten Reasons to Love Memphis
by Dr. Gerry House, superintendent of Memphis City Schools

1. Memphis City Schools
2. D'Bo's hot wings
3. Mississippi River Walk
4. National Civil Rights Museum
5. Scott Street Farmers' Market and Tomato House
6. Replica of the Mississippi River on Mud Island
7. The Peanut Shoppe downtown
8. "Zoo Lights" holiday event
9. The incredible work of the Church Health Center, a nonprofit clinic for the working poor
10. Stage productions at the Orpheum Theatre

Major Bus Lines

- *American Charters and Tours*, 5702 Summer Ave., 901/382-6366
- *Classic Charters and Tours*, 1607 E. Brooks Rd., 901/398-0566
- *Greyhound Bus Lines*, 203 Union Ave., 901/523-1184 or 800/231-2222
- *Greyhound Bus Lines*, 5260 Summer Ave., 901/683-0765
- *Memphis Area Transit Authority*, 1370 Levee Rd., 901/722-7100, 901/274-6282 (route and scheduling information), 901/274-1757 (TTY), 901/722-7171 (MATA Plus—disabled access)
- *Mid-South Charter Lines, Inc.*, 2500 Mt. Moriah Rd., 901/360-9590
- *Payne's Metro Charter and Tours*, 1551 Cameron St., 901/948-4390
- *Statewide Transportation*, 1035 Firestone Ave., 901/527-6700
- *Top Notch Travel*, 5675 Yale Rd., 901/383-9924
- *Trailways Charters and Tours*, 1607 E. Brooks Rd., 901/396-5100
- *Yellow Cab Bus/Van Service*, 581 S. Second St., 901/577-7714

Driving in Memphis

The two major east-west roads within Memphis are Poplar and Union Avenues, both of which are heavily traveled during rush hour. When approaching or departing the downtown area via Union Avenue, use extreme caution. The center lanes of this multilane thoroughfare serve as reversible, one-way express lanes. Here's how it works: In the morning rush hour, as commuters make the crush westward toward downtown, these center lanes are designated for westbound traffic only. During afternoon rush hour, these same lanes are designated for eastbound traffic leading out of the city. Traffic lights dangling above Union Avenue and displaying green arrows or red Xs help minimize the confusion.

Interstate 240, which loops around the city, is usually congested with commuters at peak times in the morning and late afternoon. Memphians consider their fellow drivers some of the worst on the planet, as a vast number of motorists seem to disregard common rules of courtesy, and more often than not speed along freeways and other thoroughfares as if they were on racetracks.

Overall, parking in downtown Memphis is not problematic. Stick with secured parking garages and clearly marked lots, and avoid areas that

Memphis's Largest Employers

Company	Employees
Federal Express	28,000
U.S. Government	14,860
Memphis Board of Education	14,000
Memphis City Government	6,600
Shelby County Government	6,500
Baptist Memorial Hospital	6,000
University of Tennessee/Memphis	4,400
Methodist Health Systems	4,300
Shelby County Board of Education	4,222
Tennessee State Government	3,900
M.S. Carriers	3,100
Wal-Mart Stores	3,100
First Tennessee Bank	2,800
Regional Medical Center	2,700
Memphis Light, Gas & Water	2,600
Kroger Co.	2,600
University of Memphis	2,400
McDonald's/Century Management	2,250
Northwest Airlines/KLM	2,200
International Paper	2,200

Source: Memphis Area Chamber of Commerce

may be "staffed" by con artists who pose as attendants until they collect your cash. Parking spaces fill up quickly, especially when there are many events taking place simultaneously in the downtown area. The best advice in Memphis, or in any other city, for that matter, is to plan ahead. Try to arrive at your destination in plenty of time to park a few blocks away, if necessary, or to park near a trolley stop and ride the remainder of the distance. Of course, don't park where it's restricted. You will be ticketed, and you might be towed.

Note: When it rains, even the most traveled Memphis roads become slippery, especially along bridges and overpasses. But Memphis drivers are notorious for plowing full speed ahead no matter what the road con-

MATA's "showboat" bus

ditions. Visitors who get behind the wheel should take extra precautions and be prepared to drive even more defensively than is normally prudent.

Biking in Memphis

Biking enthusiasts do not regard Memphis as especially conducive to the sport. Common laments are that the city's bike paths are few and far between and that vehicular traffic is too congested and drivers too inconsiderate about sharing their roadways for the city to be reasonably safe for two-wheelers.

"Avoid Poplar and Union at all costs," one Memphis bicyclist warned. "Most side streets are pretty safe, but stay off the main roads. And if you're riding in Overton Park, go slowly, because you'll have to share the trails with people, pets, and cars." Even careful bikers willing to take their chances might be disheartened to find they need to think twice about stopping in somewhere for a quick latte or a Sunday newspaper, because bike racks are scarce commodities.

Air Travel

Located almost 10 miles south of downtown (about a 20-minute drive), the Memphis International Airport (MIA) offers some six hundred departing flights per day. The largest cargo airport in the world, MIA is also the home base of Federal Express, the world's largest express transportation company. The Memphis airport also serves as a southern hub for Northwest

Major Airlines Serving Memphis

In addition to the following major airlines, MIA is home to five regional carriers. For more information call 901/922-8000.

American	*800/433-7300*	**TWA**	*800/221-2000*
Delta	*800/221-1212*	**United**	*800/241-6522*
Northwest	*800/225-2525*	**USAir**	*800/428-4322*

Airlines, which, in partnership with KLM Royal Dutch Airlines, offers daily nonstop service between Memphis and Amsterdam.

Relatively speaking, the Memphis airport is clean, modern, and compact enough that it is easy to navigate. Concourse A, the western-most of three, serves Delta, Northwest, and KLM. The central concourse, B, also serves Northwest and KLM, while Concourse C, at the far east end of the terminal, serves American and United.

Train Service

The City of New Orleans is an Amtrak train connecting Memphis with Chicago and New Orleans. It offers service six days a week. Round-trip adult fares for the 10-hour (each way) trip between Memphis and Chicago range between $124 and $232. Travel to and from Memphis and New Orleans (an eight-hour ride each way) costs anywhere from $90 to $166.

The Memphis Amtrak station, at 545 South Main Street near Calhoun, is a grand, historic building designed by the Chicago firm of Daniel Burnham and constructed in 1914 for the Illinois Central Railroad. Now badly decayed, the building has been targeted for renovation and a major urban revitalization project that's moving ahead according to schedule. Soon, the once-ominous Central Station will be restored to its former glory. Until then, visitors arriving or departing Memphis via the train station would be wise to use caution in this area. For instance, take a taxi to and from your destination, even if it's just a short distance. Walking in this neighborhood, especially after dark, is not advised. For more information call the station at 901/526-0052, or call Amtrak at 800/872-7245.

Bus Service

Popular regional bus tours out of Memphis include other music meccas such as Nashville to the east and Branson, Missouri, to the west. Prices

Memphis International Airport

vary according to length of the trip, but one operator offers day trips to Nashville priced at $55 for the four-hour (each way) drive. The trip includes some sightseeing and lunch at the Opryland Hotel. Closer to home, many of the Memphis-based tour-bus companies also offer service to the casinos in nearby Tunica, Mississippi. Even timid gamblers can beat the odds at price specials like this one: A $10 round-trip bus fare includes $20 worth of tokens or coins at two different casinos, in addition to two full meals.

Memphis Convention and Visitors Bureau

3

WHERE TO STAY

Over the years, Memphis has been associated with many famous hotels. In its heyday, the Chisca Hotel, at 262 South Main, was one of the largest in the region. Built in 1913, the Chisca gained notoriety in the late 1940s and '50s, when disc jockey Dewey Phillips broadcast his "Red Hot and Blue" radio show from the station located there. Today the massive gray stone building is used as part of the international headquarters of the Church of God in Christ, the largest African American denomination in the world.

In 1952 Memphis entrepreneur Kemmons Wilson opened his first Holiday Inn hotel on Summer Avenue, and launched the world's first international hotel chain. After four decades, the company relocated its headquarters from Memphis to Atlanta in the early 1990s.

In the days of segregation, the Lorraine Motel was one of the city's accommodations designated for blacks. Although the modest, yellow-brick building hosted such entertainers as Count Basie, Memphis-born Aretha Franklin, and Nat King Cole, the property was forever thrust into the spotlight as the place where civil rights activist Dr. Martin Luther King Jr. was assassinated in 1968. Today the Lorraine Motel, including Room 306 and the balcony where Dr. King was shot, has been preserved as part of the impressive National Civil Rights Museum.

Today the city has hotel rooms ranging from luxury suites and quaint bed-and-breakfast properties to chain hotels catering to business travelers, families, and tourists. And it seems as though new hotels are sprouting up daily throughout the metro Memphis area. Even the historic Hunt-Phelan Home, a Victorian mansion and Civil War–era museum on Beale Street, is delving into the hospitality arena, by adding a 76-room inn on the grounds.

Visitors should keep in mind that most published room rates do not include tax, which is significant. Expect to pay an additional 13.25 percent, which includes an 8.25 percent sales tax and a 5 percent hotel room tax.

DOWNTOWN MEMPHIS

Hotels and Motels

BENCHMARK HOTEL
164 Union Ave.
Memphis
901/527-4100
www.daysinn.com
$$

A less-expensive alternative to the Peabody and the Radisson across the street, this Days Inn nonetheless shares their prime location in the heart of downtown. Some of the furnishings and carpet in the spacious, light-blue lobby may have seen better days, but the hotel features 106 newly renovated rooms on five floors. In addition to an informal restaurant, small gift shop, and lounge featuring live weekend music, the hotel is also headquarters to the Blues City Tours sightseeing company. &. (Downtown)

HOLIDAY INN SELECT
160 Union Ave.
Memphis
901/525-5491 or 800/300-5491
www.holidayinn.com
$$$

This downtown hotel, located across the street from the Peabody and adjacent to the Days Inn, was until recently a Ramada. Under the new ownership, the hotel has refurbished guest rooms, banquet and meeting rooms, a lounge, and outdoor pool. The elegant lounge conveys a plush, residential atmosphere with its warm lighting, comfortable chairs, and

tasteful neutral-and-floral decor. Sekisui, Memphis's premier sushi bar, has a restaurant inside the hotel. Picture windows offer great views of the hub of downtown. &. (Downtown)

MEMPHIS MARRIOTT DOWNTOWN
250 N. Main St.
Memphis
901/527-7300
www.marriott.com
$$$

One of the fancier downtown hotels, the 18-story property recently acquired and renovated by the Marriott Corp. is connected to the Memphis Cook Convention Center and parking garage complex via an enclosed walkway and escalator. The sunny, contemporary lobby looks out onto the Main Street Trolley Line. A 200-room addition is part of Marriott's $60-million renovation project, which will make this hotel the largest in the city. &. (Downtown)

THE PEABODY
149 Union Ave.
Memphis
901/529-4000 or 800/PEABODY
www.peabodymemphis.com
$$$$

No trip to Memphis would be complete without a visit to this Southern treasure, a 12-story hotel that has built its formidable reputation on gracious service and comfortable luxury. With 468 rooms and 15 suites, including a concierge level, this is where the elite tend to cluster. The elegant lobby, with its marble fountain and world-famous live ducks, is regarded as the place to see and be seen. Guest rooms feature all the usual amenities as well as state-of-the-art phone systems. Shops, boutiques, and four fine restaurants are located on

DOWNTOWN MEMPHIS

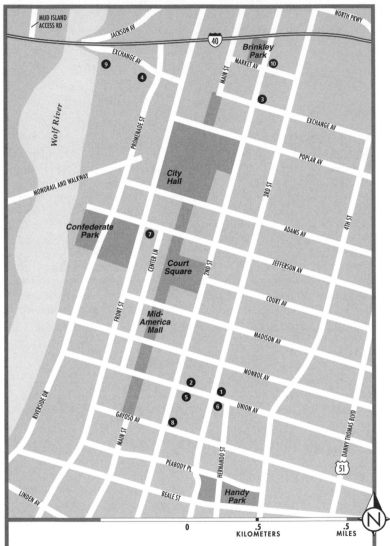

Where to Stay in Downtown Memphis

1 Benchmark Hotel
2 Holiday Inn Select
3 Memphis Marriott Downtown
4 Mississippi River RV Park
5 The Peabody
6 Radisson Hotel Memphis
7 Sleep Inn at Court Square
8 Talbot Heirs Guest House
9 Tom Sawyer's Mississippi River RV Park
10 Wyndham Gardens

the ground floor. Downstairs there is an athletic club and small indoor pool. Listed on the National Register of Historic Places, the Peabody is a Mobil Four-Star award winner, a member of Preferred Hotels and Resorts, and a member of Historic Hotels of America. ♿ (Downtown)

RADISSON HOTEL MEMPHIS
185 Union Ave.
Memphis
901/528-1800 or 800/333-3333
www.radisson.com
$$$

Hair dryers and coffeemakers can be found in most of this hotel's 280 rooms. Located downtown within walking distance of Beale Street, the Radisson has a lobby bar, a TGI Fridays restaurant, and a terrace pool. Free cable TV, morning coffee, and airport transportation are among the other amenities offered to guests. ♿ (Downtown)

SLEEP INN AT COURT SQUARE
40 N. Front St.
Memphis
901/522-9700 or 800/62-SLEEP
$$

This unassuming little gem of a chain motel caused quite a controversy when plans were announced to build it directly on the Main Street Trolley Line across from Court Square. Although to critics it might still look out of place with the turn-of-the-century elegance of the urban park at its front doorstep, the lodging facility, with 124 rooms on six floors, keeps its rooms occupied with rates in the $60 to $90 range. Free local calls, continental breakfast, parking, and in-room movies are offered to guests, along with business-class

---

Something's Fowl at the Peabody

In the 1930s, the general manager of the Peabody temporarily placed his live hunting decoys in the hotel lobby's marble fountain. Ducks have been at home there ever since. Today the pampered green and gray mallards are residents of a luxurious penthouse compound on the rooftop of the restored Peabody.

At precisely 11 every morning, the web-footed creatures are escorted into the elevator and down to the hotel's main lobby. The red carpet is rolled out, and to the strains of John Philip Sousa's "King Cotton March," the ducks waddle out to the fountain where they splash and frolic until five, when the ritual is repeated in reverse.

When the rich and famous stay at the Peabody—which they are inclined to do when passing through town—they often participate as honorary duckmasters or duckmistresses.

and nonsmoking rooms and a fitness center. & (Downtown)

WYNDHAM GARDENS
300 N. Second St.
Memphis
901/525-1800
www.wyndham.com
$$
Located near the northern end of the downtown area, within a short walking distance of the city's convention center and the Pyramid, the former Brownestone Hotel has been renovated as a four-star Wyndham Gardens property. The 11-story hotel, which opened in February 1999, offers 230 guest rooms and such homey touches as a library/meeting room with warm furnishings like Oriental rugs, comfortable chairs, bookshelves, and lamp lighting. Other nice touches resulting from the $11-million makeover include marble tile in the lobby, plantation shutters in the library and dining room, and guest rooms equipped with desks, modem connections, recliners, and large televisions. What's more, half of the hotel's 180 parking spaces are covered. & (Downtown)

Bed-and-Breakfasts

TALBOT HEIRS GUEST HOUSE
99 S. Second St.
Memphis
901/527-9772
www.talbothouse.com
$$$$
Tucked discreetly into a storefront in the Gayoso Historic District downtown, the Talbot Heirs Guest House includes nine suites. Marble floors and Oriental rugs and furniture adorn the inviting, private lobby on the ground floor. The Talbot caters to a VIP clientele. Previous guests have included film director Francis Ford Coppola, who stayed here during the

---

Bed-and-Breakfast?
Or Bed-and-Blackjack?

Getting a room is rarely a gamble in the Tunica, Mississippi, area, the nation's third-largest casino destination. Since gaming was introduced in Tunica in August of 1992, gambling revenues have soared. Revenues hit $789 million after only one year of operation. By 1998, that total had skyrocketed to $2 billion. Today the town has some 6,000 hotel rooms, and more are being built all the time. Package rates of as little as $35 per room per night, with breakfast, are not uncommon, as the competitive casino operators look for clever ways to market their properties and get warm bodies behind their slot machines and poker tables.

Bonne Terre Country Inn, p. 55

filming of *The Rainmaker*, magician David Copperfield; model Claudia Schiffer; and the consulate general of Switzerland. Advance reservations are required. (Downtown)

Campgrounds

MISSISSIPPI RIVER RV PARK
870 Cotton Gin Pl.
Memphis
800/827-1714
$
Full hookups are offered year-round at this RV park, located just south of downtown off the interstate. Fees start at $20. (Downtown)

TOM SAWYER'S MISSISSIPPI RIVER RV PARK
Exit 278 off I-40
W. Memphis, AR
901/735-9770
$
Tom Sawyer's RV Park is open year-round. Full hookups are available, and site fees start at $22 per day. (Downtown)

MIDTOWN/CENTRAL

Hotels and Motels

FRENCH QUARTER SUITES HOTEL
2144 Madison Ave.
Memphis
901/728-4000 or 800/843-0353
$$$
A bit of the Big Easy comes to Memphis in this New Orleans–style hotel that boasts oversized whirlpool tubs in each of its 105 suites. A daily breakfast buffet is included in the room rate. The hotel, which sits catty-corner from the Overton Square entertainment district, also offers a health club and an outdoor pool. &
(Midtown/Central)

HAMPTON INN– MEDICAL CENTER
1180 Union Ave.
Memphis
901/276-1175 or 800/HAMPTON
$$
Children age 18 and under stay free in rooms with their parents at this chain

GREATER MEMPHIS

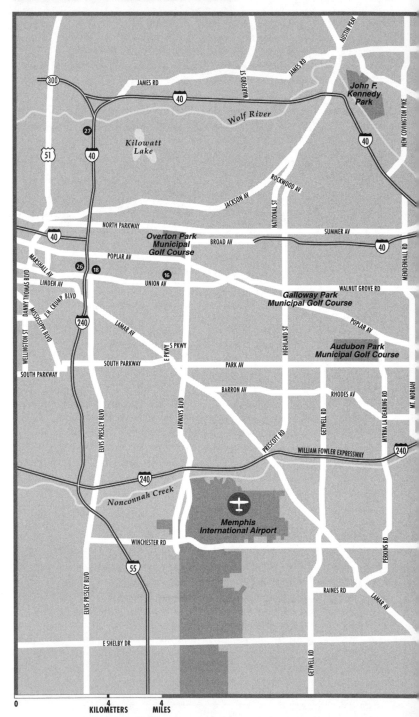

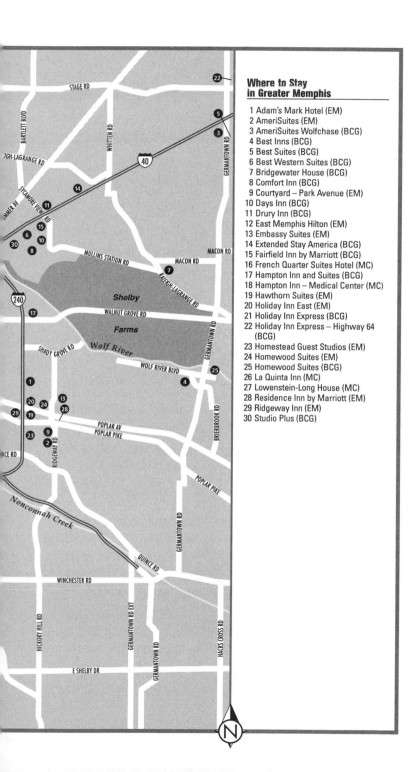

Where to Stay in Greater Memphis

1 Adam's Mark Hotel (EM)
2 AmeriSuites (EM)
3 AmeriSuites Wolfchase (BCG)
4 Best Inns (BCG)
5 Best Suites (BCG)
6 Best Western Suites (BCG)
7 Bridgewater House (BCG)
8 Comfort Inn (BCG)
9 Courtyard – Park Avenue (EM)
10 Days Inn (BCG)
11 Drury Inn (BCG)
12 East Memphis Hilton (EM)
13 Embassy Suites (EM)
14 Extended Stay America (BCG)
15 Fairfield Inn by Marriott (BCG)
16 French Quarter Suites Hotel (MC)
17 Hampton Inn and Suites (BCG)
18 Hampton Inn – Medical Center (MC)
19 Hawthorn Suites (EM)
20 Holiday Inn East (EM)
21 Holiday Inn Express (BCG)
22 Holiday Inn Express – Highway 64 (BCG)
23 Homestead Guest Studios (EM)
24 Homewood Suites (EM)
25 Homewood Suites (BCG)
26 La Quinta Inn (MC)
27 Lowenstein-Long House (MC)
28 Residence Inn by Marriott (EM)
29 Ridgeway Inn (EM)
30 Studio Plus (BCG)

hotel located near the medical center and the interstate. Free local calls and continental breakfast are other draws for travelers on a budget. ♿ (Midtown/Central)

LA QUINTA INN
42 S. Camilla St.
Memphis
901/526-1050
www.laquinta.com
$

This recently renovated chain hotel is one of the cleanest and safest hotels in the midtown area. As with other properties in the La Quinta chain, this location offers a guest laundry and outdoor swimming pool. Pets are allowed in some rooms, and children 18 and under stay free with their parents. ♿ (Midtown/Central)

Bed-and-Breakfasts

LOWENSTEIN-LONG HOUSE
217 N. Waldran Blvd.
Memphis
901/527-7174
$$

The Peabody, p. 35

Rooms at this bed-and-breakfast guest house are $60 to $85 per night for singles or doubles; additional guests are permitted for $10 each. A quiet retreat in a restored, turn-of-the-century mansion, rates include large private baths, breakfast, and parking. The first floor is available for weddings, receptions, and parties. (Midtown/Central)

EAST MEMPHIS

Hotels and Motels

ADAM'S MARK HOTEL
939 Ridge Lake Blvd.
Memphis
901/684-6664 or 800/444-ADAM
$$$$

The gleaming, rounded skyscraper hovering over the Poplar Avenue and I-240 interchange is one of the more upscale hotels in East Memphis. In addition to its 380 rooms on 27 floors, the hotel features a swimming pool, landscaped ponds, fountains, and a lounge with live music. Bravo! Ristorante is the hotel's full-service restaurant. It specializes in American and Italian cuisine (there's also a Sunday brunch), and features singing waiters who belt out show tunes, operatic arias, and everything in between. Free parking and airport transportation are included. Ask for assistance in making area golf, spa, and tennis arrangements. ♿ (East Memphis)

AMERISUITES
1220 Primacy Pkwy.
Memphis
901/680-9700 or 800/833-1516
$$

One of the newest entries in the Memphis lodging market is this 128-suite hotel, where room rates begin at $79 per night and include a complimentary

Up and at 'Em!

Bored with hotel wake-up calls? Set your bedside radio alarm clock to WEVL FM 90, Tennessee's only independent, listener-supported radio station. A true Memphis treasure, the station has a staggeringly eclectic array of offbeat and downright off-the-charts programming guaranteed to perk up the ears of even the most road-weary warrior.

Personal favorites are the Saturday morning bluegrass show, Bluff City Barn Dance, *and the weekly* Memphis Blues and Gospel Train, *whose host, local ethnomusicologist David Evans, plays vintage blues and country gospel from the early part of the century and beyond.*

There are shows devoted to everything from rockabilly and reggae to trip-hop, ambient jazz, beatnik jive, surf guitars, and show tunes. And you can count on It's Always Something, *which airs at the crack of dawn each Thursday, to come up with nifty novelty numbers. But whatever you do, don't miss WEVL's definitive radio program,* Hard Corn. *What is "hard corn," you ask? A little bit hillbilly, a little bit country-and-western rock, the genre is personified by twangy cornpone ballads by earnest singers who probably never dreamed their beer-drinkin' tearjerkers would one day become the source of so much good-humored ridicule.*

deluxe breakfast buffet, free local calls, and a daily newspaper. Rooms come equipped with 26-inch TVs, refrigerators, microwaves, wet bars, coffeemakers and coffee, and VCRs, and there's a video rental center in the lobby. Laundry and valet services are available, along with an exercise room and an outdoor pool. ♿ (East Memphis)

COURTYARD–PARK AVENUE
6015 Park Ave.

Memphis
901/761-0330 or 800/321-2211
www.marriott.com
$$$
This immaculate, centrally located inn offers a fitness facility, laundry service, restaurant, spa, and swimming pool. A small bar is open nightly from five to nine. There is no room service, but delivery is available from area restaurants. The beige and pink lobby is open and airy, with sofas and chairs and marble-topped furniture

arranged in clean, crisp lines. A brick fireplace, brass accents, plants, and a big-screen TV lend the lobby a comfortable atmosphere. The lounge-area tables overlook the pool and the garden, which includes a picturesque Victorian gazebo. ♿ (East Memphis)

EAST MEMPHIS HILTON
5069 Sanderlin Ave.
Memphis
901/767-6666 or 800/HILTONS
$$$

The city's first Hilton Hotel is located just off Poplar Avenue near dozens of shops and restaurants and some of Memphis's finest art galleries. The eight-floor hotel has six suites among its 264 rooms, including large rooms equipped with king-sized beds, two telephones, refrigerators, and work desks. Off the lobby area, a casual restaurant serves three meals a day. Other amenities include a lounge, an exercise room, and an indoor/outdoor pool. ♿ (East Memphis)

EMBASSY SUITES
1022 S. Shady Grove Rd.
Memphis
901/684-1777 or 800/EMBASSY
www.embassysuites.com
$$$

A pretty, garden-like, enclosed courtyard with gurgling stream and live, resident ducks make this all-suite hotel at the edge of East Memphis and Germantown a nice retreat for travelers. Rates start at about $100 per night, and include a cooked-to-order breakfast and a daily manager's reception. In addition to an indoor pool, whirlpool, sauna, and exercise area, there is also a game room. Frank Grisanti's, one of the best Italian restaurants in the city, is located inside the Embassy Suites. ♿ (East Memphis)

HAWTHORN SUITES
1070 Ridge Lake Rd.
Memphis
901/682-1722 or 800/527-1133
$$$

Tucked off a side street beyond the Poplar Avenue and I-240 interchange, this recent edition to the East Memphis hotel landscape is attractive to corporate clients. It's ideally situated next to such popular restaurants as Benihana and Ruth's Chris Steak House, a movie theater, shopping, and churches. One- and two-bedroom suites are available, as well as fully equipped kitchens with coffeemakers. ♿ (East Memphis)

HOLIDAY INN EAST
5795 Poplar Ave.
Memphis
901/682-7881 or 800/HOLIDAY
www.holidayinn.com
$$$

This winner of the 1989 and 1990 Superior Holiday Inn Award has 243 rooms on 10 floors. Visitors can enjoy happy hour and complimentary hors d'oeuvres at the inn's lounge Monday through Friday evenings from five to eight. On the premises are a health club, indoor pool, whirlpool, and saunas. Airport transportation, free parking, and nonsmoking rooms are included, and pets are allowed. ♿ (East Memphis)

TRIVIA

The average price for a hotel room in Shelby County is $64.84 per night. Interestingly enough, the average hotel occupancy rate also hovers near the same figure—at 64.9 percent.

The Wolfchase Boom

New hotels are mushrooming around the new Wolfchase Mall area at a rapid rate. In 1998, the area saw the introduction of a Hampton Inn and Suites near U.S. 64 and Germantown Parkway, an AmeriSuites Hotel at the northwest corner of I-40 and Germantown Parkway, and a 64-room Country Inn & Suites property on the east side of Wolfchase. In all, 10 properties and 867 rooms were added that year. In 1999 there are at least 12 more hotels and 1,500 rooms opening throughout Shelby County. In the Wolfchase area, these included a 79-room Springhill Suites by Marriott, a HomeGate Studios & Suites, a 78-suite Residence Inn, and a Fairfield Inn.

RIDGEWAY INN
5679 Poplar Ave.
Memphis
901/766-4000
$$$
The Ridgeway has 155 rooms on seven floors. Amenities include an outdoor pool with a large sundeck, free parking, valet service, a 24-hour exercise room, complimentary coffee with wake-up service, and four meeting rooms. The hotel's award-winning Café Expresso features mesquite-grilled specialties, New York deli creations, and luscious desserts. ♿ (East Memphis)

Extended Stay

HOMESTEAD GUEST STUDIOS
6500 Poplar Ave.
Memphis
901/767-5522 or 888/STAY-HSD
$$
Fully equipped kitchens with full-sized refrigerators, microwaves, and stovetops are features of the Homestead extended stay properties. Well-lit work areas with computer data ports, free local calls, and personalized voicemail telephones appeal to business travelers. Fax services and package delivery are available, and there's an on-site laundry as well. There is an additional location in the airport area, at 2541 Corporate Avenue East, 901/344-0010. (East Memphis)

HOMEWOOD SUITES
5811 Poplar Ave.
Memphis
901/763-0500 or 800/CALL-HOME
$$$
This 140-suite hotel has rooms for $119 to $169. An evening social, a fully equipped kitchen in every suite, and a complimentary breakfast are all standard. On-site are an outdoor pool, a whirlpool, and an exercise facility. The hotel provides free transportation to the airport. ♿ (East Memphis)

RESIDENCE INN BY MARRIOTT
6141 Old Poplar Pike

Memphis
901/685-9595 or 800/331-3131
www.marriott.com
$$$

This homey 105-suite inn is one of the few places in Memphis where pets are allowed. The Residence Inn requires a $125 deposit, and pets must be 25 pounds or less. Studios and two-bedroom, two-bath suites—some with kitchens and some with fireplaces—are available. Two-bedroom suites have upstairs loft bedrooms and both upstairs and downstairs baths. Other amenities include daily maid service, free newspapers, and in-room computer data ports. Evening room service is available through Café Max, which serves excellent seafood next door. The inn also has an on-site laundry facility, health-club passes, outdoor pool, indoor Jacuzzi, and a nightly social hour from 5:30 to 7. Grocery-shopping services are provided free of charge, and a free shuttle service is offered between eight in the morning and nine at night. ♿ (East Memphis)

BARTLETT, CORDOVA, GERMANTOWN

Hotels and Motels

AMERISUITES WOLFCHASE
7905 Giacose Pl.
Cordova
901/371-0010 or 800/833-1516
$$

This affordable, all-suite hotel geared toward families and business travelers features 128 suites near the new Wolfchase Galleria, off Germantown Parkway. A complimentary deluxe buffet, laundry and valet service, and newspaper are offered to guests. The inn has a fitness center and outdoor

Holiday Inn East, p. 44

pool. Rooms each have a 26-inch TV with VCR, refrigerator, microwave, and a wet bar with coffeemaker and coffee. Shuttle service is available to area attractions but not to the airport. ♿ (Bartlett, Cordova, Germantown)

BEST SUITES
8166 Varnavas Dr.
Cordova
901/386-4600 or 800/237-8466
$$$

The Best Suites is one of the newest hotels to spring up in the rapidly expanding Memphis suburb of Cordova. The hotel offers guests a free continental breakfast and a nightly manager's reception. There is also an on-site convenience store open 24 hours a day, and a copier and fax machine is available at the front desk. Each suite has a kitchenette with microwave, refrigerator, VCR, modem and fax line, sleeper-sofas, and either a recliner or armchairs. Extra-long beds are available. The sunny indoor pool, Jacuzzi, and exercise room are especially attractive. The hotel's street address is a bit misleading, because the property actually sits just off the Germantown Parkway, near Interstate 40. ⅋ (Bartlett, Cordova, Germantown)

BEST WESTERN SUITES
6045 Macon Cove Rd.
Memphis
901/385-1919 or 800/528-1234
$$

Forty guest rooms are available at this Best Western Suites. A continental breakfast is served in a tiny area, but there is no other food service. There are refrigerators and microwaves in every room, a fitness room, and an outdoor pool. ⅋ (Bartlett, Cordova, Germantown)

COMFORT INN
1335 McRee St.
Memphis
901/372-2700 or 800/228-5150
www.comfortinn.com
$$$

This new hotel offers patrons an outdoor pool, continental breakfast, a comfortable lobby, and one small meeting room. No shuttle service is provided. ⅋ (Bartlett, Cordova, Germantown)

DAYS INN
6055 Macon Cove Rd.
Memphis
901/371-0606 or 800/329-7466
www.daysinn.com
$$

Cribs and roll-away beds are available for an additional fee at this AAA-approved motel. Passes to an area gym, free local calls, and continental breakfast are included in the room rate. And, for guests with late-night cravings, some rooms come with microwaves and refrigerators. The hotel also provides free pick-up service for Blues City Tours of Memphis, but there is no shuttle to the airport. ⅋ (Bartlett, Cordova, Germantown)

DRURY INN
1556 Sycamore View
Memphis
901/373-8200 or 800/325-8300
www.drury-inn.com
$$

This clean hotel makes a nice first impression with its spacious lobby, plentiful seating, and friendly staff. Business-class kings and two-room suites with microwaves and refrigerators are available. The inn offers free continental breakfast as well as in-room movies, cable TV, and free local calls. There's an indoor swimming pool and whirlpool, and parking is free. About 80 percent of the inn's rooms are nonsmoking. ⅋ (Bartlett, Cordova, Germantown)

FAIRFIELD INN BY MARRIOTT
6010 Macon Cove Rd.
Memphis
901/384-0010 or 800/228-2800
www.marriott.com
$$

One of the newest lodging facilities in this corridor of Memphis is the Fairfield Inn, located next door to the Celebration Station kids' entertainment complex. The inn has 118 rooms on three floors. Some rooms come with microwaves, refrigerators, spas, and whirlpool tubs. Connecting rooms are also available. Room rates include the use of an indoor pool, exercise room, whirlpool, laundry, premium movie channels, and continental breakfast. Shuttle service is available to area attractions. ⅋ (Bartlett, Cordova, Germantown)

HAMPTON INN AND SUITES
33 Walnut Grove Rd. at Humphries Center

Memphis
901/747-3700
$$

This hotel offers proximity to Baptist Memorial Hospital East and other medical complexes. With an average room rate of $50 to $100 per night, the relatively new property is a good bet for travelers on a budget. & (Bartlett, Cordova, Germantown)

HOLIDAY INN EXPRESS
5225 Summer Ave.
Memphis
901/685-0704 or 800/HOLIDAY
www.holidayinn.com
$

Photocopy and laundry services are available at this hotel, which also includes 150 rooms, a two-story atrium lobby with lots of windows and a big-screen TV, and a covered walkway connected to a seafood restaurant. There's an outdoor pool and garden patio, and guests have access to the Wimbleton Sports Plex Fitness Center. & (Bartlett, Cordova, Germantown)

HOLIDAY INN EXPRESS
8635 U.S. Hwy. 64
Memphis
901/372-0000 or 800/HOLIDAY
$$

This crisp, clean, and completely remodeled hotel includes complimentary breakfast in the lobby area from 6 to 10. Passes to Wimbleton Sports Plex can be purchased, refrigerators and work desks are in every room, and microwaves are available. Children under 19 stay free in their parents' rooms. & (Bartlett, Cordova, Germantown)

Extended Stay

BEST INNS
7787 Wolf River Blvd.

Germantown
901/757-7800 or 800/237-8466
$$

A complimentary "Special K breakfast," a fax and copying service at the front desk, and fax and modem hookups in all rooms are selling points of this moderately priced inn. Queen-, double-, or king-sized beds are available, along with microwaves, refrigerators, VCRs, and baths with Jacuzzi tubs. The 80-room hotel also has an indoor pool and an in-house security system. & (Bartlett, Cordova, Germantown)

EXTENDED STAY AMERICA
5885 Shelby Oaks Dr.
Memphis
901/386-0026
$$

Newly opened in January 1997, this hotel seems more like an apartment complex than an overnight-lodging facility. Spread out within two three-story buildings are 126 suites with kitchens and appliances, queen-sized beds, and recliners. Studio apartments start at about $54 per night, while weekly rentals begin at $259. & (Bartlett, Cordova, Germantown)

HOMEWOOD SUITES
7855 Wolf River Pkwy.
Germantown
901/751-2500 or 800/225-5466
$$$

A cozy fireplace, stone floor, and country French decor set its lobby apart from other similar locations. An executive center, exercise room, sports court, and outdoor pool are among the guest amenities. There's also a sweets shop and grocery store, where guests may rent videos and purchase newspapers and other personal items. Suites come with separate kitchen, bedroom, and living areas, and guests receive a complimentary buffet breakfast. &. (Bartlett, Cordova, Germantown)

STUDIO PLUS
8110 Cordova Center Dr.
Cordova
901/754-4030 or 800/646-8000
$$$

This 71-room extended-stay inn offers guests the use of a fitness room, outdoor pool, and on-site laundry. Rooms include kitchens with microwaves and full-sized refrigerators, computer data ports, phones with voicemail service, and weekly housekeeping. Rates begin at around $259 per week, although monthly and nightly rates are available. &. (Bartlett, Cordova, Germantown)

Bed-and-Breakfasts

BRIDGEWATER HOUSE
7015 Raleigh–LaGrange Rd.
Cordova
901/384-0080
$$$

A restored schoolhouse built in the 1890s has been converted into a guest house with two large guest rooms. Private baths and full gourmet breakfasts are included in the rates. Call or write to receive a brochure with detailed directions to the inn. To reach the Bridgewater House, take the Whitten Road exit off of Interstate 40 and go south past Macon Road West to Raleigh–LaGrange South. (Bartlett, Cordova, Germantown)

SOUTH MEMPHIS

Hotels and Motels

DAYS INN RIVER BLUFF INN
340 W. Illinois Ave.
Memphis
901/948-9005 or 800/528-1234
www.daysinn.com
$

This modest hotel includes six floors, 99 rooms, and picturesque views of the Mississippi River. Located immediately south of the downtown area, convenient to the National Ornamental Metal Museum with its beautiful

Four Points Sheraton Hotel, p. 52

Memphis Convention and Visitors Bureau

SOUTH MEMPHIS

Where to Stay in South Memphis

1 Bonne Terre Country Inn
2 Comfort Inn Airport/Graceland
3 Courtyard by Marriott
4 Courtyard by Marriott – Lenox Corporate Park
5 Days Inn at Graceland
6 Days Inn River Bluff Inn
7 Elvis Presley's Heartbreak Hotel
8 Extended StayAmerica
9 Four Points Sheraton Hotel
10 Guest House Inns and Suites
11 Hampton Inn
12 Holiday Inn
13 Howard Johnson's Plaza Hotel
14 Memphis Graceland KOA
15 Memphis Marriott
16 Radisson Memphis International Airport Hotel
17 Ramada Inn Airport/Graceland
18 Skyport Inn
19 Studio Plus
20 Wilson Inn Memphis Central
21 Wilson World Hotel

grounds and picnic areas, the hotel offers guests a full-service restaurant, cable TV, and an outdoor swimming pool. & (South Memphis)

COMFORT INN AIRPORT/GRACELAND
1581 E. Brooks Rd.
Memphis
901/345-3344 or 800/228-5150
www.comfortinn.com
$$

This basic 60-room hotel sits less than two miles from both Graceland and the airport. Smoking and nonsmoking rooms are available, as is free shuttle service to and from the airport. King rooms feature recliners and remote-control TVs with full cable hook-up. An outdoor pool, continental breakfast, and local calls are included in room rates. Children under 18 stay free with their parents. & (South Memphis)

GUEST HOUSE INNS AND SUITES
4300 American Way
Memphis
901/366-9333 or 800/456-4000
$$

This tidy, redbrick inn near the Mall of Memphis offers studios and one- and two-bedroom suites—including some with full kitchens, coffeemakers and complimentary coffee, microwaves, cookware, china, flatware, and linens. There are laundry facilities, a shopping service, and a weekly cookout for guests, in addition to free continental breakfast and a nightly social hour. The inn also has a heated pool and spa. & (South Memphis)

COURTYARD BY MARRIOTT
1780 Nonconnah Blvd.
Memphis
901/396-3600 or 800/321-2211
www.marriott.com
$$$

Marriot's Courtyard, which is convenient to both the airport and the interstate, does a lot of corporate business with its meeting and banquet rooms. The modern, upscale facility features a lounge, fitness center, outdoor pool and whirlpool, laundry service, and restaurant. Children 17 and under stay free with their parents. & (South Memphis)

COURTYARD BY MARRIOTT— LENOX CORPORATE PARK
3076 Kirby Pkwy.

Memphis
901/365-6400 or 800/321-2211
www.marriott.com
$$
Opened in early 1999, this 96-room property is adjacent to the tony new Lenox Corporate Park. Area business offices include those of Arcadian-PSI, FedEx Data Center, Nike, Monsanto, and Thomas & Betts. Each room has a large work desk, sitting area, two telephones with data ports, cable TV, coffeemaker, hairdryer, iron, and ironing board. A fireplace welcomes guests in the warmly decorated lobby area. Breakfast is served daily in cheerful surroundings near the front desk. ⅃ (South Memphis)

DAYS INN AT GRACELAND
3839 Elvis Presley Blvd.
Memphis
901/346-5500 or 800/329-7466
www.daysinn.com
$$
Located half a block from Graceland,

Bridgewater House
Bed-and-Breakfast, p. 49

Memphis Convention and Visitors Bureau

this inn features an outdoor guitar-shaped pool and free in-room Elvis movies 24 hours a day. Free local calls, a beauty/barber shop, 24-hour front desk, golf, tennis, and meeting facilities also are available, as is RV and truck parking. Rates are higher in the summer than at other times of the year. Pets are allowed for a five-dollar fee. ⅃ (South Memphis)

ELVIS PRESLEY'S HEARTBREAK HOTEL
3677 Elvis Presley Blvd.
Memphis
901/332-1000 or 800/WILSONS
www.daysinn.com
$$
"As close to Elvis as you can get." With a motto like that, what else is there to know? Elvis Presley Enterprises purchased this hotel (formerly the Wilson World Hotel) in 1998. Located across the street from Graceland, the property offers spacious rooms and suites, and such commonplace extras as free continental breakfast, local calls, and microwave ovens. Die-hard fans will appreciate their 24-hour access to free Elvis movies, too. ⅃ (South Memphis)

FOUR POINTS SHERATON HOTEL
2240 Democrat Rd.
Memphis
901/332-1130 or 800/528-1234
www.sheratonfourpoints.com
$$
This renovated luxury hotel in the Nonconnah Corporate Center offers 380 rooms, most of which are nonsmoking. The expansive lobby is an aesthetic delight with its smooth, hardwood floors, bubbling fountains, and bar and lounge area strewn with leather chairs and sofas. Renovation on the five-floor hotel was completed in June of 1999. Paddleford's, a full-service

What Once Was Old Is Now New

While the Peabody is Memphis's main historic hotel, it's just about the only historic hotel. But that will change in 1999, as two historic buildings in downtown Memphis undergo transformations into new lodging and office establishments.

The old Tennessee Trust building, 79 Madison Ave., is getting an $8.5-million facelift. The 15-story high-rise, built in 1907, will house meeting rooms, commercial space, restaurant facilities, and residential amenities among its 98 luxury suites. A rooftop club that will serve complimentary gourmet breakfast, evening cocktails, and hors d'oeuvres is also planned, according to the Center City Commission. A parking structure for hotel patrons is being built near the rear entrance of the hotel.

In addition, the old Barton Cotton Warehouse, 115 S. Front St., is being revamped into the Gayoso Inn. This three-story structure next door to AutoZone's glassy high-rise headquarters will become a 27-room inn with restaurants and meeting rooms. Work on the $3.5 million project is expected to be complete by the fall of 1999.

restaurant, offers southern cuisine, and the lobby area includes a Starbucks coffee kiosk. A fitness center, outdoor pool, Tiffany-glass gazebo, two tennis courts, free parking, and complimentary shuttle service to and from the airport are among the Sheraton's many amenities. The property also offers 28,000 square feet of meeting space. ⅙ (South Memphis)

HAMPTON INN
2700 Perkins Rd.
Memphis
901/367-1234 or 800/426-7886
$
A five-story, beige stucco structure

near the Mall of Memphis and dozens of restaurants and shops, the Hampton Inn includes a large lounge area with a TV and a complimentary buffet. Same-day valet service is available, as are complimentary passes to a local athletic club. ⅙ (South Memphis)

HOLIDAY INN
2490 Mt. Moriah Rd.
Memphis
901/362-8010 or 800/HOLIDAY
www.holidayinn.com
$$$
This elegant and traditional Holiday Inn southeast of I-240 and Poplar includes 197 renovated guest rooms.

Cactus Rose is the on-site restaurant, and there's also a large, landscaped courtyard swimming pool and a recently updated fitness room. ♿ (South Memphis)

**HOWARD JOHNSON'S
PLAZA HOTEL
1441 E. Brooks Rd.
Memphis
901/398-9211 or 800/HOLIDAY
$$**

This redbrick hotel is right on Interstate 55 at Brooks Road. Included are an indoor pool and fitness center, bar, and restaurant buffet. ♿ (South Memphis)

**MEMPHIS MARRIOTT
2625 Thousand Oaks Blvd.
Memphis
901/362-6200 or 800/627-3587
www.marriott.com
$$$**

Adjacent to the Mall of Memphis at I-240 and Perkins Road, six miles east of the airport and 15 minutes from downtown, this Marriott is one of Memphis's better full-service hotels.

The Marriott is a high-rise offering 316 rooms and four suites, with individual climate control and free cable and in-room movies. The hotel restaurant serves three meals daily. In addition, there are indoor and outdoor pools; a complete health club, sauna, and whirlpool; free parking and airport shuttle; room, valet, and dry-cleaning service; and meeting rooms. ♿ (South Memphis)

**RADISSON MEMPHIS
INTERNATIONAL AIRPORT HOTEL
2411 Winchester Ave.
Memphis
901/332-2370 or 800/365-2370
$$$**

Don't blink or you'll miss the turnoff—this spacious hotel, offering 211 rooms and suites on three floors, is located at the airport entrance, on the airport grounds. There's a full-service restaurant, lounge, exercise room, outdoor pool, tennis courts, and meeting facilities for up to three hundred people. Amenities include complimentary breakfast buffet, daily newspaper, 24-hour

---

Hotel History

The first hotel in Memphis was the Gayoso House, a 150-room luxury high-rise built in 1842 as part of an extravagant and then-daring new development of homes, commercial buildings, and warehouses located south of downtown. With its own wine cellar, bakeries, gas lighting, and indoor plumbing with marble bathtubs, the Gayoso House was considered the epitome of luxury. Although it burned down on July 4, 1899, the Gayoso has found new life nearly a century later in the Peabody Place. The $121 million development includes shops, restaurants, office buildings, and tidy, redbrick apartments collectively known as Gayoso House.

airport shuttle, and parking. ♿ (South Memphis)

RAMADA INN AIRPORT/GRACELAND
1471 E. Brooks Rd.
Memphis
901/332-3500 or 800/2-RAMADA
$$
This 249-room inn, while located in the Graceland area, serves a predominantly corporate clientele. The inn's elegantly rustic lobby features lots of oak, greenery, and red brick, and the landscaped courtyard is lovely. All rooms have telephones with voicemail. ♿ (South Memphis)

SKYPORT INN
Memphis International Airport
Memphis
901/345-3220
www.skyport.com
$
Located inside the main airport terminal, the 44-room Skyport Inn is a comfortable and convenient hideaway offering free in-room movies, meeting facilities, and other amenities. ♿ (South Memphis)

WILSON INN MEMPHIS CENTRAL
2705 Cherry Rd.
Memphis
901/366-9300 or 800/WILSONS
$$
The dull beige and pink exterior of this building belies the modern, airy lobby inside. The tiled floor is strewn with rugs, and tables and chairs are clustered for private conversation. Some rooms include cooking facilities. The inn offers free transportation to the nearby airport. ♿ (South Memphis)

WILSON WORLD HOTEL
2715 Cherry Rd.

Memphis
901/366-0000 or 800/872-8366
$$
Appearing as a somewhat classier sister to the adjacent Wilson Inn, this full-service hotel was renovated in 1996. A sunken interior lounge is built around an indoor landscaped courtyard. Piano music is the forte of the Fallen Tree Lounge bar, beyond which lies an indoor pool and spa. The hotel also includes a salon, gift shop, Cajun Friday dinner and Sunday lunch buffets, and nightly dinner specials. Children 18 and under stay free with their parents. ♿ (South Memphis)

Bed-and-Breakfasts

BONNE TERRE COUNTRY INN
4715 Church Rd. W.
Nesbit, Mississippi
601/781-5100
$$$$
This newly constructed Greek-Revival home features 10 guest rooms with working fireplaces, marble Jacuzzis, and private porches overlooking a wooded landscape and five-acre lake. French and English country antiques decorate the cozy inn, where prix fixe dinners include gourmet touches. Located in a suburban country setting with other homes and properties nearby, the inn is about a 25-minute drive from Memphis, four miles west of the Interstate 55 and Church Road interchange. (South Memphis)

Extended Stay

EXTENDED STAYAMERICA
6520 Mt. Moriah Rd.
Memphis
901/362-0338
www.extstay.com
$$

Convenient to I-240 and the Nonconnah Expressway, which leads into southeast Shelby County, this extended-stay property is surrounded by apartment complexes and nearby shopping and restaurants. Suites include kitchens, beds of all sizes, and wide work desks with excellent lighting. The wheelchair-accessible rooms are especially spacious. There are coin-operated laundry machines on-site, as well. ♿ (South Memphis)

STUDIO PLUS
6085 Apple Tree Dr.
Memphis
901/360-1114
www.extstay.com

$
Built in 1991 and located within walking distance of Appletree Center, this plain facility offers laundry, full kitchens, and a workout facility with a sauna. ♿ (South Memphis)

Campgrounds

MEMPHIS GRACELAND KOA
3691 Elvis Presley Blvd.
Memphis
901/396-7125
$
The campground is open year-round. Full hookups are available, and fees start at $25 per night for two people. (South Memphis)

4

WHERE TO EAT

Pork barbecue is Memphis's primary claim to culinary fame. At last count, the city had nearly two hundred restaurants devoted to the beloved "other" white meat. But the dining scene in the home of the blues has come a long way indeed. Over the last 5 to 10 years, the city has witnessed an explosion in the number of new restaurants. Today you'll find everything from out-of-state chains and brewpubs to restaurants offering ethnic fare and traditional fine dining. A few of the town's top toques have received international acclaim in the pages of food magazines and from such prestigious organizations as the James Beard House in New York.

This chapter begins with a list of restaurants organized by the type of food each offers. For details about each restaurant, consult the pages that follow—dining spots are listed alphabetically within each geographic zone. Dollar-sign symbols indicate how much you can expect to spend per person for a meal (appetizer, entrée, and dessert).

Price-rating symbols:
$ **$10 and under**
$$ **$11 to $20**
$$$ **$21 and up**

All restaurants listed accept credit cards unless otherwise noted.

Barbecue
Blues City Café (DM) p. 61
Corky's (EM) p. 74
D'Bo's Buffalo Wings (SM) p. 84
Germantown Commissary (BCG) p. 81
Gridley's (BCG) p. 81
Interstate Bar-B-Que (SM) p. 85
Rendezvous (DM) p. 65

Breakfast
Blue Plate Café (EM, BCG) p. 72
Café Expresso (DM, EM) p. 61

Brew Pubs
Bosco's Pizza Kitchen and Brewery
    (BCG) p. 78

Burgers
Back Yard Burgers (MC) p. 66
Elliott's (DM) p. 62

Cajun/Creole
On Teur (MC) p. 70
Owen Brennan's (EM) p. 77

Casual
Grady's Good Times (EM) p. 75
Houston's (EM) p. 76
J. Alexander's (BCG) p. 81
Lulu Grille (EM) p. 76

Chinese/Vietnamese
Jasmine Chinese and Thai Restaurant
    (BCG) p. 82
Obleo's Dog House and Chinese Food
    (DM) p. 65
Saigon Le (MC) p. 71

Contemporary
Aubergine (EM) p. 72
Brushmark (MC) p. 66
Chez Philippe (DM) p. 62
Cielo (MC) p. 66
Dux (DT) p. 62
Erling Jensen's (EM) p. 74
Grove Grill (EM) p. 76
Jarrett's (EM) p. 76
La Chardonnay/Palm Court (MC) p. 69

McEwen's (DT) p. 65
Napa Café (EM) p. 77
Raji (EM) p. 77

Delicatessen
Bluff City Deli (DM) p. 61
Fino's from the Hill (MC) p. 67

French
La Tourelle/Tower Café (MC) p. 69

German
Erika's (DM) p. 63

Indian
Bombay Café (SM) p. 83
Delhi Palace (BCG) p. 81
India Palace (MC) p. 69

Italian
Bravo! Ristorante (EM) p. 72
Bolla Pasta (BCG) p. 78
Frank Grisanti's (EM) p. 73
Grisanti's (MC) p. 67
Pete and Sam's (EM) p. 77
Romano's Macaroni Grill (BCG) p. 83
Ronnie Grisanti (MC) p. 70
Spaghetti Warehouse (DT) p. 65

Japanese
Koto (MC) p. 69
Mikasa Japan (EM) p. 76
Sekisui (DM, MC, BCG) p. 71

Mediterranean
Marena's (MC) p. 69

Mexican/Southwestern
Café Ole (MC) p. 66
Cancun (MC) p. 67
Cozymel's (BCG) p. 79
Salsa (EM) p. 77

Pacific Rim
Tsunami (MC) p. 71

Russian
Café Samovar (DM) p. 62

Seafood
Café Max (EM) p. 74
Fred Gang's (SM) p. 85
Landry's (DM) p. 64
Mikasa Japan (EM) p. 76
Pappy & Jimmie's (BCG) p. 83
Sekisui (DM, MC, BCG) p. 71

Southern
Barksdale Café (MC) p. 66
Buntyn (EM) p. 72
The Cupboard (DM, MC) p. 67
Ellen's Soul Food Restaurant (SM) p. 85
Little Tea Shop (DM) p. 65
Mel's Fish Market (SM) p. 86
White Church Tea Room (SM) p. 86

Steak
Butcher Shop (DM) P. 61
Folk's Folly (EM) p. 74
Ouback Steakhouse (BCG) p. 82
Paulette's (MC) p. 70

Vegetarian
Jasmine Chinese and Thai Restaurant
  (BCG) p. 82
Wild Oats Market (MC, EM) p. 78

DOWNTOWN MEMPHIS

ARCADE
540 S. Main St.
Memphis
901/526-5757
$
Established in 1919, the Arcade has become one of downtown's most beloved institutions. The restaurant serves up hot, southern-fried breakfasts and tasty, homemade plate lunches in a vintage diner at the far end of the South Main Historic District. They also make a mean pizza. No credit cards. (Downtown)

AUTOMATIC SLIM'S TONGA CLUB
83 S. Second St.

Memphis
901/525-7948
$$
The faux zebra-skin bar stools, red chili strands, and cowboy and cacti decor contribute to Automatic Slim's reputation as the hippest restaurant in town. But it is the array of inventive salads, fresh desserts and exotic coffees, and daily fish, pasta, vegetarian, and polenta specials that keep diners and nightlife lovers alike returning to this chic urban eatery. Appetizers, soups, sandwiches, and entrées are a tantalizing mélange of Caribbean, Californian, and Southwestern cuisine. Cuban black beans and rice, Jamaican jerk chicken, cheese quesadillas, and coconut-mango shrimp are among the varied and delicious dishes served on Fiesta Ware in a rainbow of mismatched colors. Breadbaskets are filled with warm, sweet corn muffins with honeyed butter. Sandwiches are served with fiery coyote chips—thin, crisp-fried potato chips served warm with a creamy red-pepper dip. Closed for lunch Sat–Sun; reservations recommended. & (Downtown)

Chez Philippe, p. 62

The Peabody

DOWNTOWN MEMPHIS

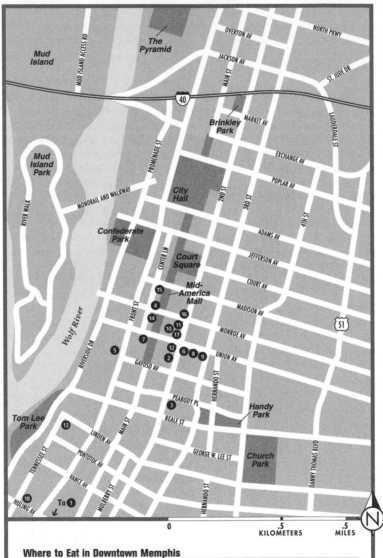

Where to Eat in Downtown Memphis

1 Arcade
2 Automatic Slim's Tonga Club
3 Blues City Café
4 Bluff City Deli
5 Butcher Shop
6 Café Expresso
7 Café Samovar
8 Chez Philippe
9 Dux
10 Elliott's
11 Erika's
12 Huey's
13 Landry's Seafood House
14 Little Tea Shop
15 Obleo's Dog House and Chinese Food
16 McEwen's
17 Rendezvous
18 Spaghetti Warehouse

BLUES CITY CAFÉ
138 Beale St.
Memphis
901/526-3637
$$

Formerly a Doe's Eat Place, Blues City Café has retained the flair, if not the name, of that legendary Mississippi barbecue joint. The nostalgic café's weathered signage, block-glass, and corrugated tin touches are reminiscent of a backwater Delta shack. Inside, cooks in crisp white caps and meat-stained aprons sear huge steaks and slabs of barbecued pork ribs over an open grill. Thick chili, beefy tamales, and cold beer round out the simple menu. In recent years, the Band Box nightclub in the adjoining room has played host to such blues greats as the late Albert King. Dinner only. & (Downtown)

BLUFF CITY DELI
80 Monroe St.
Memphis
901/525-6764
$

The matronly cooks at Bluff City Deli pack the messiest, meatiest muffalettas in town at this cheerful deli located in the Brinkley Plaza building between Front and Main Streets. The chicken salad is cold and creamy on a buttery croissant with crisp, fresh lettuce. Cucumber slices, mild peppers, red cabbage, tomatoes, green onions, olives, and feta cheese are combined in the tasty Greek salad. Bluff City also makes mean chili, and packs box lunches for business meetings. Finally, they've got the best free periodicals library around—you'll find local newspapers, *Bon Appetit*, *Gourmet*, *Newsweek*, and others. (Downtown)

BUTCHER SHOP
101 S. Front St.
Memphis
901/521-0856
$$

Two open charcoal pits allow diners to grill their own steaks at this restaurant on historic Front Street. Rustic brick walls and bookcases give the interior a comfortable appeal. Cocktails, beer, wine, a basic salad bar, and side items such as baked potatoes and sautéed mushrooms are also offered. The Butcher Shop boasts that bigger is better: Steaks range from 8- to 14-ounce filets to scale-tipping 30-ounce T-bones. Dinner seven days a week; reservations recommended. & (Downtown)

CAFÉ EXPRESSO
The Peabody
149 Union Ave.
Memphis
901/529-4160
$$

Fluffy omelets, flaky croissants, oversized muffins, and other freshly baked breads and pastries, as well as a fine selection of soups, salads, sandwiches, fish, and pasta dishes are served at this upscale delicatessen located on the ground floor of the Peabody. The towering provolone cheese, whole-wheat bread, tomato, and alfalfa sprout sandwich drizzled with Thousand Island dressing is one of the best vegetarian entrées in town. The cheerful café's bakery case is chockfull of beautifully prepared cheesecakes, fruit tarts, specialty cakes, and jumbo, two-fisted cookies, including chocolate chip, peanut butter, oatmeal-raisin, and white-chocolate macadamia nut. Reservations are not accepted. Also at the Ridgeway Inn, 5679 Poplar Avenue, 901/763-3888, in East Memphis. & (Downtown)

CAFÉ SAMOVAR
83 Union Ave.
Memphis
901/529-9607
$$

The Sadetsky family, immigrants from the Ukraine, operates this cozy downtown restaurant decorated with colorful tea samovars and brightly painted *matryoshkas*, wooden nesting dolls. Daily soup specials such as seafood chowder compete with the daily borscht, a rich beef and beet broth with shredded cabbage and carrots that tastes particularly good during the cold winter months. For around three dollars you can get the best bargain lunch downtown—a large bowl of the hot soup accompanied by a hunk of dense, freshly baked bread. *Blinis*, knishes, piroshkies, and Russian classics such as chicken Kiev are among the heartier entrées; all are served with rice, vegetables, and other trimmings. The restaurant also offers a variety of vodkas, as well as live Russian music and belly dancers on Friday and Saturday nights. Lunch and dinner; closed for lunch Sat, dinner Mon, and all day Sun. & (Downtown)

CHEZ PHILIPPE
The Peabody
149 Union Ave.
Memphis
901/529-4188
$$$

The historic Peabody Hotel's flagship restaurant has a long-standing reputation as offering one of the most elite dining experiences in all of the Mid-South. Plush decor in the multitiered dining rooms includes dramatic high ceilings, velvety drapes, and gilded mirrors. Long-stemmed peach roses in silver vases top each linen-covered table. French-born *chef de cuisine*

Jose Gutierrez has been the guiding force of Chez Philippe for more than a decade. French, Pacific Rim, and regional Southern influences are evident in such culinary creations as breast of Guinea fowl with mustard greens and gin and moonshine sauce; free-range chicken with macaroni-and-cheese spinach pancetta and smoked martini sauce; pan-braised black sea bass flavored with cinnamon and served with sassafras coulis; and smoked pork tenderloin brushed with Jack Daniels mustard and grits couscous. A jacket is required (tie optional). Dinner only, closed Sun; reservations recommended. & (Downtown)

DUX
The Peabody
149 Union Ave.
Memphis
901/529-4199
$$$

Elegant multicourse meals are served in this fine-dining restaurant, one of four eateries located inside the Peabody Hotel. A power-lunch favorite with the downtown business crowd, Dux is a quiet, understated restaurant. Prime rib, grilled seafood, chicken, and pasta entrées are served in addition to soups and generous specialty salads. Baskets of bread include cheddar-crust rolls and dense brown bread baked with sundried tomatoes. Breakfast, lunch, and dinner; reservations recommended. & (Downtown)

ELLIOTT'S
16 S. Second St.
Memphis
901/525-4895
$

Great big, greasy cheeseburgers, grilled right before your eyes while you stand in line, and piping hot French fries, golden-crisp on the outside and potato-creamy within, make the perfect late-afternoon lunch spot for downtown workers. The honest, no-fuss food, laid-back atmosphere, and convivial clientele make Elliott's what it is—a great burger joint with heart and soul. Lunch only, closed weekends; no reservations. ♿ (Downtown)

ERIKA'S
52 S. Second St.
Memphis
901/526-5522
$$

The most mouthwatering yeast rolls in all of Memphis are served warm from the oven at this tidy, unassuming German restaurant. Clientele consists mainly of people who work downtown. Daily specials include such hearty entrées as Wiener schnitzel, sauerbraten, and bratwurst, served with hot German potato salad and sauerkraut. Lunch Mon–Fri, dinner Fri–Sat, closed Sun; no reservations. (Downtown)

HUEY'S
77 S. Second St.
Memphis
901/525-4839
$

One of the most comfortable neighborhood hamburger joints in the city, Huey's operates a very popular chain of bars. Writing graffiti on the walls and shooting toothpicks up at the ceiling are two of the more childish, yet perfectly acceptable, pastimes here. Juicy cheeseburgers, golden-crisp steak fries, excellent fountain soft drinks, and beer and other spirits whet appetites and thirsts. Cream-of-the-crop live blues and jazz bands—with no cover charge—pack in music lovers on Sunday afternoons. Lunch and dinner; late-night hours all week. Also at 1927 Madison, 901/726-4372, 1771 N. Germantown Pkwy., Cordova, 901/754-3885, and 2858 Hickory Hill, 901/375-4373. (Downtown)

LANDRY'S SEAFOOD HOUSE
263 Wagner Pl.
Memphis
901/526-1966

Café Expresso, p. 61

Memphis Convention and Visitors Bureau

No Crow on the Menu?

That's not the once-jailed Whitewater figure Susan McDougal being embraced by an amorous Bill Clinton, as trumpeted in a splashy February 1999 cover story in the tabloid newspaper The Star. *It's a Memphis artist, Janet Smith, who a year earlier had sent out Christmas cards featuring those two color photos taken back in 1977, when she was a fresh-faced teenager who worked as a hostess at her parents' swank downtown restaurant, Justine's. Both snapshots showed the curvaceous Janet, dressed in a sparkling evening gown, standing alongside her father. Behind Janet, his arm cinching her waist, is the then-unknown Arkansas gubernatorial candidate, Bill Clinton. (The* Star *later ran a correction, identifying the woman in the photos as Smith, not McDougal.)*

In keeping with the flirtatious looks on their young, 1977 faces, Smith's coy greeting printed inside the 1998 Christmas card was this: "You Can't Always Get What You Want."

*Smith, who says she'd been holding onto the photos for 20 years, had resisted friends' attempts to get her to send the suggestive snapshots to the tabloids—especially as U.S. President Clinton endured the yearlong Monica Lewinsky scandal and impeachment proceedings. Instead, Smith included them in a self-published 1998 memoir and cookbook about Justine's—*Justine's: Memories and Recipes.

Old photographs, anecdotes, reprinted menus, and recipes for such popular dishes as crabmeat Justine, tournedos béarnaise, pompano papillote, and mint and lotus ice cream are included in the shrimp-pink, hardcover book. It is available at most local bookstores.

$$

Sweeping views of the Mississippi River are one of the main attractions at Landry's, a vast warehouse converted into an invitingly weathered, seaside-themed restaurant. Fried and grilled seafood with fresh coleslaw and hot French bread are specialties, although chicken, burgers, and pasta are also available. Okra is abundant in the spicy seafood gumbo, which is poured tableside over a bowl of white rice. Landry's has a lovely, landscaped patio where diners enjoy memorable views of Old Man River, especially at sunset. Lunch and dinner; reservations recommended for groups of eight or more. & (Downtown)

LITTLE TEA SHOP
69 Monroe Ave.
Memphis
901/525-6000
$

Established in 1918, the Little Tea Shop is reputedly the oldest restaurant in Memphis. Plate lunches consisting of fried catfish or chicken and dumplings come with purple hull peas and simmered greens, crumbly cornbread, and brisk iced tea. (Downtown)

OBLEO'S DOG HOUSE AND CHINESE FOOD
22 S. Main St.
Memphis
901/523-1278
$

This small, lunchtime restaurant cooks to order. Fill your plate with egg rolls; plentiful helpings of garlicky stir-fried rice with chopped veggies, chicken, or shrimp; or chili dogs, hot dogs, hamburgers, and fries. The fading orange, yellow, and lime-green decor may look dated, but the place is clean and tidy. You can phone ahead with a to-go order if you're in a hurry. & (Downtown)

McEWEN'S
122 Monroe Ave.
Memphis
901/527-7085
$

Grilled focaccia sandwiches stuffed with goat cheese, basil, and sun-dried tomatoes; hearty gourmet soups; and delicious pasta dishes such as linguine and shrimp sautéed in habanero-vanilla sauce are served in this intimate, warmly decorated storefront restaurant. Regulars rave over McEwen's crawfish pie and the

smoked oyster étouffée and "dirty" rice (that's Cajun style, for you Yankees). Contemporary local art, potted plants, and vintage jazz playing in the background make McEwen's perfect for either a romantic dinner for two or a productive business lunch. Another bonus: The entire establishment is nonsmoking. Lunch and dinner Mon–Sat, closed Sun. & (Downtown)

RENDEZVOUS
52 S. Second St.
Memphis
901/523-2746
$

When she last came to Memphis for a gourmet culinary event at the Peabody, Julia Child made a beeline for the Rendezvous the first chance she got. Antiques and vintage memorabilia cram every square inch of the vast basement establishment, where the waiters have a reputation for being good-naturedly brusque. The barbecued ribs, saucy barbecued chicken, and skillet shrimp are second to none. Cheddar cheese plates come with smoked sausage chunks and sour dill pickles, and the red beans and rice goes especially nice when washed down with cold beer. Closed Sun–Mon. & (Downtown)

SPAGHETTI WAREHOUSE
40 W. Huling
Memphis
901/521-0907
$$

Kids love sitting (and eating) in the trolley car that's parked in the center of this sprawling warehouse restaurant jammed full of quirky antiques, vintage signs, and booth seating made from brass bed frames. Traditional, family-oriented Italian food items include spaghetti with various sauces, chicken and veal dishes, and rich, layered lasagna baked with or without meat. Lunch and dinner; reservations recommended for parties of 10 or more. & (Downtown)

MIDTOWN/CENTRAL

BACK YARD BURGERS
1723 Union Ave.
Memphis
901/274-1544
$
Lean, gourmet hamburgers chargrilled to order, and plump, boneless, barbecued or lemon-pepper chicken-breast sandwiches are hallmarks of this Memphis-based fast-food franchise. Creamy, hand-dipped milkshakes, freshly squeezed lemonade, spicy or waffle-cut French fries, and toy-filled kids' "Bak-Pak" meals make BYB a tempting alternative to the more familiar burger chains. Of the more than 16 locations throughout the city, most offer double drive-through lanes as well as walk-up windows and outdoor seating areas under landscaped arbors. A few, such as the one on Union Avenue near the Medical Center, offer inside dining in-

Rendezvous, p. 65

Memphis Convention and Visitors Bureau

stead. Lunch and dinner; no credit cards. (Midtown/Central)

BARKSDALE CAFÉ
237 S. Cooper St.
Memphis
901/722-2193
$
Lookin' for some good home cookin'? "Seven days without a breakfast or lunch at Barksdale's makes one weak," or so goes the saying about this popular midtown café. Country-fried chicken and catfish, ham, and heaps of homemade biscuits are the draw at Barksdale's. Breakfast is probably the most popular meal at the site, which many years ago used to be a neighborhood grocery store. Breakfast, lunch, and dinner; no credit cards. (Midtown/Central)

BRUSHMARK
Memphis Brooks Museum of Art
1934 Poplar Ave.
Memphis
901/722-3555
$$
This restaurant, situated within the Memphis Brooks Museum of Art, offers a spicy tomato-based African peanut soup. In addition, the view from the terrace is one of the prettiest in town. With its refined decor and service, the Brushmark is the perfect place to sip a glass of wine, or indulge in a dessert and cup of coffee after a tour of the museum's impressive galleries. Lunch only, closed Mon; reservations recommended. & (Midtown/Central)

CAFÉ OLE
959 S. Cooper St.
Memphis
901/274-1504
$$

Seasoned black beans and rice, vegetarian enchiladas and burritos, and fiery salsa are best bets at this Mexican restaurant located in the Cooper-Young Historic District. With its uneven stone floors, colorful Mexican-blanket decor, and small outdoor patio behind the kitchen, the place has a distinctly informal atmosphere. Lunch and dinner; no reservations. & (Midtown/Central)

CANCUN
2094 Madison Ave.
Memphis
901/278-6608
$

Patrons return often to this festive Overton Square cantina, where cheesy enchiladas, crisp-fried tortilla chips, and chunky tomato, onion, and cilantro salsa are among the best dishes. Cancun's lunchtime buffet is a good bargain, although the quality can be inconsistent. Lunch and dinner. (Midtown/Central)

CIELO
679 Adams Ave.
Memphis
901/524-1886
$$$

Food & Wine critic Stuart Stevens said it best: "Cielo is like your crazy aunt's place with a fondness for Alice-in-Wonderland incongruities." Owned and operated by the exceptionally creative Karen Blockman Carrier (of Automatic Slim's Tonga Club), Cielo—whose name means "heaven"—serves adventurous cuisine in the historic Mollie Fontaine House. The exterior may be Victorian, but the interior is ultra-hip. Lunch and dinner. (Midtown/ Central)

THE CUPBOARD
1495 Union Ave.
Memphis
901/276-8015
$

This southern, home-style restaurant specializes in fresh-cooked vegetables, creamy mashed potatoes, and mouthwatering fried chicken. This particular restaurant proved so popular with diners that another branch (The Cupboard Too) was recently added downtown at 149 Madison Avenue, 901/527-9111. Lunch and dinner, closed for dinner weekends; no reservations. &(Midtown/Central)

FINO'S FROM THE HILL
1853 Madison Ave.
Memphis
901/272-3466
$

Breads by City Bakery in East Memphis are a big draw at this neighborhood delicatessen. Go for the dense baked breads and crusty baguettes to accompany Fino's meats, cheeses, and salads. Pizza and homemade desserts are also featured here. Lunch and dinner, closed Sun–Mon; no credit cards or reservations. & (Midtown/Central)

GRISANTI'S
220 S. Claybrook
Memphis
901/722-9363
$$

Is there a doctor in the house? Plenty, if you show up for lunch at Grisanti's, located in the busy medical-center area of midtown. Medical workers and other downtown professionals pack this friendly Italian eatery, where toasted ravioli, fresh soups and salads, and cheesy baked manicotti are house favorites. Lunch and dinner, closed weekends; no reservations. & (Midtown/Central)

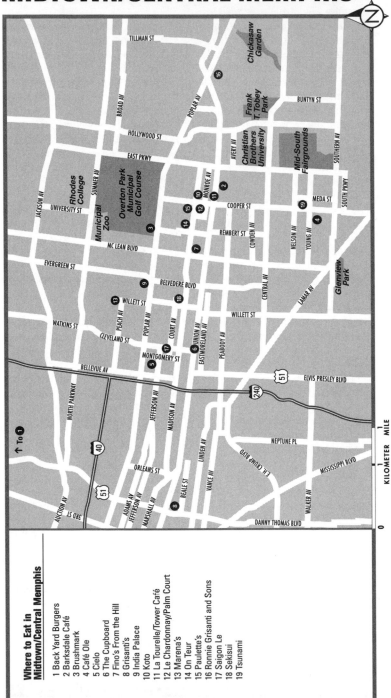

MIDTOWN/CENTRAL MEMPHIS

INDIA PALACE
1720 Poplar Ave.
Memphis
901/278-1199
$

Vegetarian curries, tandoori chicken, lamb kabobs, fragrant rice, and other Indian dishes are available at the daily buffet luncheon at India Palace. Lunch and dinner daily; reservations recommended. & (Midtown/Central)

KOTO
22 S. Cooper St.
Memphis
901/722-2244
$$$

Koto's *chef de cuisine*, Jennifer Dickerson, frequently collaborates with two other celebrated Memphis culinary kings—Erling Jensen (Erling Jensen's) and Jimmy Ishii (Sekisui)—to create memorable "East-meets-West" dinners. Courses such as foie gras teriyaki with *shemiji* mushrooms and scallions; softshell crab tempura with caviar béarnaise; veal tenderloin with wasabi consommé; and vanilla Pavlova with purple sticky rice and caramelized mango are each paired with premium sake and fine wines. Lunch and dinner; reservations recommended. & (Midtown/Central)

LA TOURELLE/TOWER CAFÉ
2146 Monroe Ave.
Memphis
901/726-5771
$$$

Elegant French cuisine, fine wines, and gracious service are focal points at La Tourelle, which is housed in a romantic, turn-of-the-century cottage near Overton Square. Upstairs in the Tower Café, the atmosphere is less formal, and the menu and prices are a bit more moderate. Dinner nightly,

Sun brunch; reservations recommended. & (Midtown/Central)

LE CHARDONNAY/PALM COURT
2100 Overton Square Ln.
Memphis
901/725-1375
$$

Gourmet pizzas baked in a wood-burning oven, one of the city's most extensive wine lists, and entrées like shrimp, smoked chicken, and pasta are outstanding features at Le Chardonnay/Palm Court. This cozy wine bar with a softly lit bistro atmosphere is tucked off of Overton Square in midtown. Closed for lunch weekends. & (Midtown/Central)

MARENA'S
1545 Overton Park Ave.
Memphis
901/278-9774
$$$

Delectable Middle Eastern, African, and Mediterranean dishes are prepared nightly in this wonderfully vibrant restaurant located in a dark neighborhood somewhat off the beaten path in midtown. Because its menu changes monthly, call ahead to make a reservation and discover whether the cuisine will be French, Moroccan, Lebanese, Egyptian, or something else. Bring your own wine to the restaurant, but be sure to order a platter of appetizers before your meal, and perhaps some Turkish coffee afterward. Dinner, closed Sun; reservations required. & (Midtown/Central)

ON TEUR
2015 Madison Ave.
Memphis
901/725-6059
$

American and Cajun specialties such

as jambalaya and fresh seafood can be found at On Teur. Although tiny, the place is loaded with quintessential midtown charm. Lunch and dinner, closed Sun; no credit cards or reservations. Restrooms are not wheelchair accessible. (Midtown/Central)

PAULETTE'S
2110 Madison Ave.
Memphis
901/726-5128
$$
Juicy, seared steaks, delicate popovers with strawberry butter, broccoli and cheese in flaky phyllo pastry, and chicken and fish entrées draw repeat customers to Paulette's. The classiest restaurant in midtown, this charming, European-style inn anchors the Overton Square entertainment district. Paulette's makes a lovely romantic getaway or a pre- or after-theater dining spot. Lunch and dinner. (Midtown/Central)

RONNIE GRISANTI AND SONS
2855 Poplar Ave.
Memphis
901/323-0007
$$

Raji's Food Favorites

by Raji Jallepalli, owner of Raji

- *La Tourelle* and *Erling Jensen's*: We, as chefs, have a unique perspective about why we choose certain restaurants. When we are not at work, we want to be entertained, amused, nourished, and nurtured with food. Contrary to popular belief, we are not being competitive.
- *Saigon Le*: Great spring rolls and egg rolls wrapped in herbs and peanut sauce, and hot chili sauce, which I particularly crave.
- *Bombay Café*: Over the past few years there has been a proliferation of Indian restaurants in town. For me, the South Indian breakfast at Bombay Café is a must. India Palace and Delhi Palace also provide a good curry fix.
- *Interstate Bar-B-Que and Corky's*: My pilgrimage to get barbecue is about as often as my pilgimage to Graceland—only when I have out-of-town company. Although I am not an aficionado of barbecue, to my taste, Interstate Bar-B-Que and Corky's are the best choices. I would probably prefer it more as a take-out option, as it can be messy, especially with wet ribs.

The Western Steakhouse and Lounge, 1298 Madison Ave., was once a regular haunt of Elvis. He loved their steaks. The place has been for sale forever, and the most recent owners auctioned off a good portion of the lounge's memorabilia. But for the time being, at least, this last-of-its-breed honky-tonk attracts Elvis fans far and near, who come to sit in the King's favorite booth and pore over photographs of him in the lounge's heyday.

The Grisantis are one of the best-loved families of restaurateurs in Memphis. This midtown restaurant, located near the Union and Poplar Avenues viaduct, is operated by friendly, gregarious Ronnie Grisanti and his family. The baked manicotti, seafood tortellini, steaks, and salads are the freshest in town. The warm, candlelit restaurant is also one of the homiest. Dinner, closed Sun. &. (Midtown/Central)

SAIGON LE
51 N. Cleveland
Memphis
901/276-5326
$

A rooster crows somewhere in the distance, and the outdoor views don't consist of much more than a mechanic's garage with junked cars, but the food at Saigon Le is inexpensive and sensational. This spotless restaurant features Chinese and Vietnamese entrées that are unparalleled in the city. Crispy spring rolls arrive with mounds of fresh, emerald-green leaf lettuce, mint, and cilantro, and are delicious wrapped and dipped in fish sauce; piles of tender lo mein are redolent of charred baby shrimp, bamboo shoots, water chestnuts, and meaty mushrooms. With a menu boasting nearly 200 items, plus an impressive array of imported and domestic beers, Saigon Le simply can't be beat. Lunch and dinner, closed for lunch Sat and all day Sun. (Midtown/Central)

SEKISUI
25 Belvedere
Memphis
901/725-0005
$$

For sushi lovers, Sekisui is the real McCoy. Not only does this discreet midtown restaurant serve some of the most authentic Japanese cuisine in Memphis, but it also offers a sumptuous *robata* bar, sumo-wrestling videos, and karaoke entertainment Friday and Saturday nights. Lunch weekdays, dinner nightly. Also in downtown Memphis at 160 Union Avenue and at 50 Humphreys Boulevard, 901/747-0001. &. (Midtown/Central)

TSUNAMI
926 S. Cooper St.
Memphis
901/274-2556
$$

Loud, colorful, and artsy describe the ambience at the Cooper-Young Historic District's hottest new restaurant. But there's no mistaking the wonderfully refreshing cuisine, which is Pacific Rim. Up-and-coming young chef Ben Smith, who honed his skills at the esteemed Three Oaks Grill in Germantown before getting his own restaurant, excels with fish and seafood dishes. Try the mussels in Thai curry sauce, the shrimp cooked with lemongrass and served with mango-chili sauce, or the fresh tuna with marinated cucumber salad and wasabi vinaigrette. Dress is casual, the crowd is hip, and there's a full bar, wine list, and daily food and drink specials. Dinner only, closed Sun. & (Midtown/Central)

EAST MEMPHIS

AUBERGINE
5007 Black
Memphis
901/767-7840
$$$
French-born chef Gene Bjorklund presides over his elegant, contemporary restaurant in East Memphis. Exquisite salads and inventive desserts, sometimes adorned with such fanciful garnishes as sugared pink rose petals, appeal to the eye as well as the appetite. Lamb, veal sweetbreads, and fresh fish are among the many entrées offered at Aubergine. It's located northeast of the Poplar and Mendenhall intersection, behind Houston's restaurant—look for the eggplant-colored awning. Lunch weekdays, dinner Tue-Sat. & (East Memphis)

BLUE PLATE CAFÉ
5469 Poplar Ave.
Memphis
901/761-9696
$
Home-style breakfasts of biscuits, sausage, gravy, and eggs, and hearty

plate-lunch dinners of meat loaf, mashed potatoes, and cooked vegetables dominate the fare at this cheerful, yellow diner. Breakfast, lunch, and dinner daily, except Sun dinner. & (East Memphis)

BRAVO! RISTORANTE
939 Ridge Lake Blvd.
Memphis
901/684-6664
$$
Arias from Verdi and Puccini, and show tunes by everyone from Stephen Sondheim to George Gershwin are belted out by the singing waiters at Bravo! Ristorante. The cuisine is an above-average assemblage of American and Italian favorites, but the musical skill of the singing waiters and waitresses is excellent. And the atmosphere is anything but ordinary. Blue and white clouds painted on the arched, overhead ceilings reflect the soft lighting in the dining room, and some of the tables look out over pretty landscaped gardens and a placid pond. The restaurant is tucked beyond a staircase at the lower level of the towering Adam's Mark Hotel. Breakfast, lunch, and dinner. & (East Memphis)

BUNTYN
Park Ave. at Mt. Moriah Rd.
Memphis
901/458-8776
$
Homemade yeast rolls to die for, warm banana pudding that would make Elvis moan from the grave, and plate lunches of such Southern comfort foods as fried catfish, meat loaf, macaroni and cheese, and seasoned greens, have for years been attracting construction workers, little old ladies, white-collar workers, and even the city's celebrity elite to this genuine,

EAST MEMPHIS

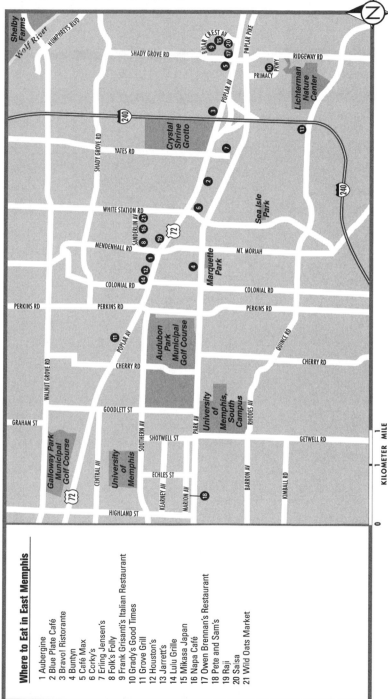

Where to Eat in East Memphis

1 Aubergine
2 Blue Plate Café
3 Bravo! Ristorante
4 Buntyn
5 Café Max
6 Corky's
7 Erling Jensen's
8 Folk's Folly
9 Frank Grisanti's Italian Restaurant
10 Grady's Good Times
11 Grove Grill
12 Houston's
13 Jarrett's
14 Lulu Grille
15 Mikasa Japan
16 Napa Café
17 Owen Brennan's Restaurant
18 Pete and Sam's
19 Raji
20 Salsa
21 Wild Oats Market

old-time diner. Lunch and dinner, closed weekends; no credit cards or reservations. ♿ (East Memphis)

CAFÉ MAX
6161 Poplar Ave.
Memphis
901/767-3633
$$
Fresh seafood, including shrimp and crab delicacies, are cooked in an open kitchen at Café Max. It's a popular place for cocktails and dinner. Dinner daily; no reservations. ♿ (East Memphis)

CORKY'S
5259 Poplar Ave.
Memphis
901/685-9744
$
Dan Quayle, assorted Miss Americas, and a host of other celebrities have all made the obligatory pilgrimage to the city's most popular pork parlor. You'll have ample time to ogle the framed, 8-by-10 photos that line the lobby area, where hour-long waits to get inside are common. What's the attraction? Slow-cooked pork pulled from the bone in tender shreds, doused in tangy barbecue sauce, and piled on steamed buns with a mound of ice-cold coleslaw for garnish. The Memphis-based eatery, which has franchised its highly successful enterprise over the last few years, sells bottled barbecue sauces and ships its products worldwide. Corky's also has a drive-through window and recently opened a second location in Cordova. Lunch and dinner daily. ♿ (East Memphis)

ERLING JENSEN'S
1044 Yates Rd.
Memphis
901/763-3700
$$$

La Tourelle Restaurant, p. 69

Alan Howell/Memphis Business Journal

One of the newest restaurants in Memphis is also one of its best. Erling Jensen, a Danish-born chef who worked for many years at La Tourelle in midtown, opened this eponymous eatery in 1996 in a quiet neighborhood of East Memphis. Response to date has been overwhelming, with well-heeled diners flocking to this elegant restaurant for such delicacies as pecan-crusted grilled lamb and filet mignon topped with tender foie gras. Palate-cleansing sorbets come in a variety of stimulating flavors such as champagne, passion fruit, and mulberry. Service is very professional, and the atmosphere is pristine. Dinner nightly, except Sun; Sun brunch; reservations recommended. ♿ (East Memphis)

FOLK'S FOLLY
551 S. Mendenhall Rd.
Memphis
901/762-8200
$$$
Legend has it that Memphis contractor Humphrey Folk opened his own restaurant because he couldn't find a

good steak. People laughed, so he named the enterprise Folk's Folly. No one's laughing any more, unless it's happy hour at this traditional, elegantly furnished home that's been transformed into one of Memphis's best steak houses. The restaurant won the *Memphis Business Journal*'s Small Business of the Year award in 1998. Lobster, salmon, crab legs, and other seafood specialties are on the menu along with prime rib, T-bones, filets, and every cut of beef imaginable. The wine list is extensive, the piano bar serene. Dinner nightly; reservations recommended. ♿ (East Memphis)

FRANK GRISANTI'S ITALIAN RESTAURANT
Embassy Suites Hotel
1022 Shady Grove Rd.
Memphis
901/761-9462
$$

Italian spinach, sausage casserole, and delectable, thin-crust pizzas are some of the specialties offered at this Grisanti family eatery in the Embassy Suites Hotel. But almost anything ordered in this revered restaurant is likely to be outstanding. Dark, polished

wood, fine linen, and upholstered chairs in mauves and deep greens lend posh elegance to the dining room. Another option is to sit "outside," in the hotel's lushly landscaped, enclosed atrium. Cushioned chairs and umbrellas are positioned amidst the greenery. A gurgling stream, and pools with goldfish and ducks contribute to the atmosphere. Lunch and dinner daily. ♿ (East Memphis)

GRADY'S GOOD TIMES
6080 Primacy Pkwy.
Memphis
901/763-4663
$$

Plump, grilled chicken breasts served in a variety of ways are one of the many specialties at Grady's, a Tennessee-based chain that always seems to have a crowd. Brass railings, dark, polished woodwork, an abundance of greenery, and exposed brick interiors give the multilevel dining rooms a clubby, informal atmosphere. Appetizers such as garlic toast topped with melted cheese, and plentiful green salads are among Grady's more popular items. There's also a full bar. Lunch and dinner. ♿ (East Memphis)

TRIVIA

India-born chef Raji Jallepalli likes to dine out when she's not cooking at her namesake East Memphis restaurant. Her French and Indian fusion cuisine has attracted rave reviews in such lofty culinary journals as *Gourmet* and *Bon Appetit*, as well as in *Vanity Fair*, *Elle*, the *New York Times*, and other publications. Invitations to cook have taken her around the world, from the White House to European chateaux to the most noted restaurants of Paris and New York. Honored by the James Beard Foundation, she has also been a guest chef at the prestigious Masters of Food and Wine event in Carmel, California.

GROVE GRILL
4550 Poplar Ave.
Memphis
901/818-9951
$$

With its excellent location in the Laurelwood shopping center, adjacent to Ledbetter Lusk art gallery and fine apparel stores, the relatively new Grove Grill lures an upscale clientele. Grilled salmon entrées, fried oysters, cool gazpacho, and fruit sherbets ensconced in freshly baked cookie cups are best bets here. The restaurant is also earning a reputation for its array of extraordinary vegetable side dishes. & (East Memphis)

HOUSTON'S
5000 Poplar Ave.
Memphis
901/683-0915
$$

One of the most popular chain restaurants in town, Houston's draws huge crowds to its busy East Memphis restaurant. The atmosphere is festive and informal, and the service is friendly and attentive. Food specialties include fresh fish, prime rib, baby-back ribs, and delicious appetizers such as a hot artichoke dip. Houston's also serves excellent homemade soups and large salads. Lunch and dinner. & (East Memphis)

JARRETT'S
5689 Quince Rd.
Memphis
901/763-2264
$$

Chef Richard Farmer has a fiercely loyal customer base that has followed him to the various restaurants at which he's cooked over the years. Since he and his wife, Barbara (who runs the front of the house) opened Jarret's in the early 1990s, the restaurant has delighted diners with California- and French-influenced cuisine with Southern flourishes. Gulf crab cakes, lamb, and seafood entrées are among Farmer's specialties. Frequent, Monday-night wine and martini tastings are held at the East Memphis restaurant. Lunch and dinner, closed Sun; reservations recommended for groups of six or more. & (East Memphis)

LULU GRILLE
565 Erin Dr.
Memphis
901/763-3677
$$

Intimate and informal in atmosphere, but holding to high standards of service and food presentation, Lulu Grille is regarded by locals as a cozy neighborhood bistro. Wild game, hearty steaks, and pasta, poultry, and seafood options are on the menu, along with rich desserts including great chocolate cake. Lunch and dinner, closed Sun; reservations recommended for groups of five or more. & (East Memphis)

MIKASA JAPAN
6150 Poplar Ave.
Memphis
901/683-0000
$$

Sushi and other traditional Japanese dishes reign supreme at this unique East Memphis restaurant, where the dining experience is always an adventure. Guests may sit at the sushi bar or cook their own meals at a smokeless grill table. Spartan decor, including bamboo screens and tasteful Oriental touches, lends atmosphere to Mikasa. Lunch and dinner, closed for lunch weekends; reservations recommended. & (East Memphis)

NAPA CAFÉ
5101 Sanderlin Ave.
Memphis
901/683-0441
$$

Napa Café is operated by the same gastronomically savvy proprietors of Paulette's and Three Oaks Grill, two of Memphis's best and most beloved restaurants. If walnut-Dijon chicken salad, barbecued catfish, and shrimp wrapped with basil and pancetta tempt your appetite, and if desserts along the lines of praline pecan ice cream pie or chocolate Kahlua crème brûlée make your mouth water, you'll want to check out the Napa Café. As the name implies, there's a commendable wine list. Lunch and dinner. ⅙ (East Memphis)

OWEN BRENNAN'S RESTAURANT
6150 Poplar Ave.
Memphis
901/761-0990
$$

Perhaps best known for its festive Sunday brunch that features champagne, Cajun and Creole food, and live jazz, Owen Brennan's is also a popular happy-hour destination and special-occasion restaurant. Gumbo, turtle soup, fresh seafood, chicken, and pasta dishes all can be found on the menu, along with such definitive desserts as woozy bread pudding and flaming bananas Foster. Lunch and dinner, closed for dinner Sun; no reservations. ⅙ (East Memphis)

PETE AND SAM'S
3886 Park Ave.
Memphis
901/458-0694
$

If you don't mind feeling like one of the family—a very large, extended family, at that—step into this homey Italian eatery that recalls the restaurants of days gone by. This rather plain, decades-old Memphis establishment serves huge portions of such traditional Italian dishes as spaghetti and meatballs and meaty ravioli. Side dishes include cooked spinach and simple green salads. Dinner; reservations recommended weekends. (East Memphis)

RAJI
712 W. Brookhaven Circle
Memphis
901/685-8723
$$$

Raji's warm, chocolate crème brûlée is heavenly; the wine list, exclusively French; the wait service, second to none in the city. But the main attraction at this quiet, beautifully appointed restaurant is its personable and talented chef/owner herself. Raji Jallepalli is an internationally acclaimed, award-winning chef who has built her reputation on fusion cooking. Traditional French techniques and interesting Indian spices flavor her inventive, exotic dishes such as tandoori quail salad and spice-crusted tuna with sesame-turmeric sauce. What's more, Raji's artistic culinary presentations are as pleasing and elaborate as the cuisine is delectable. Dinner, closed Sun–Mon; reservations recommended. ⅙ (East Memphis)

SALSA
6150 Poplar Ave.
Memphis
901/683-6325
$

Salsa is arguably the best, and definitely the most upscale Mexican restaurant in Memphis. The restaurant's chips and salsa, along with everything else on the menu, are made daily from scratch. The margaritas

Four-Course Serving Suggestion: Memphis Music Menu

"Funky Chicken," by Rufus Thomas
"Green Onions," by Booker T. and the MGs
"Poke Salad Annie," by Elvis Presley
And for dessert . . . a big ol' *"Hunka Hunka Burnin' Love"*

complement such specialty items as *carnitas*, fajitas, and enchilada platters accompanied by rice and beans. Stuffed breast of chicken with cheese and *poblano* peppers, and fresh grilled snapper flavored with lime and cilantro are also terrific. Lunch and dinner, closed Sun. Reservations recommended for groups of six or more. & (East Memphis)

WILD OATS MARKET
5022 Sanderlin Rd.
Memphis
901/685-2293
www.shopwildoats.com
$
Fresh tabouli salads, pasta dishes, vegetarian lasagna, and hearty cheese sandwiches with thick Muenster, provolone, alfalfa sprouts, cucumbers, sliced tomatoes, and shaved carrots are among the myriad of options available. Sushi is sliced and arranged while you watch. Herbal teas, exotic coffees, and fruit ices and yogurt shakes are refreshing year-round. The midtown location also features occasional acoustic music in its pleasant dining room, filled with abstract art and lush tropical plants. Also at 1801 Union Avenue, 901/725-4823. Lunch and dinner. & (East Memphis)

BARTLETT, CORDOVA, GERMANTOWN

BOLLA PASTA
2200 Germantown Pkwy.
Cordova
901/384-7988
$
From the esteemed Grisanti family comes this casual Italian restaurant, where a respectable variety of pastas and sauces may be ordered in endless combinations. Sweet Italian sausage, pepperoni, and other tasty Italian staples top the nine-inch appetizer pizzas, built on delicious cracker-crisp crusts. Large salads come topped with a bracing vinaigrette and pungent Gorgonzola and are garnished with marinated peppers. The jumbo beef ravioli are tender, toothsome, and slathered in a thick and meaty tomato sauce, and dusted with snipped parsley and grated Parmesan. The popular restaurant also offers a nice selection of wine. & (Bartlett, Cordova, Germantown)

BOSCO'S PIZZA KITCHEN AND BREWERY
Saddle Creek Shopping Center
7615 W. Farmington Blvd.
Germantown

901/756-7310
$$

With 16 selections of gourmet pizzas baked in a wood-fired oven, as well as pasta, salads, and grill specials, Bosco's has a lot going for it. The sophisticated Germantown bistro also offers a wide variety of freshly brewed beers. Kick back, relax, and admire the vast copper cauldrons as diners and late-night revelers come and go at this trendy nightspot. Lunch and dinner; no reservations. ৬ (Bartlett, Cordova, Germantown)

COZYMEL'S
6450 Poplar Ave.
Memphis

901/763-1202
$$

For diners who want to experience the flavor as well as the atmosphere of a Mexican shack on the Yucatán, kitschy Cozymel's is your place. Mariachi music is piped into the noisy, riotously colorful restaurant, where twinkling lights and chicken wire are draped over the entryway. Inside, burlap sacks and mountains of produce—green peppers, yellow lemons, red tomatoes—double as decor. Entrées are huge, with enchiladas, fajitas, and other traditional dishes buried beneath mounds of creamy black beans and rice, and dusted with freshly chopped cilantro and perhaps

Tennessee Turnip Greens

2 bunches (about 3 pounds) of fresh turnip greens
6–8 cups of water
2 large pork neck bones
Crystal hot sauce for seasoning

Wash greens thoroughly by tearing off stems, rinsing and submerging each leaf under clean, cold water. Rinse, drain, and rinse again. Pat dry with paper towels and set aside.

Bring the water to a boil in a deep pot over high heat. Add the neck bones and bring back to a full boil. Turn heat down to medium-low and simmer for about an hour, or until the water has been reduced to about a cup. The broth that remains is the delicious pot liquor, or "pot licker." Add the rinsed greens to this rich broth, bring to a full boil, then reduce the heat to low. Cover and cook for an hour, or until the greens are tender but still bright.

Serve with a splash of spicy Crystal hot sauce. The greens go great with fried chicken or catfish, mashed potatoes, and crisp cornbread.

BARTLETT/CORDOVA/GERMANTOWN

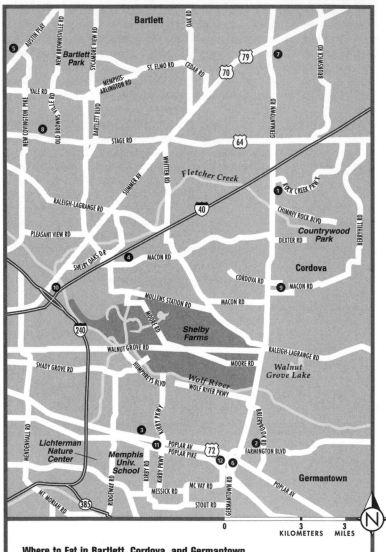

Where to Eat in Bartlett, Cordova, and Germantown

1 Bolla Pasta
2 Bosco's Pizza Kitchen and Brewery
3 Cozymel's
4 Delhi Palace
5 Germantown Commissary
6 Gridley's
7 J. Alexander's
8 Jasmine Chinese and Thai Restaurant
9 Outback Steakhouse
10 Pappy and Jimmie's
11 Romano's Macaroni Grill
12 Three Oaks Grill

a sprinkling of lime juice. Festive and almost infectiously fun, Cozymel's invites diners to order their margaritas by color—they swirl in a margarita flotilla at the front entrance. Lunch and dinner. & (Bartlett, Cordova, Germantown)

DELHI PALACE
6110 Macon Rd.
Memphis
901/386-3600
$$
Northern Indian cuisine is the focus of this consistent, informal restaurant located in a busy shopping center in the northeastern suburbs of Memphis. Creamy lentil *dhal*, vegetable curries, and tandoori chicken, along with yogurt, mint, and cucumber garnishes, are part of the popular lunchtime buffet. The tasty nan is served in pliable, slightly puffed rounds, warm from the oven. Lunch and dinner; reservations recommended. & (Bartlett, Cordova, Germantown)

GERMANTOWN COMMISSARY
2290 S. Germantown Rd.
Germantown
901/754-5540
$
One of ritzy Germantown's more humble and unpretentious restaurants is this popular barbecue spot. The rustic, nostalgic general store specializes in simple pork-shoulder barbecue with all the trimmings. Lunch and dinner; no

reservations. & (Bartlett, Cordova, Germantown)

GRIDLEY'S
3624 Austin Peay Hwy.
Memphis
901/388-7444
$
One of the oldest barbecue establishments in Memphis, Gridley's offers the same kind of shredded-pork sandwiches served elsewhere in the city—juicy meat slathered in smoky barbecue sauce, plopped on a bun, and topped with creamy coleslaw. Diners who aren't as pork crazy as the rest of Memphis seems to be should consider the barbecued chicken—moist, white meat roasted and basted in a delicious, tangy barbecue sauce. Icebox lemon pie is Gridley's signature dessert. Also at 6430 Winchester Rd., 901/794-5997. Lunch and dinner. & (Bartlett, Cordova, Germantown)

J. ALEXANDER'S
2670 N. Germantown Pkwy.
Memphis
901/381-9670
$$$
The potent Maytag blue-cheese coleslaw may be your first indication that J. Alexander's is not your typical suburban mall-area restaurant. Resembling a Pacific Northwest lodge, the spacious stone-and-timber establishment stands out amid the southern

The Viking Culinary Arts Center recently opened in Pembroke Square. The cooking school, located at 119 South Main in downtown's Peabody Place development, offers culinary demonstrations and instruction for all skill levels. Viking stoves and other kitchen appliances are used, of course. For details call 901/578-5822.

A Meal Fit for the King

For a hilarious and irreverent look at the life of Elvis Presley—as viewed through the food he ate—check out David Adler's The Life and Cuisine of Elvis Presley *(Crown Trade Paperbacks, 1993). The author calls the King's food his "first and most lasting love." Chock-full of finger-lickin' photos and gut-busting recipes, from the buttermilk and cornbread "soaks" on which baby Elvis was weaned, to the infamous "Fool's Gold Loaf," which contained a jar each of peanut butter and grape jelly, and a pound of burnt bacon, this book's got it all. (Helpful hint: Don't look for the chartreuse, softcover tome on your next pilgrimage to Graceland. It's not among the titles to be found in the souvenir shops run by the discriminating Presley estate.)*

urban sprawl around the Wolfchase Galleria mall. The Nashville-based chain has become hugely popular since opening in Memphis a few years ago. It's easy to taste why: Try the hardwood-grilled cilantro black-tiger shrimp or the eight-ounce prime rib sandwich, served on a toasted sourdough roll. For southwestern kick, you can't beat the spicy Rattlesnake Pasta, which blends linguine with peppers in a cream sauce. Desserts are kept to a powerful few: Snicker's ice cream pie in an Oreo-cookie crust, chocolate cake served with vanilla ice cream and hot fudge, and carrot cake with cream cheese icing. (Bartlett, Cordova, Germantown)

JASMINE CHINESE AND THAI RESTAURANT
3024 Covington Pike, Suite 6
Memphis
901/386-2974
$

Chinese and Thai specialties such as almond chicken and green-pepper beef are popular at this restaurant in the Raleigh-Bartlett area. Lunch and dinner, closed Mon; reservations recommended weekends. & (Bartlett, Cordova, Germantown)

OUTBACK STEAKHOUSE
1136 N. Germantown Pkwy.
Cordova
901/751-9800
$$

This steakhouse chain with the Australian "outback" theme has become one of the area's most popular destinations for beef-lovers. Appetizers such as the deep-fried "blooming" onions go great with the nightly drink specials and beer selections. Crisp iceberg-lettuce salads, and grilled seafood and chicken specialties all arrive in huge portions with warm loaves of bread. Also at 5956 Winchester Road, 901/365-3444. Dinner;

no reservations. & (Bartlett, Cordova, Germantown)

PAPPY AND JIMMIE'S
5225 Summer Ave.
Memphis
901/763-3946
$$

The neon, lobster-head sign that illuminates this long-standing seafood restaurant is your first clue that this place has personality. Lobster and other fresh seafood, served in enormous portions, are featured along with steaks, prime rib, and other entrées. Lunch and dinner; no reservations. & (Bartlett, Cordova, Germantown)

ROMANO'S MACARONI GRILL
6705 Poplar Ave.
Germantown
901/753-6588
$$

Italian specialties such as soups, pasta dishes, and fresh breads are prepared from an open kitchen in this roomy, whitewashed restaurant. Desserts such as tiramisu are baked fresh daily. Lunch and dinner; no reservations. & (Bartlett, Cordova, Germantown)

THREE OAKS GRILL
2285 S. Germantown Rd.
Germantown
901/757-8225
$$

Crackling fireplaces, stone-tile floors, and paintings and antiques give the Three Oaks Grill a cozy, Northern California ambiance. The restaurant is owned and operated by the proprietors of Paulette's, one of midtown's best and most established restaurants, and offers a similar menu. Juicy steaks, delicate pastries, salmon, lamb, and duck are among the varied entrées. Superior service and soothing, classical music make this restaurant an endearing favorite. Lunch and dinner. & (Bartlett, Cordova, Germantown)

SOUTH MEMPHIS

BOMBAY CAFÉ
3700 Ridgeway Rd.

Corky's, p. 74

Memphis Convention and Visitors Bureau

SOUTH MEMPHIS

WALNUT GROVE RD

Wolf River

Shelby Farms Recreation Area

Germantown

FOREST HILL-IRENE RD

Forest Hill

Olive Branch Municipal Airport

HACKS CROSS RD

Nonconnah Creek

72

GERMANTOWN RD

HICKORY HILL RD

Mineral Wells

30

OLD US HIGHWAY 78

LAMAR AV

Olive Branch

Nolehoe Creek

Camp Creek

240

Fox Meadows Park

WINCHESTER RD

38

MT. MORIAH RD

MENDENHALL RD

Jones Creek

AMERICAN WAY

PERKINS RD

78

PLEASANT HILL RD

Capleville

Johns Creek

GOODLETT RD

GETWELL RD

Plum Point

POPLAR AV

PARK AV

Nonconnah Creek

McKellar Park

TCHULAHOMA RD

GOODMAN RD

LAMAR AV

Memphis International Airport

Days Creek

7

Cane Creek

SOUTH PKWY

240

4

AIRWAYS BLVD

E.H. CRUMP BLVD

3

240

MALLORY AV

5

ELVIS PRESLEY BLVD

6

BROOKS RD

SHELBY DR

HOLMES RD

51

Horn Lake Creek

LAKE RD

30

55

55

MITCHELL RD

61

Harbor Canal

Cypress Creek

WEAVER RD

30

Lynchburg

5   MILES

5   KILOMETERS

0

Where to Eat in South Memphis

1 Bombay Café
2 D'Bo's Buffalo Wings
3 Ellen's Soul Food Restaurant
4 Fred Gang's
5 Interstate Bar-B-Que
6 Marlowe's Ribs and Restaurant
7 Mel's Fish Market
8 White Church Tea Room

Memphis
901/368-1002
$

Crispy, deep-fried *samosas* (hand-wrapped fried puffs filled with potatoes and peas), *bhel puri* (puffed rice topped with dates, cilantro, and garlic chutney), meat, and other traditional Indian dishes are served at this inexpensive restaurant. Neat and immaculate, it's tucked between a huge home-improvement store and a pet-supply store in a corner of a busy shopping center in southeast Shelby County. Lunch and dinner; no reservations. & (South Memphis)

D'BO'S BUFFALO WINGS
3279 Kirby Pkwy.
Memphis
901/363-8700
$

One bite of these mouthwatering, spicy chicken wings and you'll be hooked. D'Bo's started out as a concession stand that its owner parked alongside one of the city's main thoroughfares. The crispy, deep-fried poultry drums and tips, accompanied by thick blue cheese or ranch dip

with celery and carrots, attracted such regular crowds that the proprietor was able to open a storefront. Today there's a second D'Bo's in South Memphis at 4407 Elvis Presley Blvd. Lunch and dinner. & (South Memphis)

ELLEN'S SOUL FOOD
RESTAURANT
601 S. Parkway East
Memphis
901/942-4888
$

There's nothing fancy about Ellen's. That's why the regulars love it. Ellen's serves up good, Southern soul food like fried chicken, mashed potatoes, and greens, in a storefront restaurant that recalls diners of days gone by. Lunch and dinner; closed Mon. & (South Memphis)

FRED GANG'S
2872 Airways Blvd.
Memphis
901/345-3693
$$

Prime rib, filets, and fresh seafood selections are the focus of the menu at Fred Gang's Restaurant, which draws diners to the airport area for its broad selection of food and its friendly atmosphere. Sandwiches, soups, and other American fare round out the offerings. Lunch weekdays, dinner seven days a week. & (South Memphis)

INTERSTATE BAR-B-QUE
2265 S. Third St.
Memphis
901/775-2304
$

One of the few local restaurants to receive the prestigious *Memphis Business Journal* Small Business Award (in 1995), this South Memphis barbecue joint consistently rates among residents' all-time favorites. Juicy, shredded-pork sandwiches and toothsome barbecued ribs, as well as tangy, chopped-beef barbecue, barbecued spaghetti, sausage, and even fried bologna are on the menu. Desserts include pecan pie and "sock-it-to-me cake." Lunch and dinner daily. & (South Memphis)

MARLOWE'S RIBS AND RESTAURANT
4381 Elvis Presley Blvd.
Memphis
901/332-4159
$$

A mile up the street from Graceland, Marlowe's serves up some of the best steaks, ribs, and chicken in South Memphis. Entertainment is featured on weekends, and delivery service is available to area hotels. Marlowe's also functions as a late-night hangout—it doesn't close until three in the morning. Lunch and dinner. & (South Memphis)

MEL'S FISH MARKET
1796 Lamar Ave.
Memphis
901/274-6523
$

Fried catfish is the specialty of the house at this down-home, southern-style fish market. 12–10 daily. & (South Memphis)

WHITE CHURCH TEA ROOM
196 N. Main St.
Collierville
901/854-6433
$$

Bring your own wine to this charming little restaurant nestled inside an antique-filled church in Collierville's old-time town square. Fine teas and classic French quiches and crepes are items on the light menu. Classical music is performed on Saturday nights. Lunch Mon–Sat, dinner Fri–Sat. & (South Memphis)

5

SIGHTS AND ATTRACTIONS

Any tour of the sights and sounds of Memphis is best begun along the banks of the picturesque Mississippi River. Start at the new Memphis Welcome Center, where you can pay your respects to a couple of musical heavyweights—larger-than-life bronze statues of Elvis Presley and B. B. King— and pick up brochures and maps that will help you navigate your way across downtown and toward the eastern suburbs.

Stroll Confederate Park, with its interesting historic markers and sprawling, ancient trees, and then walk across the rough cobblestones at the mouth of the river, where countless bales of cotton have been unloaded over the years. It's possible to continue walking south along the riverfront all the way through Tom Lee Park, a newly improved recreation area with paved trails, freshly planted trees, and park benches overlooking the water. The same stunning view is accessible by car from Riverside Drive.

Day or night, plan to spend at least several hours on legendary Beale Street, with its wide assortment of clubs, souvenir shops, museums, and historic architecture. The visitors center at the eastern end of the brick-lined road is a tourist headquarters, where travelers can get answers to questions and pick up hundreds of brochures and maps. Downtown's other primary attractions are the National Civil Rights Museum and the Pyramid. Sun Studio lies within a mile or so of the downtown business district, but walking to the area is not advisable. Just northeast of the downtown area is the quaint, antebellum neighborhood known as Victorian Village.

South Memphis is where you'll find Elvis Presley's mansion, Graceland, arguably the city's top tourist attraction. Dozens of other sites are scattered throughout metropolitan Memphis, from the centrally located midtown area to such densely populated and commercially developed suburbs as East Memphis, Hickory Hill, Germantown, and Cordova.

DOWNTOWN MEMPHIS

AUCTION SQUARE
N. Main St. at Auction Ave.
Memphis
Now a small park on North Main Street, this is the site of Memphis's first food market. The fenced-in granite marker supposedly commemorates the auction block where slaves were bought and sold prior to the Civil War. (Downtown)

BEALE STREET BAPTIST CHURCH
379 Beale St.
Memphis
901/527-4832
This weathered, white church near the edge of the Beale Street Historic District was the first church in the city built for an African American congregation. On a trivial note, the church, with its towering cross and statues, also has an interesting history. Once, in the 1880s, the tall cross was blown into the church sanctuary during a strong windstorm. And, in 1938, the statue of John the Baptist that topped the church's east tower

Memphis Welcome Center, p. 87

Tennessee Photographic Services

was struck by lightning. The blast reportedly decapitated John's head, which then rolled across Beale Street. (Downtown)

BEALE STREET
HISTORIC DISTRICT
Beale St. between Second
and Fourth Sts.
Memphis
901/526-0110
The Beale Street Historic District is known as the home of the blues because it was here, shortly after the turn of the century, that bandleader W. C. Handy wrote and published the first blues song. In the early 1900s the street was an economic center for the black community, and bustled with blues and jazz. Today the street is lined with historic stores such as A. Schwab Dry Goods, the unusual Beale Street Police Substation and Museum, and many restaurants, nightclubs, and souvenir shops. (Downtown)

BURKLE ESTATE/SLAVEHAVEN
826 N. Second St.
Memphis
901/527-3427
A German immigrant named Jacob Burkle is said to have harbored runaway slaves in this home north of downtown Memphis. Haunting photographs such as one of a slave's whipped and welted bare back, along with such poignant artifacts as shackles and receipts for the sale of human beings, are among the items on display. The most moving part of any tour of this recently discovered historic treasure, however, is in the cellar. Slaves seeking freedom on the Underground Railroad hid for days in this tiny room connected to the nearby river by dirt tunnels. Open by appointment only. Tour prices vary; call for details. (Downtown)

DOWNTOWN MEMPHIS

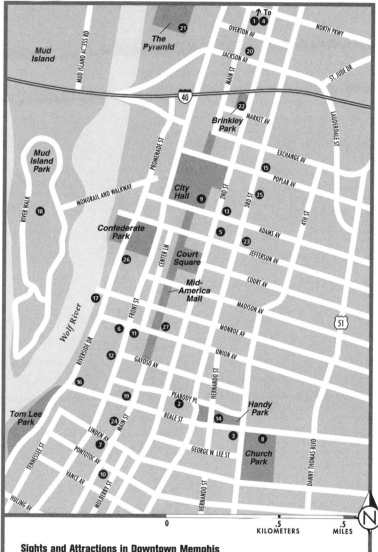

Sights and Attractions in Downtown Memphis

1 Auction Square
2 Beale Street Baptist Church
3 Beale Street Historic District
4 Burkle Estate/Slavehaven
5 Calvary Episcopal Church
6 Carter Seed Store
7 Chisca Hotel Building
8 Church Park
9 Civic Plaza
10 Clayborn Temple AME Church
11 Cotton Exchange Building
12 Cotton Row
13 County Courthouse
14 Daisy Theatre
15 First Presbyterian Church
16 Gibson Guitar Corp.
17 Memphis Queen Riverboats
18 Mud Island River Park
19 Orpheum Theatre
20 Pinch District
21 The Pyramid
22 St. Mary's Cathedral and Grotto of Lourdes and Meditation Church
23 St. Peter's Catholic Church
24 South Main Historic District
25 Trinity Lutheran Church
26 U.S. Post Office
27 WDIA Radio

Ida B. Wells was a woman ahead of her time. In the late 1800s, as an associate editor of the *Memphis Free Speech*, she crusaded against the lynchings of three black businessmen. Wells's newspaper office on Beale Street was subsequently burned down, and her enemies vowed that if she ever dared return to Memphis, she herself would be lynched. Wells moved to Chicago in 1892, where she continued her work as a Civil Rights pioneer and helped to found such organizations as the NAACP.

CALVARY EPISCOPAL CHURCH
102 N. Second St.
Memphis
901/525-6602
Founded in 1832, this church is the city's oldest continuously used public building. The present church was built in 1844, and a tower was added in 1848. Among other treasures of the parish are the Flemish stained-glass windows, the custom-carved marble altar, and the organ built in 1935 by G. Donald Harrison of the Aeolian-Skinner Organ Co. (Downtown)

CARTER SEED STORE
85 S. Front St.
Memphis
901/527-8856
Today you can get a hot ham biscuit, eggs, and coffee at the adjoining, homespun storefront within view of the Mississippi River, and there's a *New York Times* rack out on the corner. But in the old days, Carter Seed Store was the place where farmers brought their produce to market in Memphis. True to its name, Carter's still sells seeds in addition to antique knickknacks and old-fashioned candies. (Downtown)

CHISCA HOTEL BUILDING
Main St. and Linden
Memphis
The Church of God in Christ now has its world headquarters here, but this building, the Chisca Hotel, was once the site of WHBQ Radio. Disc jockey Dewey Phillips and the *Red Hot and Blues* show first aired Elvis's record *That's All Right Mama* and the flip side, *Blue Moon of Kentucky*, on July 10, 1954. Elvis was brought to the station for an interview, but was so shy they had to trick him into talking by telling him the microphone was off. (Downtown)

CHURCH PARK
Fourth and Beale St.
Memphis
Robert Church, a former slave who became Memphis's first African American millionaire, gave this park to the African American citizens of the city. The site once included a 2,000-seat auditorium. Built in 1899, the civic and entertainment hall attracted such diverse and distinguished guests as W. C. Handy, Booker T. Washington, and President Theodore Roosevelt, who spoke there in 1902. (Downtown)

CIVIC PLAZA
Adams Ave. to Poplar Ave., and

Front St. to Second St.
Memphis
A central stop on the Main Street Trolley line, this spacious government plaza features a striking, 60-foot water fountain and open areas where ethnic festivals such as Africa in April and Oktoberfest are held. The mayors of both Memphis and Shelby County have their offices here.

Bill and Hillary Clinton and Al and Tipper Gore drew a crowd of about 10,000 supporters and impromptu "macarena" dancers to the plaza in the final months of the 1996 presidential reelection campaign. Amy Carter, daughter of former president Jimmy Carter, staged a one-woman demonstration on the same plaza in 1991—when George Bush was president. Then a student at Memphis College of Art, she draped herself in a black body bag and sat motionless in defiance of Desert Storm. (Downtown)

CLAYBORN TEMPLE
AME CHURCH
294 Hernando
Memphis

901/527-7283
Originally dedicated in 1893 as the Second Presbyterian Church, historic Clayborn Temple became an African Methodist Episcopal Church in 1949. Dr. Martin Luther King Jr. led peaceful demonstration marches to and from this downtown church. In 1996 the congregation and its new pastor began an ambitious social outreach program to feed, clothe, house, and counsel the homeless. A vital component of that ministry is the rousing worship service held here on Saturday and Sunday. The public is welcome to step inside and view the gracefully aging sanctuary. (Downtown)

COTTON EXCHANGE BUILDING
84 S. Front St.
Memphis
A bronze plaque honoring best-selling author John Grisham may be the most immediately recognizable characteristic of this beautifully restored historic structure and modern-day office building. Originally organized in 1874, the Memphis Cotton Exchange was the center of the cotton

Sam & Dave and Isaac & David

Sam Moore and Dave Prater, better known as Sam & Dave, had a slew of soul hits at Memphis's Stax Records beginning in the late 1960s. Such sing-alongs as "Soul Man," "Hold On I'm Coming," "Thank You," and "When Something Is Wrong with My Baby" were written by the legendary Stax team of two stalwart Memphis residents, David Porter and Isaac Hayes. "Stax," by the way, is derived from the last names of Estelle Axton and Jim Stewart, the brother-and-sister duo that founded the now-demolished South Memphis studio.

Robert Gordon's Memphis Primer

Gordon is a music critic, filmmaker, and author of the book It Came From Memphis *(Faber & Faber, 1994). He was also nominated for a Grammy in 1998 for his liner notes on an Al Green CD package that* Rolling Stone *honored with a five-star review. Currently, he's at work on a biography of Muddy Waters.*

- **It Came from Memphis**: My book and companion CD lay out an approach to the city's present and past that the Chamber of Commerce will never tell you about.
- **Mud Boy and the Neutrons**: This Memphis supergroup is the missing link between Delta blues and the Rolling Stones. Their recordings are rare, but a recent compilation, *They Walk Among Us*, is more readily available. Also look for solo projects from the core members: albums by Jim Dickinson, Sid Selvidge, and Lee Baker's Agitators; and Jimmy Crosthwait's puppet shows at the Pink Palace Museum.
- **O'Landa Draper and the Associates**: The late charismatic leader of this large choir was the one who finally brought gospel music to the mainstream. *All the Bases* and *Live: A Celebration of Praise* are two excellent CDs.
- **Alex Chilton**: This Memphian was a pop celebrity at the age of 16,

---

trade. This particular building, with its classical arches and Gothic architectural features, was built between 1924 and 1925. (Downtown)

COTTON ROW
Front St. from Gayoso
to just north of Monroe Ave.
Memphis
Since the 1850s, the Memphis area has been the center of the cotton-trading industry. Even though the cotton warehouses along Front Street have been placed on the National Register of Historic Places, the cotton industry has not been put out to pasture. Memphis is still the leading cotton-trading market in the world. (Downtown)

COUNTY COURTHOUSE
N. Adams between Second
and Third Sts.
Memphis

when he fronted the Box Tops and their number-one hit, "The Letter." After that, he led the power pop group Big Star, which has become one of the primary influences for both alternative rock and no-depression country. His brilliantly chaotic album, *Like Flies on Sherbet*, anticipated cow-punk, and his soulful, more recent albums package all these influences into something suave and accessible.

- **The Panther Burns (and various descendants)**: Inspired by Memphis greats like rockabilly's Charlie Feathers and blues diva Jesse Mae Hemphill, photographer Tav Falco (who died in 1997) adopted punk's DIY approach to these roots sounds. He, in turn, inspired other groups, which continue to dot the Memphis scene: The Hellcats, Lorette Velvette, the Chiselers, the Young Seniors, and many more.
- **William Eggleston's *Ancient and Modern***: This collection of the pioneering color photographer's works makes the everyday wonder of the South plain for all to see.
- **Stanley Booth's *Rhythm Oil***: In this compilation of the elegant southern writer's essays, Stanley Booth ties together B. B. King, the BarKays, Phineas Newborn Jr., and Gram Parsons.
- **Fat Possum CDs**: This Oxford, Mississippi, label is releasing blues albums that sound like the music in the juke joints. Look for the gritty greats from R. L. Burnside, the late Junior Kimbrough, and CeDell Davis.

This sprawling, stately courthouse is regarded as one of the finest examples of neoclassical revival architecture in the United States. (Downtown)

DAISY THEATRE
329 Beale St.
Memphis
901/527-6008
Sam Zerilla, who in 1909 built the Pastime Theatre, the first Memphis movie house for African Americans, also built the Daisy Theatre. The theater now houses blues memorabilia. (Downtown)

FIRST PRESBYTERIAN CHURCH
166 Poplar Ave.
Memphis
This church's present site at the corner of Third and Poplar was deeded by the city in 1832, but the congregation wasn't organized until 1928. First the Civil War, then the yellow

Howlin' Wolf (Chester Arthur Burnett) was born in Mississippi and discovered in Memphis by a talent scout named Ike Turner (Tina Turner grew up in nearby Nutbush, not far from Memphis). Sam Phillips recorded Howlin' Wolf at Sun Studio before the singer moved north to help transform the Chicago blues scene.

fever epidemics interrupted the early years of the church. The church burned and was rebuilt in 1884. (Downtown)

GIBSON GUITAR CORPORATION
Off Beale St.
Memphis
Nashville-based Gibson Guitar is nearing completion of its long-awaited, 75,000-square-foot manufacturing facility one block south of Beale Street. Tours of the $11.2 million plant, where the company plans to make its ES-series guitars (like B. B. King's "Lucille" model), will be offered to the public by mid-1999. A family-oriented Gibson Café and Gallery will include an outdoor performance stage and serve as a prototype for a national chain of Gibson-themed cafés. It's been designed to give tourists an alternative to other Beale Street clubs that serve alcohol. In May of 2000, Gibson also plans to debut a traveling exhibition on Memphis music, *Smithsonian Rock & Soul*, which the Smithsonian Institute in Washington, D.C., has been working on since the early 1990s. (Downtown)

MEMPHIS QUEEN RIVERBOATS
45 Riverside Dr.
Memphis
901/527-5694 or 800/221-6197
www.memphisqueen.com

One of the most definitive Memphis experiences may be enjoyed aboard the *Memphis Queen* riverboats, which operate from March through December, weather permitting. The gracious boats invoke images of bygone days as they slowly glide up and down the Mississippi River for 90-minute sightseeing excursions. Gift shops and snack bars are on board.

The sloped, cobblestone landing along Riverside Drive is used as a parking lot for patrons about to board the paddle wheelers. A century ago, these cobblestones were used as ballast by boats coming up the river to pick up cargoes of cotton.

Dinner cruises May–Sept and weekends in Oct; moonlight music cruises weekends May–Sept; dockside brunch served Easter–early Sept Sun 11 –2. $11 adults for sightseeing cruises, $35 per person for dinner cruises. (Downtown)

MUD ISLAND RIVER PARK
125 N. Front St.
Memphis
901/576-7241 or 800/507-6507
www.mudisland.com
This 18-gallery Mississippi River museum shows river life through legends, models, and folklore. Free guided tours of the Mississippi River Walk, a five-block-long scale model of the river, are

available. The tour includes a stop at a pavilion devoted to the *Memphis Belle*. The plane was World War II's most famous B-17 bomber and was the first such plane to complete 25 missions against Nazi targets without a casualty. The bomber is named for the pilot's wartime Memphis sweetheart and was the subject of a 1943 film by William Wyler as well as a modern-day remake. Mud Island also has a swimming pool, beach, 5,000-seat outdoor concert amphitheater, gift shops, and restaurants. Open spring–late fall; call ahead for hours. $8 adults, $6 children 4–11, free for children 3 and under. (Downtown)

Memphis Convention and Visitors Bureau

Orpheum Theatre

ORPHEUM THEATRE
203 S. Main St.
Memphis
901/525-3000

The Orpheum Hopkins Grand Opera House was built on this site in 1889. It was bought by the Orpheum Vaudeville Theatre Circuit in 1908, but burned down in 1923 and was replaced by the present building in 1928. Performers such as John Philip Sousa and Burns and Allen have appeared here. (Downtown)

Gone but Not Forgotten

It's a lament worthy of the blues itself that the site where the late, great Stax record label once stood has been allowed to deteriorate into a vacant lot with only a vandalized historic marker as evidence of its past glory. The movie theater-turned-studio that churned out soul classics by Otis Redding, Sam & Dave, Booker T. and the MGs, Isaac Hayes, and Albert King was demolished in the late 1980s. Broken glass, discarded beer bottles, and other trash litter the gravelly, potholed lot. The Stax site sits in a crime-ridden area of South Memphis near College and McLemore, within the shadow of Al's Tasty Burger and a few hair salons. If the spirit moves you, swing by the place.

Keith Sykes

He may not be a household name, but one of Memphis's most successful songwriters is Keith Sykes. After rising to fame as a folk singer/songwriter with Jimmy Buffett, Sykes continues to reap royalties from his 135 songs that have been recorded by himself and others. The best-selling Buffet album Volcano *remains Sykes's biggest commercial success. The 1979 album has sold almost 9 million copies to date.*

Advanced Medication for the Blues, *released in the fall of 1998 on his own Syren Records, is Sykes's latest solo effort. In addition to that record label, Sykes owns and operates Woodshed recording studio in Memphis, as well as a production company and various publishing companies affiliated with both BMI and ASCAP.*

His publishing catalogs list his own songs and others, including titles by his friend, Todd Snider, another local singer/songwriter who has garnered national attention.

PINCH DISTRICT
N. Main St. between Jackson and Overton Park
Memphis
A turn-of-the-century neighborhood first settled by Irish immigrants and Jewish merchants, the Pinch district is now a late-night center for food and live entertainment. Antiques shops are also located in the area. (Downtown)

THE PYRAMID
1 Auction Ave.
Memphis
901/521-9675
The 32-story, stainless steel, 22,500-seat, multipurpose riverfront arena is a tribute to Memphis's Egyptian namesake. The Pyramid was built in 1991 at a cost of $65 million. Tours are available year-round at noon, 1, and 2. $4 adults, $3 seniors and ages 4 to 11. (Downtown)

ST. MARY'S CATHEDRAL AND GROTTO OF LOURDES AND MEDITATION GARDEN
115 Market St.
Memphis
901/522-9420
This Gothic Revival church with handmade brick exterior walls and limestone buttresses was established by German immigrants and dedicated in 1870. In 1860 the city's first Catholic mass was held in a little house on this street corner. In 1864 the present site was bought, and a two-story frame house already on the property was

Burkle Estate, p. 88

used as a temporary church, school, and parsonage. The marble altar in the church is a memorial to the Episcopalian sisters and priests who died in the 1878 yellow-fever epidemics. (Downtown)

ST. PETER'S CATHOLIC CHURCH
190 Adams Ave.
Memphis
In one of the more bizarre construction stories relating to historic architecture, this church, the oldest Roman Catholic Church in Memphis, was built around an already existing church. The original building was then dismantled and carried out in pieces. Dedicated in 1858, the present-day church features elements of Gothic design, striking octagonal towers, and stained glass dating from the early 1900s. (Downtown)

SOUTH MAIN HISTORIC DISTRICT
Main Street south of Beale St.
Memphis
Whether explored by horse-drawn carriage, trolley, car, or on foot, the South Main Historic District is an interesting place to visit. Historic structures, galleries, businesses, and apartments are helping to revitalize the area. (Downtown)

TRINITY LUTHERAN CHURCH
210 Washington Ave.
Memphis
Organized in 1855, this church is the

Notable Quote

Composer George Gerswhin, to W. C. Handy, Father of the Blues: "Your work is the grandfather of mine."

Have Heart

Because the Variety Children's Charities of Memphis in 1998 purchased the antebellum Lowenstein Mansion (Jefferson and Manassas in Victorian Village) for use as the headquarters of the Memphis-based International Children's Heart Foundation, the former mansion is now known as the Variety Heart House.

Founded in 1990 by Dr. William Novick, M.D., the ICHF provides lifesaving heart surgery for children of needy families around the world. When a full renovation of the main house and an 11-bedroom annex is completed, the facility will be able to provide accommodations for children and their families undergoing surgery at nearby Le Bonheur Children's Medical Center.

With both parents' and physicians' libraries, the Variety Heart House serves an educational role as well. The parents' library, one of the first of its kind, helps parents seeking in-depth, understandable information about congenital heart disease and pediatric cardiac surgery. It's a great resource for worried parents looking for answers.

Since 1994 the foundation has provided educational scholarships to more than 20 international doctors and nurses, allowing them to visit Le Bonheur for intensive training and study in pediatric cardiac surgery. The third floor of Variety Heart House accommodates these medical professionals. By eliminating the costs of apartment rentals for these doctors, a significant amount of money can be redirected to provide surgery for needy children.

In 1998 alone, Dr. Novick and his medical team made eight international trips to perform cardiac surgery on more than 100 children in Croatia, Nicaragua, Yugoslavia, Bosnia, Israel, and China. For more information contact the International Children's Heart Foundation at 901/527-3237 or www.babyhearts.com.

oldest Lutheran congregation in Memphis and one of the oldest in Tennessee. The interior retains its original character, and includes stained-glass windows imported from Dresden, Germany. The first floor of the present building was completed in 1874, and the sanctuary was finished in 1888. Each Christmas the church is filled to the rafters with faithful worshipers who attend a service sung and spoken entirely in German. (Downtown)

U.S. POST OFFICE
1 S. Front St.
Memphis
The Custom House portion of this building was built of white Tennessee marble, and was completed in 1885. Though largely obscured by more modern construction surrounding it, the historic architecture is visible from various angles in the vicinity. (Downtown)

WDIA RADIO
112 Union Ave.
Memphis
901/529-4300
Any tourist with even a passing interest in Memphis music should be familiar with the history of WDIA radio. The station was the first—and it remains the oldest continuing—black-oriented radio station in the country. Musicians, advertising pitchmen, and DJs such as B. B. King, Nat D. Williams, Bobby "Blue"

Bland, and Rufus Thomas all started out here. Even Elvis himself graced the station's airwaves.

In 1948 WDIA, under white ownership, became the nation's first radio station to adopt an all-black format. Today the offices and studios are home to four radio stations, including WHRK 97.1 FM, WDIA 1070 AM, KJMS 101.1 FM, and KWAM 99 AM. Visitors to the station will see a busy, contemporary radio enterprise at work. They can peer into some of the historic sound booths and other rooms cluttered with dusty turntables, antique microphones, plaques, gold records, newspaper clippings, photographs, and other archival materials documenting the station's past. Be sure to call several days ahead of time to set up an appointment if you want to take a free, informal tour of the premises. (Downtown)

MIDTOWN/CENTRAL

ARDENT RECORDING STUDIO
2000 Madison Ave.
Memphis
901/725-0855
Although no public tours are offered, fans of popular music will surely want to know about one of the city's oldest and most successful recording studios. Over the past 30 years Ardent has played host to such top-name acts as the Gin Blossoms, R.E.M., Cracker, the Spin Doctors, the Allman Brothers,

A downtown Elvis-Style walking tour begins Saturday mornings at 10 at the King's statue on Beale Street. The three-hour tour includes more than 30 sites and costs $10 per person, plus 50¢ for the trolley fare. For details call 901/274-7187.

GREATER MEMPHIS

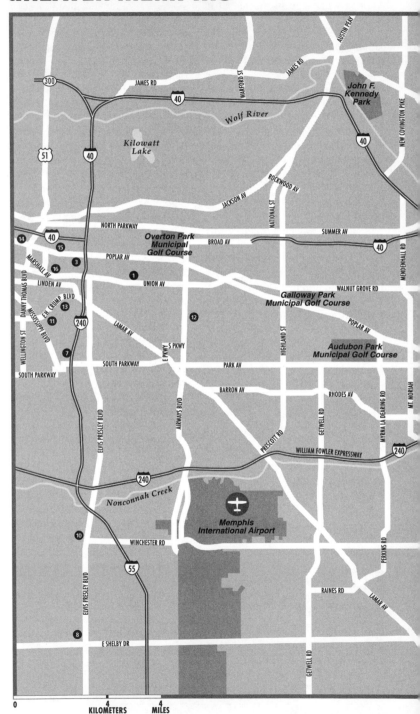

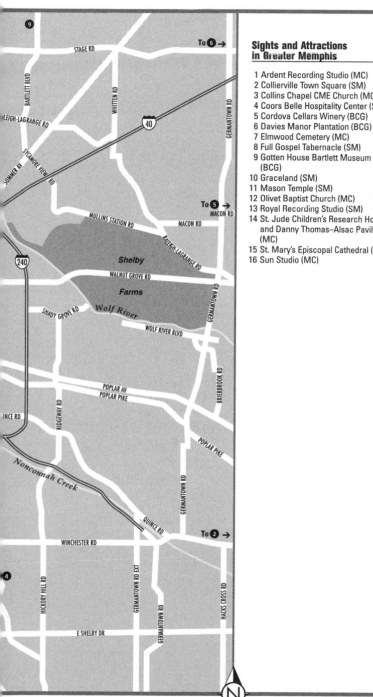

Sights and Attractions in Greater Memphis

1 Ardent Recording Studio (MC)
2 Collierville Town Square (SM)
3 Collins Chapel CME Church (MC)
4 Coors Belle Hospitality Center (SM)
5 Cordova Cellars Winery (BCG)
6 Davies Manor Plantation (BCG)
7 Elmwood Cemetery (MC)
8 Full Gospel Tabernacle (SM)
9 Gotten House Bartlett Museum (BCG)
10 Graceland (SM)
11 Mason Temple (SM)
12 Olivet Baptist Church (MC)
13 Royal Recording Studio (SM)
14 St. Jude Children's Research Hospital and Danny Thomas–Alsac Pavilion (MC)
15 St. Mary's Episcopal Cathedral (MC)
16 Sun Studio (MC)

"Go, Cat, Go!"

You can ask them anything, but don't step on their blue suede shoes! They're the Blue Suede Brigade, a corps of spirited tour guides who walk the streets of downtown Memphis in search of lost tourists, puzzled passersby, and residents looking for a good restaurant recommendation. You'll recognize the Blue Suede Brigade by their white shirts and blue shoulder sashes, khaki pants, hard-hat helmets, and blue suede shoes—in this case, blue suede Nikes. When they're not out pounding the pavement, they're at the Center City Commission at 114 North Main Street. For more information, call them at 901/575-0540.

ZZ Top, Stevie Ray Vaughan, the Replacements, Robert Cray, Big Star, Alex Chilton, Led Zeppelin, Al Green, and many more. Most recently, Ardent/Forefront (Forefront Communications is Ardent's marketing and distribution partner) has focused on the burgeoning contemporary Christian music genre, recording such artists as Big Tent Revival, DC Talk, Audio Adrenaline, Rebecca St. James, Grammatrain, and others. (Midtown/Central)

COLLINS CHAPEL CME CHURCH
678 Washington Ave.
Memphis
901/525-2872
This small redbrick church in the Victorian Village area predates the founding of the CME movement and serves as mother church to all others in the city. Incidentally, the church's gospel choir was featured in the baptism scene in the 1996 movie *The People vs. Larry Flynt*. (Midtown/Central)

ELMWOOD CEMETERY
824 S. Dudley
Memphis
901/774-3212
Founded in 1852 and shaded by giant oak trees, Elmwood is the final resting place of some of the city's most celebrated citizens, including its first black millionaire, Robert Church, and Mayor E. H. "Boss" Crump. There are also several mass graves for the victims of the yellow-fever epidemic. (Midtown/Central)

OLIVET BAPTIST CHURCH
3084 Southern Ave.
Memphis
901/454-7777
Rev. Kenneth T. Whalum Sr. is one of Memphis's more visible clergymen. In addition to being an ordained Baptist minister, Whalum is a former Memphis City Council member. His home church in the Orange Mound area of central Memphis has been visited by such luminaries as President Bill Clinton, who addressed voters here during his first

term in office. One of Whalum's sons, incidentally, is the internationally acclaimed jazz saxophonist Kirk Whalum. (Midtown/Central)

ST. JUDE CHILDREN'S RESEARCH HOSPITAL AND DANNY THOMAS–ALSAC PAVILION
332 N. Lauderdale
Memphis
901/495-2305
Actor and humanitarian Danny Thomas founded this hospital and spent the better part of his life supporting its efforts to help sick children. The pavilion now serves as the late entertainer's final resting place. Sun–Fri 8–4, Sat 10–4; closed holidays. (Midtown/Central)

ST. MARY'S EPISCOPAL CATHEDRAL
672–692 Poplar Ave.
Memphis
901/527-3361
St. Mary's is the oldest Episcopal cathedral in the South, and the present building replaces an earlier wooden Gothic Revival church erected in 1857. The altar memorializes the sisters who died during the yellow-fever epidemic of 1878, when the church was a center of relief services. The adjoining chapel, built in 1887, has an impressive Gothic Revival interior. (Midtown/Central)

SUN STUDIO
706 Union Ave.
Memphis
901/521-0664
Sam Phillips opened this small recording studio in 1950, specializing in blues sung by black artists. Elvis Presley became a superstar after recording some early rock 'n' roll records here. Others, including Jerry Lee Lewis, B. B. King, Rufus Thomas, Howlin' Wolf, Johnny Cash, Carl Perkins, and Roy Orbison, also launched successful recording careers here. Amazingly, the tiny studio is still in operation, and has been sought out by bands such as U2 for its particular Memphis "vibe." Tours are offered seven days a week. $7.50 adults, free for children under 12

Graceland, p. 106

Memphis Convention and Visitors Bureau

with parents, and free to all Memphis residents. (Midtown/Central)

BARTLETT, CORDOVA, GERMANTOWN

CORDOVA CELLARS WINERY
9050 Macon Rd.
Cordova
901/754-3442
The gently rolling countryside, symmetrically aligned vineyards, and fruity vintages make Cordova Cellars Winery a popular picnic site. Tours of this family-owned and -operated winery are available, as are wine tastings, lectures, occasional art exhibitions, and classical music and bluegrass concerts. Tue–Sat 10–5, Sun 1–5; call for winter and holiday hours. (Bartlett, Cordova, Germantown)

DAVIES MANOR PLANTATION
9336 Davies Plantation Rd.
Brunswick
901/386-0715
Shelby County's oldest home, built in 1807, is an original, two-story, log frontier structure furnished with early family furniture and artifacts and operated by the Davies Manor Association. Tue–Fri 12–4; call for group tours and special hours. $4 adults, $2 students. (Bartlett, Cordova, Germantown)

GOTTEN HOUSE BARTLETT MUSEUM
2969 Court (off Stage)
Bartlett
901/373-8433
First settled in the late eighteenth century, the town of Bartlett was officially incorporated in 1866. Its history is displayed in the home of Nicholas Gotten, which dates back to 1871. Tours are offered the first and third Sundays of each month. Call ahead

for tour times. Free. (Bartlett, Cordova, Germantown)

SOUTH MEMPHIS

COLLIERVILLE TOWN SQUARE
101 Walnut
Collierville
Collierville is Tennessee's fastest-growing city, but its residents have fiercely fought to preserve the small-town charm of its quaint downtown square. Dating back to 1850, the area includes antiques stores, arts-and-crafts galleries, and an old train depot. (South Memphis)

COORS BELLE HOSPITALITY CENTER
5151 E. Raines Rd.
Memphis
901/368-BEER
The fascinating Coors Brewery facility is open year-round for free 40-minute tours. Adults may sample the brewery's products at the conclusion

W.C. Handy statue in
W.C. Handy Park, p. 88

Memphis Convention and Visitors Bureau

Top Ten Places to Be in Memphis
by Adrienne and D'Army Bailey

Adrienne is executive director of Big Brothers–Big Sisters of Greater Memphis. D'Army is a judge, author, and actor, last featured in the 1998 screen adaptation of Terry McMillan's *How Stella Got Her Groove Back*. Prior to that, he appeared in the 1996 Milos Forman film, *The People vs. Larry Flynt*.

1. Sharing some hot wings and having cocktails at **Neil's** on Madison. This is a great neighborhood bar with a fun-loving group of folks.

2. Not that we hang out in bars all the time, but the Sunday jazz set at **Huey's** is one of our favorites, too.

3. Like all health-conscious people in Memphis, we have to make our weekly trek to the **Wild Oats Market** for lunch. D'Army likes the rice and beans. I fancy the sushi. We both love the frozen yogurt. It's a great way to nourish your body without all the guilt. Hopefully this makes up for the occasional plate of hot wings.

4. To experience the best Chinese food in the Memphis area, we drive to Bartlett to **Chang's House Restaurant**. All the food is packed for take-out, but you can eat there. It's simply the best.

5. To broaden our musical taste, we like to visit **Blockbuster Music**. We can listen before we purchase—it's like test-driving a CD. What a user-friendly place!

6. We love to take out-of-town guests to **Automatic Slim's**. Even the well-traveled visitor enjoys the ambiance at Slim's. Their art exhibits are interesting, and on occasion they have great live entertainment.

7. The place to be on Friday for happy hour is the bar at the Days Inn Downtown. **Memphis Sounds** attracts the young (and young at heart), black, "in" crowd. It's the place for good music, good drinks, and good people.

8. For the best catfish in town, there's no better place than **Mel's** on the corner of Lamar and McLean. Not only do they have great fish, but they also have a wonderful photo collection.

9. OK, we have to talk barbecue. From time to time, we have to go to the **Rendezvous** for an order of dry ribs. You've just gotta have them. Cozy Corner is a must, too.

10. We always enjoy the scenic drive along **Riverside Drive** and the Mississippi River.

of the tour, from the comfortable sur-roundings of the tasting room. Known as the Coors Belle, this lounge area is designed to resemble an old paddle wheeler riverboat. (South Memphis)

FULL GOSPEL TABERNACLE
787 Hale Rd.
Memphis
901/396-9192

In a small, redbrick church in the suburb of Whitehaven, the world's greatest living soul singer still preaches the Gospel on Sunday mornings. Al Green's touring sched-ule prevents him from being there every week (services are held, re-gardless), but those who have been blessed enough to sit amidst the con-gregation as the charismatic rev-erend fires up the pulpit with shouts and praises of joy know it as a truly transcendent experience.

Whether heard fronting the choir at Full Gospel Tabernacle, where he has ministered for the past 20 years; onstage in Cleveland where, in 1995, he was inducted into the Rock 'n' Roll Hall of Fame; or through the enduring records made in producer Willie Mitchell's Hi Records studio in South Memphis in the early 1970s, Green's voice is the mortal embodiment of soulful spirituality.

Full Gospel Tabernacle is located just south of Graceland, about a mile west of Elvis Presley Boulevard on Hale Road. Sunday-morning services begin at 11 and usually last for at least two hours. Although Rev. Green and his friendly church staff are warm and welcoming toward all worshipers, including visitors and tourists, make no mistake: This is first and foremost a church—not a sightseeing attraction. Visitors should be respectful of that fact. Ab-solutely no photography or other similar intrusions are allowed. Amen. (South Memphis)

GRACELAND
3734 Elvis Presley Blvd.
Memphis
901/332-3322 or 800/238-2000
www.elvis-presley.com

There's no other home like it. But then there was no one quite like Elvis Pres-ley, as a tour of his beloved Memphis mansion and final resting place clearly illustrates. You'll witness lots of gaudy 1970s decor and such bizarre decorat-ing schemes as the daring Jungle Room, with its ceramic monkey fig-urines and fake tropical waterfall. You'll also find a dazzling display of Presley's gold records, costumes, and jewelry. Tours end at the Meditation Garden, where he is buried along with other family members. Separate tours are offered of Elvis's airplane, the *Lisa Marie*, and of museums showcasing his cars and motorcycles.

It cost the owners about $500,000 to open Graceland to the public in 1982—an investment they recouped in a mere 38 days. What's even more

Elmwood Cemetery, p. 102

Memphis Convention and Visitors Bureau

Order in the Court!

Controversial Memphis Judge Joe Brown is the star of a syndicated TV show featuring real-life cases of the local criminal court judge. The program airs locally weekday mornings at 11 on WLMT-TV 30. Known for his outlandish sentences, Judge Brown has ordered law-breakers to do such things as apologize to one another, make charitable donations, and to read and discuss the autobiography of Malcolm X. He once gave a thief a taste of his own medicine by allowing the burglary victim to take something from the intruder's home. Who says two wrongs don't make a right?

remarkable is that Elvis Presley's estate, valued at roughly $4.5 million at the time of the entertainer's death in 1977, has, according to industry estimates, taken in more than $500 million in sales, licensing, and worldwide royalties of Elvis merchandise. Graceland ticket sales alone account for as much $25 million annually.

Memorial Day–Labor Day daily 8–6; rest of the year daily 9–5; closed Tue Nov–Feb, and on New Year's Day, Thanksgiving, and Christmas. $9 adults, $8 seniors, $4.75 children 5–12, free for children under 5; ticket packages including all attractions range from $11–$17. (South Memphis)

MASON TEMPLE
930 Mason
Memphis
901/578-3800

The first international headquarters of the 4 million members of the Church of God in Christ, this temple is also the site of Dr. Martin Luther King Jr.'s final speech. He delivered "I've Been to the Mountain Top" the night before his assassination in 1968. Celebratory services are held here each January, in honor of Dr. King's birthday. (South Memphis)

ROYAL RECORDING STUDIO
1320 S. Lauderdale
Memphis

Willie Mitchell's recording studio still stands in this bleak, run-down neighborhood. Even the most intrepid urban travelers might be advised to think twice before venturing into the vicinity. Nevertheless, the dilapidated little building where Mitchell and Al Green recorded some of the best soul music in the world is indeed an important part of Memphis's rich musical history. Although the recording equipment is high-tech, the studio remains as it must have looked 30 years ago, when Green and Mitchell laid down such classic tracks as "Let's Stay Together" and "Tired of Being Alone." Though not open to the public, the studio is still in use by recording artists, both local and from around the world. (South Memphis)

6

MUSEUMS AND GALLERIES

First-time visitors expecting the Memphis arts scene to hold little of interest beyond black-velvet Elvis paintings may be in for a culture shock. To be sure, there's enough kitsch to fulfill the expectations of those who crave it, but Memphis also supports a relatively young and vibrant fine-arts scene that includes regionally renowned museums and a growing number of commercial galleries, as well as a few fledgling, nonprofit spaces devoted to more experimental, cutting-edge art.

Over the past decade, the city's artistic identity has been boosted exponentially by a government initiative known as Wonders: The Memphis International Cultural Series. Established by civic leaders in 1989, Wonders has produced "blockbuster" exhibitions such as those on Napoleon, Catherine the Great, and the Imperial Tombs of China, which have collectively drawn millions of visitors to Memphis. One of the premier international cultural arts organizations of its kind, Wonders is being emulated by other U.S. markets eager to duplicate its successes.

ART MUSEUMS

DIXON GALLERY AND GARDENS
4339 Park Ave.
Memphis
901/761-5250 or 901/761-2409
www.dixon.org
French and American Impressionist paintings are hallmarks of the Dixon Gallery and Gardens, widely regarded as one of the country's finest small, private museums. Secluded in a wooded oasis in the heart of Memphis, the Dixon also houses important collections of eighteenth-century porcelain and major traveling exhibitions. Visitors encounter anything from Rodin sculptures or Cezanne landscapes to bejeweled Faberge eggs and shimmering installations by contemporary

glass artist Dale Chihuly. The Dixon's lush, formal gardens and neatly manicured lawns serve as seasonal backdrops for community picnics, symphony and blues concerts, and even Shakespeare under the stars. Tue–Sat 10–5, Sun 1–5, closed Mon (gardens open for half-price). $5 adults, $4 seniors, $3 students, $1 children under 12. ♿ (Downtown)

MEMPHIS BROOKS MUSEUM OF ART
Overton Park
1934 Poplar Ave.
Memphis
901/722-3500
www.brooksmuseum.org
The Memphis Brooks Museum of Art, opened in 1916, is Tennessee's oldest and largest museum. European and American artworks of the eighteenth through twentieth centuries are its strengths, although the museum boasts an encyclopedic permanent collection of world art dating from antiquity to the present. Paintings by artists such as Mary Cassatt and Henri Matisse, as well as sculpture, prints, and decorative arts, are displayed chronologically in a series of stunning galleries. Located in lovely Overton Park, the Brooks lies within a few steps of the esteemed Memphis College of Art, where exhibits in the Tobey Gallery are free and open to the public. Tue, Thu, Fri 9–5, Wed 9–8, Sat 9–5, Sun 11:30–5. $5 adults, $4 seniors, $2 students, additional fees for special exhibitions. ♿ (Downtown)

NATIONAL ORNAMENTAL METAL MUSEUM
374 Metal Museum Dr.
Memphis
901/774-6380
Even if the tree-shaded bluffs overlooking the majestic Mississippi River didn't constitute the most picturesque spot in all of Memphis, the National Ornamental Metal Museum located there would be well worth a visit. As the country's first and only museum dedicated to preserving the art and craft of metalworking, the NOMM has presented exhibitions on such diverse subject matter as ornamental teapots, gem-encrusted fine jewelry, silver spoons, and swords. Among the more tongue-in-cheek displays is the one devoted to functional pork-barbecue cookers. The display is staged annually during the Memphis in May World Championship Barbecue Cooking Contest. The cozy museum has interior gallery space on two floors, outdoor sculpture including architecturally unique wrought-iron gates, and a working blacksmith shop. Tue–Sat 10–5, Sun 12–5. $2 adults; $1 seniors, students, and children; free for children under 5. Wheelchair-accessible on the first floor only. (Midtown/Central)

PEABODY PLACE MUSEUM AND GALLERY
119 Main St.
Memphis
901/523-ARTS
www.belz.com
Touted as one of the country's most extensive and rare collections of Chinese artistry, the new, 7,500-square-foot gallery that opened in 1998 features Chinese art from the private collection of Memphis businessman Jack Belz and his wife, Marilyn. Belz is chairman and CEO of Belz Enterprises, a real estate development company that owns such properties as the Peabody Hotel and Peabody Place. While most of the artworks, including those of jade and ivory, are from the nineteenth century and later, there are a few rare pieces dating

The International Conference on Elvis Presley

The International Conference on Elvis Presley, launched at the University of Mississippi in Oxford, moved to Memphis in 1997. Founded by former Ole Miss professor Vernon Chadwick, author of In Search of Elvis: Music, Race, Art and Religion, *the conference has received international media attention for its highly academic and decidedly offbeat approach to "Elvisology." The annual conference, held each August during the anniversary of the King's death, varies in location from year to year.*

Recent conference themes have included 1998's "Are You Lonesome Tonight? Elvis and the Dysfunctional Family," which explored the entertainer's well-documented battles with drugs, loneliness, and obesity. In 1999 the conference theme was "Politics and the Presidency, 1970–2000." Discussions explored the strange correlation between Presley and the presidency and included talks on such events as Elvis's Oval-Office meeting with President Richard Nixon and the phone call a reportedly stoned Presley made to President Jimmy Carter. The correlation between Elvis and President Bill Clinton, whose well-known Secret Service code name is "Elvis," was also discussed.

For more information, contact Chadwick's Institute for the Living South at 601/236-4693 or www.members.xoom.com/livingsouth.

---

back to the Manchu Dynasty (1644 to 1911). Tue–Fri 10–8, Sat 9–5, Sun 10:30–5. $5 adults, $4.50 seniors, $4 children under 12. & (Downtown)

SCIENCE AND HISTORY MUSEUMS

HUNT–PHELAN HOME
533 Beale St.

Memphis
800/350-9009
Opened in March 1996 after an extensive refurbishment, the Hunt–Phelan Home is one of the newest historic attractions in Memphis. This stately, antebellum mansion is filled with period furnishings dating back to the early 1600s. Slave labor built this imposing, redbrick structure, which served as a headquarters to General Ulysses S.

Grant during the Civil War. After the war the former residence was used as a school in which Northern teachers educated blacks. Summer Thu–Mon 10–5; call for winter hours. $10 adults, $9 students and seniors, $6 children 5–12, free for children under 5. (Downtown)

MEMPHIS PINK PALACE MUSEUM AND PLANETARIUM AND UNION PLANTER'S IMAX THEATER
3050 Central Ave.
Memphis
901/320-6320 or 901/320-6362
www.memphismuseums.org

With enough exhibitions and attractions to engage a visitor for an entire day, the Memphis Pink Palace is one of the most diverse museums in the city. This hands-on science and learning center features changing exhibits on natural and cultural history, laser shows set to rock music, and a planetarium offering educational programs on astronomy. The Pink Palace Mansion wing of the museum complex is the original home of Clarence Saunders, founder of the Piggly Wiggly supermarket chain. Museum exhibits include one on medical history and another on Memphis's African American heritage. The Union Planter's IMAX Theater presents new films every few months on a screen four stories high. Summer Mon–Wed 9–5, Thu–Sat 9–9, Sun 12–5; winter Mon–Wed 9–4, Thu 9–8, Fri 9–10, Sat 10–10, Sun 12–5. $6 adults, $5.50 seniors, $4.50 children 3–12; tickets to IMAX theater and planetarium are additional. (Midtown/Central)

NATIONAL CIVIL RIGHTS MUSEUM
450 Mulberry St.
Memphis
901/521-9699

This impressive museum, dedicated to the American Civil Rights movement, opened in 1991 at the historic Lorraine Motel, where Dr. Martin Luther King Jr. was assassinated in April 1968. Interactive multimedia exhibits and realistic scene recreations trace the history of segregation, from the days of slavery to the present. Among the powerful exhibits is one dedicated to Rosa Parks. Racial discrimination can also be felt at a recreation of the Greensboro, North Carolina, lunch counter that was boycotted by Southern blacks. More uplifting are the presentation devoted to the March on Washington and the video of Dr. King's "I Have a Dream" speech. $5 adults, $4 seniors and students, $3 children 6–12, free for children 5 and under. Summer Mon and Wed–Sat 10–6, Sun 1–6; winter Mon and Wed–Sat 10–5, Sun 1–5; closed Tue and major holidays. (Downtown)

VICTORIAN VILLAGE
Magevney House, 198 Adams

Hunt-Phelan Home, p. 110

Ave., 901/526-4464
Mallory-Neely House, 652 Adams
Ave., 901/523-1484
Woodruff-Fontaine House,
680 Adams Ave., 901/526-1469
Clustered together in a stately, tree-shaded neighborhood known as Victorian Village are three nineteenth-century homes. The most lavish of the trio is the 25-room Mallory-Neely House, a three-story Italianate mansion built in the 1850s and furnished with period antiques, many of which are original to the dwelling. Nearby is the Woodruff-Fontaine House, an 1870s French-style mansion featuring mannequins dressed in elaborate Victorian-era clothing. The Magevney House, built in the 1830s, is one of Memphis's oldest homes. Mallory-Neely: $4 adults, $3 seniors and students. Woodruff-Fontaine: $5 adults, $4 seniors, $2 students. Magevney: free. Hours vary, so call ahead for details. (Downtown)

SPECIALTY MUSEUMS

**BEALE STREET SUBSTATION
POLICE MUSEUM
159 Beale St.
Memphis**

901/525-9800
This active police substation houses a museum that documents some of Memphis's most notorious crimes. It's open 24 hours a day. Admission is free. ⅚ (Downtown)

**CENTER FOR SOUTHERN
FOLKLORE
209 Beale St.
Memphis
901/525-3655**
The casual Center for Southern Folklore, a private, nonprofit organization documenting the people and traditions of the South, exhibits changing and permanent displays on topics relating to historic Memphis music, art, and daily life. The center also operates a gift shop showcasing regional folk art, books, and recordings emphasizing Memphis music and such seminal Southern delights as chocolate moon pies and bottled barbecue sauce. They've recently added a coffee bar that also offers beer and pizza. Sun–Thu 10–8, Fri–Sat 10 a.m.–1 a.m. Suggested donation $2 adults, $1 students and seniors. ⅚ (Downtown)

**ELVIS PRESLEY AUTOMOBILE
MUSEUM (AT GRACELAND)
3734 Elvis Presley Blvd.**

TRIVIA

One of the South's most distinguished African American photographers is Ernest C. Withers. A former Memphis policeman who gave up crime-fighting to become a full-time photographer, Withers is an important researcher as well as an artist. His intensely journalistic, black-and-white photographs document the history of the Civil Rights movement in the Memphis area. He also photographed many of the black musicians who toured the circuit. Withers still works in Memphis.

Wonders

Wonders: The Memphis International Cultural Series was established in 1989 to continue the success of the 1987 *Ramesses the Great* exhibition. Since then, Wonders has produced seven blockbuster exhibitions, each lasting four to five months:

Catherine the Great (April–September 1991): With the Hermitage Museum in St. Petersburg, Russia, Wonders organized an exhibition about the life and reign of the Russian empress Catherine II. The 287-object exhibition included crowns, jewels, costumes, and Catherine's grand coronation carriage, restored especially for the Memphis exhibit.

Splendors of the Ottoman Sultans (April–August 1992): The centerpiece of the 275-object show was the famous emerald-encrusted Topkapi dagger, which had never before been exhibited in the Western Hemisphere.

The Etruscans (May–August 1992): From the Vatican's *Gregorian Etruscan Music*, Wonders presented a 175-object exhibition on the Etruscan civilization, which existed in Italy prior to the Roman Empire.

Napoleon (April–September 1993): Nearly 50 museums and private collections from France, the Vatican, Switzerland, England, and the United States loaned approximately 175 objects for the largest exhibition on Napoleon Bonaparte ever presented in North America.

Imperial Tombs of China (April–September 1995): More than 250 objects comprised the largest and most significant exhibition of tomb treasures ever seen outside of China. Among the many objects were four life-size terra-cotta warriors from the tomb of the first Chinese emperor; a jade burial suit sewn with gold thread; and the Dragon and Phoenix Empress Crown from the Ming Dynasty.

Titanic (April–September 1997): The largest exhibition of artifacts ever recovered from the wreck site of the *Titanic* drew more than 600,000 visitors to Memphis. Galleries replicated portions of the *Titanic*, transporting visitors back to the elegant Edwardian era of 1912.

Ancestors of the Incas: The Lost Civilizations of Peru (April–September 1998) Human mummies and skulls, delicate textiles, pottery, and other artifacts from such ancient populations as the Nazca Indians of Peru were focal points of this exhibition.

Heart House located in Victorian Village, p. 111

Memphis
800/238-2000
This museum is devoted to the King's many vehicles. Portions of the display are arranged to replicate a drive-in movie theater where weary tourists may sit and watch big-screen videos of some of Elvis's Hollywood movies of the 1960s. The King's 1955 pink Cadillac is a centerpiece, but various other sports cars and motorcycles are also present. Summer daily 8–6; winter daily 9–5; closed major holidays and Tue Nov–Feb. Mansion tour: $9 adults, $8.10 seniors, $4.75 children 5–12, free for children under 5. Package including all main attractions: $17 adults, $15.30 seniors, $11 children 5–12. (South Memphis)

FIRE MUSEUM OF MEMPHIS
118 Adams Ave.
Memphis
901/452-9973

This museum—located at historic Fire Engine House No. 1—opened to the public in 1998. Exhibits of antique fire-fighting equipment and uniforms, along with photographs, videos, and a reference library, are part of this privately operated $3.75 million museum. There's also a poignant memorial to city firefighters who died in the line of duty. Tue–Sat 9–5, Sun 1–5. ♿ (Downtown)

MEMPHIS MUSIC HALL OF FAME
97 S. Second St.
Memphis
901/525-4007
Memphis music from the 1950s to the present is the focus of this extensive museum. Videos, photographs, musical instruments, and other memorabilia document the city's famed forays into rock 'n' roll, rockabilly, and soul. Vintage recording equipment is also prominent, particularly that used in such well-known Memphis studios as Stax and Sun. Mon–Thu 10–6, Fri–Sat 10–9, Sun 10–6. $7.50 adults, $2.50 children 7–14, free for children 6 and under. ♿ (Downtown)

W. C. HANDY HOME
Beale St. at Fourth St.
Memphis
901/522-1556 or 901/527-3427
William Christopher Handy (1873–1958) was born in Florence, Alabama, but it was in Memphis that he fathered a new style of music known as the blues. Enlisted by mayoral candidate E. H. Crump to write a campaign song, Handy composed "Memphis Blues," first published in 1912. Exhibits focus on Handy's career as a trumpeter, composer, and black bandleader, and on his lasting contributions to American music after the turn of the century. Mon–Sat 10–4, Sun 1–5. $2 adults, $1 students. ♿ (Downtown)

GALLERIES

ALBERS GALLERY
1102 Brookfield Rd.
Memphis
901/683-2256

In the 15 years since she opened her business, Kathy Albers has established herself as one of the most respected gallery owners in Memphis. With an increasing emphasis on artists from New York and other parts of the United States, Albers Gallery continues to showcase well-established local and regional artists working in a variety of media, including painting and drawing, sculpture, and fine crafts such as functional and decorative furniture and glass. This sophisticated and immaculate gallery is tucked at the far end of Brookfield Road, off of Poplar Avenue, just yards west of the busy I-240 interchange. Tue–Fri 9:30–5:30, Sat 11–3. Free. & (East Memphis)

COOPER STREET GALLERY
964 S. Cooper St.
Memphis
901/272-7053

Among the more steadfast tenants in the artsy, bohemian intersection known as the Cooper-Young Historic District, is Jay Etkin's Cooper Street Gallery. A native New Yorker, Etkin is an award-winning artist whose works have been exhibited in Soho, Greenwich Village, and beyond. In the tidy space he also uses as his working studio, Etkin champions the works of up-and-coming local and regional artists. Wed, Fri, Sat 11–5, or by appointment. Free. & (Midtown/Central)

DELTA AXIS CONTEMPORARY ARTS CENTER
901/327-5917

Delta Axis Contemporary Arts Center, a nonprofit organization showcasing the works of new and/or neglected Southern artists, is arguably the most alternative or avant-garde of the art spaces within the Memphis metro area. After moving from previous locations in the Cooper-Young district and on Front Street downtown, Delta Axis's latest home was inside the Marshall Arts Studio. At this writing, however, Delta Axis was on the move again while continuing to schedule a full slate of often surprising exhibitions at various locations. Their May 1998 "drive-through" exhibit, in which artworks were wrapped "to go," was a

---

TRIVIA

Vivid southern images ranging from urban dumpsters and blossoming wisteria vines to tar-paper Mississippi shacks and Graceland's "Jungle Room" are framed for posterity by one of Memphis's best-known artists. William Eggleston, who pioneered the use of color photography as a fine art form, has exhibited his works in such venues as the Museum of Modern Art in New York. Born in 1939, Eggleston is a world traveler who lives and works in Memphis and Mississippi. Among his various coffee-table books are the excellent *William Eggleston: Ancient and Modern* (New York, Random House, 1992).

---

hit. Patrons drove through the Marshall Arts gallery space—a former mechanic's garage—to purchase their pieces before driving ahead with them. Wed–Sat 12–5. Free. (Midtown/Central)

GESTINE'S
156 Beale St.
Memphis
901/526-3162
African American art, primarily colorful framed prints and paintings, dominate this commercial gallery and gift shop. In addition, the boutique sells drawings, photographs, and other items. Wedged between blues clubs, bars, and souvenir shops along Beale Street, Gestine's stays open late by gallery standards—until 10 p.m. Friday and Saturday. Free. & (Downtown)

LEDBETTER LUSK GALLERY
4540 Poplar Ave.
Memphis
901/767-3800
www.llg.com
One of the newest galleries in Memphis was opened three years ago by

Dixon Gallery and Gardens, p.108

Memphis Convention and Visitors Bureau

partners Baylor Ledbetter and David Lusk, two young entrepreneurs with a flair for commercially viable fine art. Many of the region's best-known artists, including painters Mary Sims and Nancy Cheairs, exhibit in this chic gallery space with its dramatic high ceilings and contemporary decor. Among the up-and-coming local artists periodically shown here is photographer Huger Foote, son of Civil War historian and Memphis resident Shelby Foote. Tue–Fri 10–5:30, Sat 11–5, or by appointment. Free. & (East Memphis)

LISA KURTS GALLERY
766 S. White Station Rd.
Memphis
901/683-6200
www.lisakurts.com
Gallery owner Lisa Kurts operates one of the premier commercial art galleries in Memphis. The gallery, which has won acclaim as one of the South's finest, displays the creations of regional and national artists working primarily in the media of painting and sculpture. Among the best-known artists here are San Francisco watercolorist Gary Bukovnik, sculptor Manuel Neri, and the legendary Southern photographer William Eggleston. The gallery can be found just north of the Poplar Avenue and White Station intersection in East Memphis. Mon–Fri 10–5:30, Sat 11–4. Free. & (East Memphis)

MEMPHIS COLLEGE OF ART
1930 Poplar Ave.
Memphis
901/272-5100
Admission is free to most of the exhibitions presented in the Tobey Gallery of the Memphis College of Art, a highly respected private institution whose former students have included

Amy Carter. Student exhibitions are always interesting, as are frequent faculty shows and other special events. The gallery is open daily. (Midtown/Central)

RAINBOW STUDIO AND STAINED GLASS, INC.
387 S. Main St.
Memphis
901/521-0400
Rainbow Studio is a commercial enterprise located in the South Main Historic District along the Main Street Trolley line. Billed as the South's largest stained glass and decorative arts studio, Rainbow also retails antique and American windows, lamps, and decorative glass objects. Mon–Fri 8–5, Sat 9–3. Free. (Downtown)

SHAINBERG GALLERY
Memphis Jewish Community Center
1930 Poplar Ave.
Memphis
901/272-5100
Exhibitions by outstanding local artists hang in this art gallery located inside the Memphis Jewish Community Center complex. Sun–Thu 9–5. Free. & (East Memphis)

PUBLIC ART

FIRST TENNESSEE HERITAGE COLLECTION
First Tennessee Bank
165 Madison Ave.
Memphis
901/523-4291

The First Tennessee Heritage Collection, on view in the lobby of this downtown bank building, features colorful, dramatic murals and sculpture of Tennessee artists. Mon–Thu 8:30–4, Fri 8:30–5, tours by appointment. Free. (Downtown)

RAMESSES THE GREAT
The Pyramid
1 Auction Ave.
Memphis
901/521-9675
Memphis's signature statue is the stone *Ramesses the Great* before the entrance of the Pyramid sports and entertainment arena. The piece is identical to the statue that guards the tombs in Egypt. The Memphis statue, however, is hollow, and weighs a mere 5,000 pounds. The original tips the scales at nearly twice that. (Downtown)

DRAMATIS PERSONAE
Theatre Memphis
630 Perkins Ext.
Memphis
901/682-8323
One of the largest outdoor public sculptures in the entire region is *Dramatis Personae.* Theatre Memphis commissioned Rhodes College art professor Lon Anthony to create these larger-than-life lawn ornaments. The nine animated steel sculptures represent heroic mythological and literary characters and thespians, including Medea, Cleopatra, Cyrano de Bergerac, Sarah Bernhardt, and Samuel Beckett's Hamm. (East Memphis)

7

KIDS' STUFF

With its wealth of cultural, educational, and recreational organizations, special events, and festivals, Memphis offers ample opportunities for family recreation. Spring and fall are ideal times to explore the great outdoors, including the city's beautiful parks. In inclement weather, look indoors to world-class museums that allow kids to explore everything from abstract art to astronomy. From kid-friendly galleries and interactive concert performances to spacious parks and play areas, there is plenty to do year-round.

ANIMALS AND THE GREAT OUTDOORS

LICHTERMAN NATURE CENTER
5992 Quince Rd.
Memphis
901/767-7322
www.memphismuseums.org
Kids can participate in a variety of educational nature hikes and crafts activities through ongoing programs at the first accredited nature center in the United States. Lichterman features 65 acres of woods, fields, and marshes in the heart of East Memphis. Youngsters especially seem to enjoy the wildlife hospital, where injured animals receive care. Tue–Sat

9:30–5, Sun 1–5. $2 adults, $1 seniors and children 4–18, free for children 3 and under. (East Memphis)

MEMPHIS BOTANIC GARDEN
750 Cherry Rd.
Memphis
Audubon Park
901/685-1566
Children enjoy watching the goldfish swim beneath the bridges in the Japanese garden, and hiking the secluded woodland trails that seem far beyond the hustle and bustle of central Memphis. New in 1999 is the Four Seasons Garden, which provides year-round color. Nov–Feb Mon–Sat 9–4:30, Sun 11–4:30; Mar–Oct

Mon–Sat 9–6, Sun 11–6. $2 adults, $1.50 seniors, $1 children, free for children under 6; free for everyone Tue after 12:30 p.m. (East Memphis)

MEMPHIS ZOO AND AQUARIUM
2000 Galloway
Memphis
901/276-WILD
www.memphiszoo.org

Monkeys, lemurs, and bears are among the more than four hundred species of animals, birds, and reptiles at the world-class Memphis Zoo and Aquarium. Located in Overton Park, the zoo features exhibits on the African veldt, Asian temple ruins, Peruvian rain forests, and Jamaican caverns. Regal tigers, lions, and panthers roam freely in their new environmentally correct *Cat Country* exhibit, while the apes and monkeys hang out in *Primate Canyon*.

Younger children may find the *Animals of the Night* exhibit on bats and other nocturnal creatures a bit too intense, while older children may find it "awesome." Another popular kid-friendly area includes the *Once Upon a Farm* exhibit where city kids can acquaint themselves with such farm animals as cows.

Trams that carry passengers throughout the zoo operate seasonally, as do the children's amusement rides. The zoo also has a snack bar, gift shop, and strollers and wheelchairs available for rent. Mar–Oct daily 9–5; Oct–Feb 9–4:30. $8.50 adults, $7.50 seniors, $5.50 ages 2 to 11. (Midtown/Central)

ST. NICK FARMS ZOOLOGICAL PARK
10928 E. Shelby Dr.
Collierville
901/850-0275

This private, 27-acre zoo, located in the suburbs of southeastern Shelby County, is a cross between a park and a petting zoo. It is home to some 135 exotic animals, including the University of Memphis's striped mascot, Tom. This huge, handsome tiger is trucked to and from home basketball games at the downtown Pyramid—a 45-minute drive along the freeway—in an elaborate, well-lit white cage, and accompanied by at least two police cars. Guided tours weekdays by appointment, and Sat at 1, 2, and 3 p.m. $3. (South Memphis)

ART AND MUSEUMS

CHILDREN'S CENTER FOR THE ARTS
2183 Young Ave.
Memphis
901/272-1677

Creative arts and after-school programs are available at this locally owned neighborhood arts center, which opened as a for-profit daycare program in the summer of 1998. Classes are offered in all the visual and performing arts. (Midtown/Central)

CHILDREN'S MUSEUM OF MEMPHIS
2525 Central Ave.
Memphis
901/458-2678
www.cmom.com

Fire engines for climbing and exploring, a police motorcycle with all the bells and whistles, and a kid-sized skyscraper eight stories tall encourage children to use their imaginations while exploring the Children's Museum of Memphis. Located in a large warehouse structure near the fairgrounds, the museum includes a kid-sized city complete with a grocery

Best Pizza Places with Video Arcades

by Justin Romine-Wykoff, age 7, a pepperoni pizza–eating machine and video-game expert

1. **Mazzio's:** *The pizza is great, and it's cheap, too! The games are cool. You can also listen to great tunes on the jukebox or watch a game on one of their televisions.*
2. **Cici's Pizza:** *Yes! Very cheap, very good pizza. The games are so cool—the first time you play them you'll jump out of your britches!*
3. **Celebration Station:** *The go-karts are fast and fun! The games are unlimited. The pizza, honey, is so good!*
4. **Chuck E. Cheese's:** *Oh! The games are cool and exciting. The "play-pen," for kids age seven and under, has slides and balls, and is a place kids can just hang out. You don't have to pay to get in, either! The pizza is the best in town.*
5. **Hickory Ridge Mall:** *Their arcade has lots of action-packed games. After a hard afternoon of playing games, you can go to the nearby food court for delicious pizza, hot dogs, or nachos.*

store where children can push carts and collect a variety of produce and pantry staples, and a bank where they can practice writing checks. Tue–Sat 9–5, Sun 12–5. $5 adults and teenagers, $4 seniors and children 1–12; all children must be accompanied by an adult; groups by reservation only. (Midtown/Central)

CHUCALISSA ARCHAEOLOGICAL MUSEUM
1987 Indian Village Rd.
Memphis
901/785-3160
A reconstructed, prehistoric Native American village, Chucalissa, which means "abandoned village," dates

back to the fifteenth century. Outdoor trails, a museum, and on-site demonstrations of the crafts, skills, and games of the period are featured attractions. Tue–Sat 9–4:30. $3 adults, $2 seniors and children, free for children under 4. (South Memphis)

MEMPHIS ARTS COUNCIL FAMILY SERIES
85 Third St.
Memphis
901/578-2787
www.memphistravel.com/memphisarts
Parents won't find a better bargain for culture than the Memphis Arts Council's Sunday afternoon Family

Series, unique programs that aim to be entertaining and affordable to families.

Music, theater, dance, and story-telling programs designed to appeal to both adults and children are held three or four times a year at various venues throughout the city. After each 60-minute performance, refreshments are served and an informal question-and-answer session between artists and audience is held. $10 per family (for up to five members), $1 extra per additional person; season tickets to entire series cost $30. Call the arts council for information on specific performance schedules, times, and locations. (varying locations)

MEMPHIS BROOKS MUSEUM OF ART
Overton Park
1934 Poplar Ave.
Memphis
901/722-3500
www.brooksmuseum.org
In addition to the exhibition galleries filled with fine oil paintings, sculpture, and decorative arts, the museum offers kids a hands-on gallery that encourages them to actually (gasp!) touch the art. The museum also has special workshops and Saturday events designed to give kids fun and educational art experiences. Most events include tours of museum exhibitions from a child's perspective. Call for details. Tue, Thur, Fri 9–4, Wed 9–8, Sat 9–5, Sun 11:30–5. $5. (Midtown/Central)

MEMPHIS PINK PALACE MUSEUM AND UNION PLANTER'S IMAX THEATER
3050 Central Ave.
Memphis
901/320-6320
www.memphismuseums.org
During the dreary winter months, as an appealing alternative to movies or video arcades, the Pink Palace offers extended hours on Friday and Saturday nights. The museum's first-rate natural- and cultural-history exhibits, planetarium, and IMAX theater are popular with kids of all ages.

The recently restored "pink-marble" mansion, built in 1923 for Piggly Wiggly founder Clarence Saunders, includes such treasures as a shrunken head. Older kids should tune in to the hip laser shows in the plane-

Chucalissa Archaeological Museum

Memphis Convention and Visitors Bureau

tarium, which are set to loud recorded music by the day's top alternative and classic-rock artists. In recent years these astrologically oriented videos have been orchestrated to music by bands like Pearl Jam and the Grateful Dead. Each August there's also an Elvis show. Memorial Day–Labor Day Mon–Wed 9–5, Thu–Sat 9–9, Sun 12–5; Labor Day–Memorial Day Mon–Wed 9–4, Thu 9–8, Fri 9–10, Sat 10–10, Sun 12–5. $6 adults, $5.50 seniors, $4.50 children 3–12. (Midtown/Central)

WONDERS: THE MEMPHIS INTERNATIONAL CULTURAL SERIES
255 N. Main St.
Memphis
800/263-6744 or 901/576-1231
Along with the informational, narrated audiocassette guides that accompany patrons through each Wonders exhibition, there are separate guides made just for children. Written and recorded with young students in mind, these self-directing tours enliven exhibit subject matter with dramatizations, music, and other special sound effects.

Teachers' guides, lesson plans, children's brochures, and other materials stress the educational component of the exhibits, making world-class art accessible to patrons of all ages. A walk through any Wonders exhibition is a great opportunity for parent-child interaction and discussion of art, history, and culture. Hours and fees vary with each exhibition. (Downtown)

THEATER

EWING CHILDREN'S THEATRE
2635 Avery
Memphis
901/452-3968
Led by an energetic staff of professional actors and teachers, this theater company is named for Lucille Ewing, a beloved Memphis thespian. The theater specializes in stage productions that allow area children to act upon the lessons they've learned in drama, clowning, and dance classes. There's also a young-playwrights' showcase in which student writers get a chance to cast and stage some of their works. (Midtown/Central)

Pink Palace Museum, p. 121

Memphis Convention and Visitors Bureau

Top Things for Kids to Do in Memphis
by Zakary Romine-Wykoff, age 11

1. **East End Skating Rink:** It's a fun place just to hang out and have fun.
2. **Putt-Putt Golf and Games:** A hole-in-one wins you a free game of miniature golf, plus there are video games inside.
3. **The Pink Palace Museum:** The museum is really interesting—especially the dinosaur exhibit and the mansion with the shrunken head. And the IMAX theater is really awesome.
4. **Children's Museum:** It lets children use their imagination. You can climb into a real fire truck or shop at a grocery store.
5. **Malco's Appletree Cinema:** Terrific movies for low prices.
6. **Circuit/Playhouse on the Square:** They have plays like *The Lion, the Witch and the Wardrobe*, and a lot of comedies. For instance, at Christmas you can go see *A Tuna Christmas*, which is really, really funny—I highly recommend it!
7. **Libertyland:** The "Revolution" is a roller coaster that reaches high speeds and turns you sideways and upside down. Do not eat any food before you go on this ride. If you do, it wouldn't be a pretty sight.
8. **Malco's Majestic Theater:** It offers a wide variety of movies on 20 screens, all with stadium, rocking-chair seating, plus concession stands and an arcade room.
9. **Wolfchase Galleria:** A fancy name for a huge new mall. The big-screen movie theater with stadium seating rocks.
10. **The Melting Pot:** If you're into fondue, this restaurant (across the street from Wolfchase) is for you.

MORGAN WOODS CHILDREN'S THEATRE
7771 Poplar Pike
Germantown
901/757-7206
Instruction in audition preparation, movement, voice, theater etiquette, and other areas is offered at this children's theater company at the new Germantown Performing Arts Centre.

Youths participating in the program perform in periodic productions at the state-of-the-art facility. In addition, several children's theater performances are staged throughout the year at other locations. (Bartlett, Cordova, Germantown)

PLAYHOUSE ON THE SQUARE
51 S. Cooper St.

Memphis
901/726-4656
In addition to offering a theater school with a full range of acting and other theater-related classes, as well as theater programs for the deaf, Playhouse on the Square offers a Saturday morning kids matinee program. Storytellers such as Annie McDaniel, a local resident who recalls growing up on the Mississippi River, spin tales suitable for children ages six and over. Admission is on a "pay-what-you-can" basis. No reservations are accepted. (Midtown/Central)

STORES KIDS LOVE

BELLA NOTTE
2172 Young Ave.
901/726-4131
Unusual toys, sterling rattles, celestial candles, picture frames, chenille bibs, and cotton sleepers are among the items sold at this kids' store. Mon–Sat 11–7, Sun 1–6. (Midtown/Central)

CHOCOLATE SOUP
7730 Hwy. 72 E., No. 6
Germantown Village Square

Germantown
901/754-7157
Colorful threads for newborns to boys' size 7 and girls' size 14 are the focus of this delightful store that's been designing and manufacturing clothing for a quarter-century. The store's stock in trade is its matching sibling outfits, and everything's designed to be easy to care for. Toys will keep the kids occupied while parents shop for them. Mon, Thu, Fri 10–8; Tue, Wed, Sat 10–6; Sun 1–5. (Bartlett, Cordova, Germantown)

DAVIS-KIDD BOOKSELLERS
397 Perkins Ext.
Memphis
901/683-9801
Saturday morning group storytelling sessions and creative children's activities are offered periodically at this terrific East Memphis bookstore.

In addition to its large selection of children's books, Davis-Kidd also sells fun, educational toys. There are enough floor displays to let your children test-drive a few of the blocks, books, and computerized games for sale. The David-Kidd Kids Events hotline number is 901/682-0042. (East Memphis)

HICKORY RIDGE MALL'S CAROUSEL
Winchester Ave. at Hickory Hill Rd.
Memphis
901/367-8045
An old-fashioned carousel dominates the sunny, central area of Hickory Ridge Mall. Rides are 50¢ each on this enchanting, double-decker Venetian merry-go-round. Adults should be forewarned, however, that the aromas of freshly baked cookies and cinnamon rolls are inescapable in this area, and inevitably entice riders to explore the mall and picnic square around the corner. (South Memphis)

ONLY KIDS (OK)
6105 Poplar Ave., No. 124
Poplar at Ridgeway Rd.
Memphis
901/683-1234
Located inside the Regalia shopping center, this specialty store features competitively priced clothing for kids ranging from newborns to teenagers. Lines such as Gund, Polo, and Esprit de Corp are carried in the store, which is designed as "a department store from a kid's point of view." Educational toys are featured in addition to fine clothing. Mon–Sat 10–6, Thu 10–9. (East Memphis)

THE VILLAGE TOYMAKER
4615 Poplar Ave., Ste. 14
Memphis
901/761-1734
Kids' creativity kits, and brand-name toys by Brio, Playmobil, and others are among the merchandise offered at these stores. Stuffed toys, costumes, dolls, and toy race cars are also for sale. A second location is at 7850 Poplar Ave., Suite 12 (901/755-3309). (East Memphis)

THEME PARKS AND ENTERTAINMENT

BOGEY'S
7800 Fischer Steele
Cordova
901/757-2649
www.bogeys.com
With more than one hundred acres of grass driving range, Bogey's Golf and Family Entertainment Center is a family-oriented attraction offering go-karts, bumper boats, miniature golf courses, children's rides, and batting cages. Bogey's also boasts a video arcade, company picnic area, and corporate meeting facilities. Summer daily 8:30 a.m.–12 a.m.; winter daily 8:30 a.m.–9:30 p.m. Armbands for unlimited

"If you like flowers and bugs and twigs and slugs, birds and bees and rocks and trees, colors and smells and ponds and trails, you will love the Caterpillar Club!" So goes the pitch for the Memphis Botanic Garden's popular classes developed especially for "preschool ecologists," ages five and under. Each class focuses on a different topic and includes lessons, crafts, and outdoor exploration.

Sessions are held Tuesday and Wednesday mornings from 10 to 11 and 11 to noon. The fee is $4 per student. Check the calendar in the monthly *Memphis Parent* (free at area newsstands) or register by calling the gardens at 901/685-1566.

play range from $10 and $12.50 for youths to $15 for adults; price is based on participant's height. (Bartlett, Cordova, Germantown)

CELEBRATION STATION
5970 Macon Cove Rd.
Memphis
901/377-6700
Two 18-hole miniature golf courses, six batting cages, a go-kart track, a bumper-boat lake, a play area for small children, and an indoor arcade and restaurant are among the attractions at this play-station complex. In its effort to attract families, Celebration Station offers a "Value Pak," which includes a large, single-topping pizza, soft drinks, and 40 game tokens for $21.99. Summer Mon–Thu 10 a.m.–11 p.m., Fri–Sat 10 a.m.–12 a.m., Sun 12 p.m.–11 p.m.; winter Mon–Thu 4–8, Fri 4–10, Sat 11 a.m.–10 p.m., Sun 12–8. (Bartlett, Cordova, Germantown)

CORDOVA SKATING CENTER
7970 Club Center Dr.
Memphis
901/755-0221
Cordova Skating Center is one of the newest and nicest roller-skating rinks in town. It's a large, well-managed rink in which skaters are closely super-vised and safety rules are enforced. Regular roller skates, as well as in-line skates, are available for rent. There's also a pro shop that sells socks and other skating accessories. A popular birthday party destination, the Cordova Skating Center serves pizza, hot dogs, and ice cream in its snack bar. Lockers are also available. Call for hours. (Bartlett, Cordova, Germantown)

EAST END SKATING RINK
5718 Mt. Moriah Rd.
Memphis
901/363-7785
Just off the I-240 Mt. Moriah exit, this well-maintained roller-skating rink has become especially popular with the junior high school set. A DJ plays the day's favorite Top 40 hits, and there's a snack bar, video and arcade games, and several semiprivate birthday-party rooms. $5 includes standard skate rental, $4 additional for in-line skates, $3 additional for racing skates (or skaters may bring their own). Call for open hours. (South Memphis)

ICE CHALET
Mall of Memphis
Perkins Rd. at American Way
Memphis
901/362-8877

The city's largest mall also features Memphis's only indoor ice-skating rink. Ice skates may be rented, or skaters may bring their own. The rink area also features an arcade with video games. It's adjacent to the mall's huge food court. Mon and Wed 11–3; Tue, Thu, Fri 11–5:30 and 7–9; Sat 12:30–9; Sun 1–6. $6, $2.25 additional for skates. (South Memphis)

LIBERTYLAND
Mid-South Fairgrounds
940 Early Maxwell Blvd.
Memphis
901/274-1776

The nostalgic, turn-of-the-century Grand Carousel, built in 1909, is one of the more sedate pleasures at this bicentennial-themed park, which is now entering its third decade of operation. Among the more modern thrill rides are the log flume, Sea Dragon, and the Kamikaze, not to mention the corkscrewing Revolution roller coaster. Libertyland's "Zippin' Pippin" is the oldest operating wooden roller coaster in America. Elvis, who used to love to rent the amusement park after hours, reportedly rode this rattling, high-speed beast just days before he died at Graceland.

Arcade games, live stage shows, and other attractions are also part of Libertyland Amusement Park. When the Mid-South Fair kicks off in late August, this is where it's held. April 26–Labor Day. $17. (Midtown/Central)

Wonders Cultural Series, Titanic Exhibit, p.122

MUD ISLAND RIVER PARK
125 N. Front St.
Memphis
901/576-7241

The big thrill for kids is to walk the three-quarter-mile, to-scale replica of the mighty Mississippi River, which spills out over Mud Island. Boys and girls alike may also delight in climbing aboard the famous World War II B-17 bomber *Memphis Belle.* Open seasonally, usually Apr–Oct. $8 adults, $6 seniors and children 4 and older. Season passes $25 adults, $45 families. (Downtown)

8

PARKS, GARDENS, AND RECREATION AREAS

While it's true that Memphis boasts one of the largest urban park systems in the country, it's also a sad fact that not all 179 of those parks, spread out over 5,312 acres, are properly maintained and reasonably safe for tourists.

Among the better parks in the city are those with playgrounds, basketball and tennis courts, soccer fields, and picnic grounds. Tom Lee Park, along the riverfront, is a nice place for watching the boats, taking a brisk walk, or simply admiring the view of the downtown bridges that arc over the Mississippi River. In midtown and East Memphis, Overton and Audubon are among the parks most frequented by local residents.

Out in the suburbs, Shelby County maintains some of the nicest, cleanest parks in the metropolitan area. You'll have to venture beyond downtown to reach such areas as Germantown, Collierville, and Bartlett, but the drive will generally pay off in the form of spacious, litter-free grounds, neat ball fields, and playgrounds in family-centered neighborhoods.

MUNICIPAL PARKS

AUDUBON PARK
Park Ave. and Goodlett
Memphis
Centrally located in East Memphis near the Dixon Gallery and Gardens, Memphis Botanic Gardens, and the University of Memphis, Audubon Park features a recently renovated playground area, a lovely, 18-hole golf course, tennis center, soccer and baseball fields, shaded picnic areas, outdoor grills, and a shelter house. The park's easy access, and stately trees that provide some of the most picturesque autumn foliage in town, are among the reasons Memphis residents cluster at this park. (East Memphis)

CAMERON-BROWN PARK
E. Farmington Blvd.
at Farmington Ext.
Germantown

This 55-acre park boasts a one-and-a-half-mile hiking trail and a large family picnic pavilion nestled beside a three-acre lake. The park also includes five baseball/softball fields, a batting cage, and a combination football/soccer field. In addition to the family picnic area, there are 32 picnic sites with tables, grills, and waste containers, two playgrounds, and two tennis courts. Much of the park is lighted at night. (Bartlett, Cordova, Germantown)

C.O. FRANKLIN PARK
Germantown

Located south of Poplar Pike and east of Germantown Road, this park consists of 50 acres with such amenities as baseball and softball fields, two football/soccer fields, two playgrounds, and an ADA-designed playground. Also on the grounds are six tennis courts, the Pickering Community Center, the Morgan Woods Children's Theatre, and the Germantown Charity Horse Show Arena and Stables.

Adjacent to this area is the Morgan Woods Park, a 14-acre park between C.O. Franklin Park and Oaklawn Gardens. The heavily wooded park is laced with hiking trails, and includes 10 pristine picnic sites complete with tables and grills. (Bartlett, Cordova, Germantown)

COURT SQUARE
Court between Main St.
and Second Ave.
Memphis

Tom Cruise and Gene Hackman strolled through this downtown park during the filming of *The Firm*, but the grounds have a history that can be traced back long before Hollywood. Townsfolk have gathered at this historic square since the late nineteenth century for parades, civic celebrations, and such somber occasions as watching local men and boys march off to battle in the Mexican, Civil, and Spanish-American Wars, as well as World War I.

Today, the Main Street Trolley glides past this nostalgic, turn-of-the-century park. Tourists may have to fend off panhandlers, pigeons, and the feisty, fat-bellied squirrels that have become accustomed to handouts from strollers resting on the park benches.

A small, elevated gazebo and a lovely bronze fountain are focal points of Court Square. The fountain,

---

TRIVIA

Tennessee trivia buffs may already know that the state bird is the mockingbird, the state flower is the iris, and the state tree is the tulip poplar. But what about the state insect? There are two: the ladybug and lightning bug. The state animal is the raccoon, but we have our own horse, too: the Tennessee walking horse. The Volunteer State's motto, "Agriculture and Commerce," is reflected in the state seal, adopted in 1801,which features a bundle of wheat and a plow, a cotton plant, and a sailboat.

---

a statue of Hebe, cup-bearer to the gods, is a replica of the original in St. Petersburg, Russia. The Court Square statuary was first dedicated on May 28, 1876. (Downtown)

GERMANTOWN MUNICIPAL PARK
1801 Exeter St.
Germantown
The park's lush, meticulously landscaped 17 acres are part of Germantown Municipal Square, which encompasses multiple municipal buildings and the Germantown Centre. The park offers outdoor enthusiasts six tennis courts, a tennis pro shop, two lakes for fishing, clean restrooms, a playground, a pavilion, a softball/soccer field, six picnic sites with tree-shaded tables and grills, and a historic building known as the John Gray House.

Germantown Centre (1801 Exeter St., Germantown) is worth a look if you're anywhere near the park. The center is part of a 70,000-plus-square-foot recreational complex that includes a 40-meter swimming pool, three basketball courts, four

locker rooms, saunas, a whirlpool, three racquetball courts, meeting rooms, and game rooms. What's more, the Germantown Performing Arts Centre is next door. (Bartlett, Cordova, Germantown)

HOUSTON LEVEE PARK
9777 Dogwood
Germantown
This 37-acre park, adjacent to Houston High School in Germantown, has a brand-new skateboarding center in addition to a myriad of other pleasing amenities. The park includes a four-acre lake with three baseball/softball fields, four tennis courts, jogging and walking trails, a fountain, pine-shaded picnic areas, benches, grills, a pavilion, a concession stand, two restroom facilities, and a vast general recreation area. (Bartlett, Cordova, Germantown)

MARQUETTE PARK
Park Ave. at Mt. Moriah Rd.
Memphis
Marquette Park is located in the heart of East Memphis. A residential area

Lichterman Nature Center, p. 134

Lions and Tigers and Bears . . .

A parade of pretend beasts greets visitors along a 40-foot path that leads from a cave at the Peabody Place Museum (see Chapter 6). The animals, ranging from three to five feet in height, include pairs of horses, tigers, camels, and sheep, all created from a variety of precious stones, ivory, cloisonne, and other materials. Their colorful backdrop is an enormous mural painted by local artist Elinor Hawkins. Two cloisonne Temple Shizi guardian lions, known as "Foo Dogs," guard the moon-shaped gallery entrance. They tower almost six feet tall and once stood watch over the Forbidden City in Beijing, China

to the east and a commercial development directly to the west border the park, which includes ball fields, swings, and other playground equipment, as well as wide-open spaces ideal for tossing Frisbees. There is also a restroom facility here. (East Memphis)

OVERTON PARK
Poplar Ave. at Parkway
Some of the oldest and most beautiful trees in Memphis dot the verdant landscape at Overton Park. Aptly described as an urban oasis in the heart of midtown Memphis, Overton Park features a nine-hole golf course, softball fields, a playground, soccer fields, picnic areas, and wooded nature trails. It's also home to the zoo and art museum.

On July 30, 1954, Elvis performed at the outdoor amphitheater in Overton Park. "That's All Right (Mama)" was a hit with the large crowd. Other entertainers, from Furry Lewis to ZZ Top, have played there as well. The amphitheater, known locally as the Shell, still occasionally serves as the stage for local bands in search of an audience. You'll recognize it by the pastel rainbow that's painted across its acoustically concave backdrop. With its weathered but utilitarian benches, the amphitheater sits beneath a grove of towering shade trees, just behind the Memphis College of Art and near the entrance to the Memphis Zoo. (Midtown/Central)

TOM LEE PARK
Riverside Dr.
Memphis
A river workman named Tom Lee became a national hero in 1925, when he rescued dozens of survivors after the steamboat *Norman* overturned and sank in the Mississippi River just south of Memphis. His efforts were especially remarkable because Lee could not swim. The beautiful riverside park named in Lee's honor today bears a memorial to that brave man.

Hugging the wide, broad banks of

the Mississippi River, with a grassy, magnolia-covered bluff rising high above it to the east, the park along Riverside Drive offers one of the most picturesque views in all of Memphis. A leisurely drive along this smooth, paved road allows for breathtaking panoramas of Old Man River and the graceful bridges that extend over the vast waterway. (Downtown)

MAYWOOD BEACH AND POOL
8100 Maywood Dr.
Olive Branch, Mississippi
601/895-2777
Imported white sand provides clean beachfront property for this well-maintained lake just south of the Hickory Hill area and across the Tennessee-Mississippi state line. Picnic areas with tables and grills are among the amenities. Mid-May–Labor Day Tue–Sat 9–5 (and weekends thereafter as long as the weather permits). $6.75 adults, $4.75 children 3–9, free for children 2 and under. (South Memphis)

MUD ISLAND RIVER PARK
280 Island Dr.
Memphis
576-7223
Although Mud Island is best known as a tourist attraction, visitors also embrace it as a park. After all, the site consists of 52 acres of parkland bordered by the Wolf River Harbor to the East and the Mississippi River to the west. The park has been open since 1982, and offers gorgeous views of the river as well as the Memphis skyline.

Legend has it that Mud Island formed when river silt piled up around the hull of a sunken Union gunboat, but maps show it in existence—sometimes called City Island—long before that. And, despite its name, it's not an island since it's connected to the mainland at its northern end. (Downtown)

MUNICIPAL PARK
6400 Stage Rd.
Bartlett
Another popular Bartlett-area park is

Top Ten Reasons to Love Memphis
by U.S. Congressman Harold Ford Jr.

1. The great people of Memphis
2. The city's rich music history, especially Beale Street
3. Our museums, especially Brooks, the Civil Rights Museum, and the Pink Palace
4. Memphis barbecue
5. Memphis in May
6. Federal Express
7. The Memphis skyline
8. St. Jude Children's Research Hospital
9. Libertyland
10. Our future!

located behind the city hall. The park includes tennis courts, a beautiful Japanese tranquillity garden with a bridge imported from the Orient, and picnic areas, a playground, and restroom facilities. (Bartlett, Cordova, Germantown)

POWELL ROAD PARK
350 W. Powell Rd.
Collierville

Located on the same grounds as the state-of-the-art Harrell Theatre and the Collierville Community Center is this inviting suburban park that boasts four baseball diamonds, a five-field soccer complex, and a sand volleyball court. Powell Road Park also offers visitors four lighted tennis courts, a 1.2-mile exercise trail, two playground areas, picnic facilities, a concession stand, and restrooms. (South Memphis)

W. C. HANDY PARK
Beale St. between Third and Fourth Sts.
Memphis

Although it isn't the kind of park for tossing a Frisbee or playing catch, W. C. Handy Park is a must-see site. In 1960, two years after Handy, the father of the blues, passed away, this park was renamed in his honor. Today the paved park is where contemporary blues and jazz musicians go to play for tips. A terrific statue of Handy, trumpet in hand, makes a great photo opportunity. (Downtown)

W. J. Freeman Park
2629 Bartlett Blvd.
Bartlett

One of the nicest suburban recreation areas in the Bartlett area, W. J. Freeman Park offers large, open playing areas, walking trails and a jogging track, and ball fields. Picnic facilities include tables and a gazebo. There's also a playground and restrooms. The park hosts the annual Autumn Folk Festival during the last week of September. (Bartlett, Cordova, Germantown)

GARDENS

DIXON GALLERY AND GARDENS
4339 Park Ave.
Memphis
901/761-5250

Inside, the art is outstanding, but the Dixon Gallery and Gardens also

Memphis Botanical Garden, p. 134

Memphis Convention and Visitors Bureau

Park City

The Germantown Greenway Master Plan is a nature-lover's delight. The plan, which calls for 20 linear miles of contiguous parkland to run along the perimeter of Germantown, includes land along the Wolf River to the north, along the power easements to the east and west, and along the railroad tracks to the south.

Areas already developed are Nashoba Park, the Miller Farms section, and the Houston Levee section. Still under construction is the swath from Miller Farms to Poplar Estates.

happens to be one of the most beautiful outdoor spots in all of Memphis. Meandering trails, exquisite sculpture, and a profusion of flowers and year-round foliage blanket acres of sun-dappled woodlands and neatly manicured lawns. Tue–Sat 10–5, Sun 1–5; Mon gardens open only. $5 adults, $4 seniors and groups with advance reservations, $3 students, $1 children under 12. (East Memphis)

LICHTERMAN NATURE CENTER
5992 Quince Rd.
Memphis
901/767-7322
This 65-acre environmental education facility and wildlife sanctuary is listed on the National Register of Historic Places. There's a three-mile hiking trail, a picnic area, and a 10-acre lake, as well as a forest, field, marsh, greenhouse, and wildlife hospital. Tue–Sat 9:30–5, Sun 1–5. $2 adults, $1 children and seniors, free for children 3 and under. (East Memphis)

MEMPHIS BOTANIC GARDEN
750 Cherry Rd.
Memphis

901/685-1566
This 96-acre complex includes a Japanese tranquillity garden as well as sensory, sculpture, daylily, rose, herb, wildflower, perennial, cactus, dogwood, and azalea gardens. The Goldsmith Civic Garden Center features a Boehm porcelain collection, art exhibitions, horticultural shows, and a plant information library. The Hardin Hall is a 5,500-square-foot facility used for weddings and receptions, banquets, meetings, corporate parties, seminars, special events, and fundraisers. Tram rides are available at various times. Nov–Feb Mon–Sat 9–4:30, Sun 11–4:30; Mar–Oct Mon–Sat 9–6, Sun 11–6; closed Thanksgiving, Christmas, New Year's Day. $2 adults, $1.50 seniors, $1 children, free for children under 6. (East Memphis)

STATE PARKS AND RECREATION AREAS

MEEMAN-SHELBY STATE PARK
Rte. 3
Millington
901/876-5215

A 15-mile drive north of Memphis is the Meeman-Shelby State Park. Boats with electric motors may be launched at the park's lake. Rental johnboats are available at the boat dock, but fishing may also be enjoyed from the pier or riverbanks. Swimming, hiking, and camping are other pursuits available throughout the heavily wooded, 14,500-acre site. (Downtown)

SHELBY FARMS
7171 Mullins Station Rd.
Memphis
901/382-2249
Shelby Farms is a haven for all sorts of outdoor activity, including horseback riding, hiking, and windsurfing. At 4,500 acres and the largest park of its kind in an urban setting, Shelby Farms is also home to a variety of birds, reptiles, deer, bobcats, and other wildlife—including bison, which roam freely on the animal range.

Other park attractions include the Showplace Arena, where several equestrian events are held each year; Ducks Unlimited's international headquarters, which boasts a scenic waterfowl propagation lake; and Agricenter International, which displays advances in farming technology. (Bartlett, Cordova, Germantown)

9

SHOPPING

From fuzzy press-on sideburns and amber-tinted aviator sunglasses that evoke the King's later years, to autographed first-edition novels by such southern authors as William Faulkner and Kaye Gibbons, to fine antiques and works of art, the offerings in Memphis's retail scene are wildly eclectic and vast. In fact, metropolitan Memphis has nearly 55 square feet of retail space for every person. That's about triple the national average.

Most of the city's best shopping lies in the eastern suburbs, in areas such as Hickory Hill, Germantown, and Cordova. Outlet shopping can be found about a 20-minute drive east of downtown Memphis at the Belz Factory Outlet Mall.

Downtown, once the weakest of the city's shopping areas, is on the brink of a long-awaited renaissance. A plethora of new hotels, restaurants, brewpubs, boutiques, and even a grocery store are among the businesses that have followed suit with moves into the once-vacant downtown area. Most recently, developers announced plans to build a 24-screen movie theater that will include an IMAX theater. Scheduled to open in 1999, the downtown cineplex will be one of only seven of its kind in the United States. And Hard Rock Café is the latest tenant to move into the Beale Street Historic District.

Souvenirs are plentiful along Beale Street and at virtually all of the city's museum and gallery gift shops. For Graceland goods, the shopping complex across the street from Elvis's mansion corners the market with an astonishing array of mostly tasteful, and rarely irreverent, Elvis memorabilia. For the tackier stuff, go no farther than midtown, where you'll find new and used merchandise in the Cooper-Young Historic District and Overton Square.

SHOPPING DISTRICTS

Downtown and Beale Street

Not so long ago, downtown was an abysmal place, with more vacant storefronts than viable businesses. Today, however, downtown is in the midst of a phenomenal comeback, and the shopping selection is improving every day. Beale Street is the main magnet for tourist dollars, but businesses along the Main Street Trolley line are gradually coming back, as well. You won't find name-brand department stores along the trolley line, but rather small mom-and-pop-type businesses and boutiques that cater to customer's individual needs.

CENTER FOR SOUTHERN FOLKLORE
209 Beale St.
Memphis
901/525-3655
While it's primarily a museum, coffee bar, and hot spot for live acoustic blues, folk, and gospel music, the one-of-a-kind Center for Southern Folklore also contains a killer gift shop. It's filled with "Southern stuff," including tapes, CDs, books on musical and cultural history, folk art, photographs, posters, and other unique items. Their Southern sampler box includes Goo Goo Clusters, barbecue sauce, a Memphis-music cassette or CD, and real bolls of cotton neatly baled in hand-sized souvenirs. The center publishes a newsprint catalogue that makes ordering easy. (Downtown)

MEMPHIS MUSIC
149 Beale St.
Memphis
901/526-5047
CDs and cassettes by the likes of W. C. Handy, Blind Lemon Jefferson, and other blues greats line the shelves and display racks in this Beale Street store. Music-related souvenirs, T-shirts depicting famous jazz musicians, and other items may be found here. (Downtown)

PEANUT SHOPPE
24 S. Main St. Mall
Memphis
901/525-1115
"You name it, we have it," is the owner's proud boast. That may not be entirely true, but this nostalgic candy counter with the blue and gold Mr. Peanut in the window sells pound after pound of freshly roasted peanuts—shelled, unshelled, salted, unsalted, and blanched—as well as cashews, pecans, pistachios, chocolate, hard fruit candies, and other snacks. There's also a cooler full of cold drinks and a movie-house popcorn machine. (Downtown)

PINCH ANTIQUE MALL
430 N. Front St.
Memphis
901/525-0929
Located in the Pinch Historic District across from the Pyramid, this antique mall is the most convenient to downtown Memphis and is full of great collectibles. (Downtown)

POP TUNES
308 Poplar Ave.
Memphis
901/525-6348
Elvis, who used to live around the corner in the Lauderdale Courts housing project, loved this record store. Today the shelves are stuffed with vintage '50s rock, country, and rockabilly recordings, along with photomurals of the King in his early years. The

store has a good selection of urban and rap music, as well as blues. This locally owned and operated record-store chain, the city's oldest, has other locations throughout the Memphis metro area, but none with the palpable historic richness of this American original. (Downtown)

ROD & HANK'S VINTAGE GUITARS
97 S. Main St.
Memphis
901/525-9240
www.rhguitars.com

Look for the Bob Marley posters, pink guitar, and vintage amps in the window of this cool guitar shop, where you can watch instruments being repaired and buy new and vintage instruments. The owners boast they offer the city's finest selection of used and antique Martin, Fender, Gibson, and Gretsch guitars, old amps, and other effects. Judging by the brisk business they seem to do, who are we to question that assertion? (Downtown)

A. SCHWAB'S
163 Beale St.
Memphis
901/523-9782

Operating on Beale Street since 1876, this old-time dry-goods store is truly one of a kind. The scuffed, hardwood floors still creak underfoot, as do the stairs leading up to the mezzanine and second floor. Voodoo potions, candles, incense, and good-luck charms, including bottled "Curse Remover," are among the more eye-catching curios offered here. This store sells absolutely everything, from oversized overalls and white cotton petticoats to canes and straw hats, house slippers, and moccasins. The store's apt motto is, "If you can't find it at Schwab's, you're better off without it." Closed Sunday. (Downtown)

STRANGE CARGO
172 Beale St.
Memphis
901/525-1516

Humorous and adult-oriented gag gifts, cards, and T-shirts are sold in this Beale Street souvenir shop. (Downtown)

WE'RE NUTS PECAN CO.
62 S. Front St.
Memphis
901/521-6887 or 800/254-7768

One of downtown's newest businesses also holds the distinction of being the city's only pecan-cracking, shelling, sorting, and bagging outfit as well. Guests may purchase pecans by the pound or in gift packages for mailing. They can also walk through this historic warehouse and watch the circa-1940s pecan machinery in action. (Downtown)

Cooper-Young Historic District

This historic neighborhood prides itself on its artsy, bohemian atmosphere. While several of the area's anchor establishments folded or changed hands around 1998, new owners/operators have stepped in to take their place—evidence that the district still has a lot of life left. Look for unusual and handcrafted gift items, artwork, vintage clothing, and pet supplies in this laid-back shopping area. Cooper-Young makes for some of Memphis's best window-shopping— as well as people-watching.

DEL CORAZON
2172 Young Ave.
Memphis
901/725-7647

Quartz-crystal hearts, wishing stones, leather-bound writing journals with handmade paper and writing pens, and wax stamps are among the many items pleasingly arranged within this relatively new boutique in the Cooper-Young Historic District. Birdhouses, candles, antique children's toys, and Elvis refrigerator-magnet "paper dolls" are other fascinating finds. (Midtown/Central)

MEMPHIS DRUM SHOP
878 S. Cooper St.
Memphis
901/276-2328

Drums, cymbals, and Latin, ethnic, and other hand-percussion instruments are the stocks in trade at the Memphis Drum Shop. Sales, service, repairs, and rentals on new, used, and custom instruments are offered. The store owner likes to encourage customers to "visit our vintage vault!" (Midtown/Central)

SCOTT'S COSMIC CLOSET
2093 Madison

Proprietors of A. Schwab's, p. 138

Memphis Convention and Visitors Bureau

Memphis
901/278-2259

Furniture and decorative arts and gifts are among the finds at this fabulous shop in Overton Square. From hand-painted tableware to leopard-print chairs shaped like platform shoes, the store is as unusual as it is fun. (Midtown/Central)

Graceland Plaza

Graceland Plaza, across the street from Elvis Presley's mansion (see Chapter 5: Sights and Attractions), is a treasure trove of shopping opportunity for fans of the King, and a shopping district in and of itself. The Good Rockin' Tonight store sells tapes, CDs, cards, and posters, while the ritzier Elvis Threads sells T-shirts, jackets, and other apparel. Other shops in the area include an ice-cream parlor, Chrome Grille, and Rockabilly's Diner.

Hickory Hill

This area of southeast Shelby County is booming with commercial development. Virtually every big discount store or nationwide chain you might care to mention probably has stores in the area. From Best Buy with its CDs, computers, and appliances to Bed Bath and Beyond, Office Max, and Babies R Us, the area is wall-to-wall parking lots teeming with shoppers. While that's great for bargain hunters and shoppers visiting Memphis from smaller, rural areas without such extensive commercial development, it could be frustrating to a person trying to seek out small or independently owned gift shops or one-of-a-kind boutiques. A few exceptions are noted below.

A Good Read

Phineas Poe, an ex-cop just released from a psychiatric hospital, wakes up in a hotel room in a bathtub full of ice. A day or two after being drugged and lured into bed by a vixen named Jude, Poe must be rushed to the hospital, for Jude has cut him open and stolen one of his kidneys to sell on the black market.

So begins Kiss Me, Judas *(Viking, 1998), the seductive first novel by Will Christopher Baer that's been hailed as a "fine and dangerous work." Author Madison Smartt Bell (*All Soul's Rising*) calls it "ingeniously plotted . . . a perfect noir novel, right up there with Chandler's* The Big Sleep.*"*

Born in Mississippi, Baer lived in Canada and Italy before moving to Memphis, where he attended Rhodes College and the University of Memphis. A Generation Xer with a penchant for spoken-word performances at Memphis's notorious (and defunct) Antenna Club, he also played in a grunge band called The Scam. Now living in California, Baer is working on his next novel, Penny Dreadful.

HOBBY LOBBY
3661 Hickory Hill Rd.
Memphis
901/367-0144
The Hobby Lobby, an enormous discount store featuring items of interest to arts-and-crafts enthusiasts, has everything from silk flowers and pincushions to oil paints, sable-haired brushes, and sketchpads. Within the store is a full-service fabric department. Although Hobby Lobby is a national chain, its stores retain a distinctive atmosphere not unlike old-time department stores. Other locations are at 1991 Exeter Road,

Germantown (901/757-4419); and 3252 Austin Peay Highway (901/388-8740). (South Memphis)

XANADU
7235 Winchester Ave.
Memphis
901/757-9885
This pleasantly cluttered neighborhood bookstore in southeast Shelby County carries interesting gift items, new and used books, domestic newspapers, magazines, and literary journals. Independently owned and operated, Xanadu has a friendly, knowledgeable staff. (South Memphis)

Poplar Avenue Corridor

A nightmare of a thoroughfare if you're a motorist in a hurry, multi-lane Poplar Avenue between Highland and I-240 is also a shopper's dream come true. Retail establishments of every stripe line the congested east-west artery that connects downtown Memphis with the suburbs. From convenience stores to shopping centers, hair salons to hardware dealers, grocery stores to gas stations, Poplar Avenue has a bit of it all.

BOOKSTAR AND STARBUCKS CAFÉ
3402 Poplar Ave.
Memphis
901/323-9332
Books, books, and more books fill this converted movie theater in a central Memphis shopping center. Many books are marked down 20 to 30 percent, including the latest *New York Times* hardcover and paperback bestsellers. There's also a Starbucks Café inside. (East Memphis)

DAVIS-KIDD BOOKSELLERS
397 Perkins Rd. Ext.
Memphis
901/683-9801
The largest bookstore in Memphis offers shoppers a broad selection of note cards, calendars, writing journals, and other gift items, as well as an extensive collection of children's books and toys, and a terrific café. (East Memphis)

DIVE SHOP
999 S. Yates Rd.
Memphis
901/763-3483
This is the place for scuba equipment and accessories. The Dive Shop has an on-site pool designed specifically for scuba, and instruction is available privately or in a class setting. Call for their next group trip to the Caribbean. (East Memphis)

JAMES DAVIS
Laurelwood Center
400 Grove Park
Memphis
901/767-4640
Designer names such as Giorgio Armani, Hugo Boiste, Zanella, and Bricker for Men are sold in this upscale men's apparel store. Additionally, James Davis offers casual lines and high-end women's dresses. (East Memphis)

JOAN FRANKS
434 Grove Park S.
Memphis
901/767-4640
Designer women's fashions are the specialty of this upscale boutique in the Laurelwood Center in East Memphis. Jewelry and other accessories, including beautiful hand-painted silk scarves, round out the accessories options. (East Memphis)

Starbucks Café

Alan Howell/Memphis Business Journal

Top 10 Memphis Shopping Spots
by Nicky Robertshaw, Memphis business writer and shopper

1. **Graceland Plaza**, 3700 block of Elvis Presley Blvd., 901/332-2233. This is the international mecca for those seeking official Elvis souvenirs in every price range. The plaza (also the starting point for Graceland Mansion tours) has several general souvenir shops with all things Elvis, including postcards, posters, CDs and tapes, address books, license plates and T-shirts. Don't miss the boutiques: Threads (from Elvis socks to silk ties), Good Rockin' Tonight (huge selection of the King's CDs, tapes, and videos), Gallery Elvis (collectibles including a $5,000 limited-edition replica of Elvis's Gibson J-200 guitar and $250 commemorative posters) and Elvis Kids (3-D puzzle of Graceland Mansion). Want more? Next door is Graceland Crossing, a cluster of general souvenir shops.

2. **Williams-Sonoma Clearance Outlets**, 4718 Spottswood Ave. (Audubon Shopping Center), 901/763-1500. Great shopping is one outcome of Williams-Sonoma locating its warehouse in Memphis. A variety of discounted merchandise turns up here from recent Williams-Sonoma, Pottery Barn, Chambers, Hold Everything, and Gardeners Eden catalogs. There are two stores: one for furniture and rugs, one for everything else. The stores don't ship, so to send purchases home, check with Mail Boxes Etc., across the parking lot.

3. **ICBs**, 137 E. Calhoun St., 901/529-1476. This smaller retailer of closeout merchandise, mainly furniture and decorative items, is located in a big downtown warehouse. Ask about other, smaller ICB locations around town if you want more.

4. **A. Schwab**, 163 Beale St., 901/523-9782. Operating on Beale Street since 1876, this historic general store with its creaking hardwood floors and old-fashioned fixtures is a trip back in time. Merchandise includes a large selection of suspenders, over-sized overalls, and a huge assortment of sub-five-dollar items. No connoisseur of kitsch will want to miss the voodoo corner (featuring Jinx Removal Spray for $2.95) or the array of one-dollar souvenirs.

JOSEPH
418 Grove Park S.
Memphis
901/767-1609
Joseph offers footwear, handbags, jewelry, and complete ladies' wardrobes, and includes the finest designers from America and Europe. Located in the Laurelwood Center, the store specializes in high-end

5. **Center for Southern Folklore**, 209 Beale St., 901/525-3655. The center, also a café and entertainment venue, sells CDs and tapes of blues and other regional music. But the real reason to shop here is the "Southern stuff," including folk art portraits, local ceramics, and a variety of local handmade crafts. A painted bowling-pin figure of Elvis is $40; a birdhouse made from beer tops is $100. Ask about the center's newsprint catalog for easy ordering.

6. **Wolfchase Galleria**, 8359 Hwy. 64, just off I-40, in Cordova, 901/373-4514. The newest and shiniest of Memphis's malls houses Dillard's, Goldsmith's, Ann Taylor, Disney Store, Pottery Barn, and dozens of others.

7. **Burke's Book Store**, 1719 Poplar Ave., 901/278-7484. Known for its new, used, and collectible books, this friendly and literate shop is one of the few places where author John Grisham does book signings. Visitors will find that Southern writers and Civil War history are particularly strong here.

8. **Rod and Hank's Vintage Guitar Store**, 45 Main St. (just off Monroe Ave.), 901/525-9240. This buyer and seller of vintage guitars recently moved from its tiny corner at the Memphis Music Hall of Fame to its own digs on Main Street. This is where a collector could buy, say, a 1950s Gibson J45 acoustic guitar for $1,500, or a guitar once owned by a famous rocker. Be sure to check out the art gallery upstairs.

9. **Shangri-La Records**, 1916 Madison Ave., 901/274-1916. Vintage music (vinyl as well as CDs and tapes) and souvenirs such as bricks from Stax Recording Studio are sold here. Pick up a copy of the store's alternative tourist guide, a bargain at $2.50. Or order the guide before you get to town—they'll send it to you for three dollars if you want to use it to help plan your trip.

10. **Bella Notte**, 2172 Young St. (Cooper-Young Historic District), 901/726-4131. This is the town's best retailer of unique gifts. Candles, hip baby gifts, European bath products, notes, seasonal items, and jewelry can be found here. While in the neighborhood, walk south toward Cooper Street to check out other shops and the many hip restaurants.

fashionable women's shoes. (East Memphis)

REGENCY TRAVEL AND INTERNATIONAL MARKET

**397 Perkins Ext.
Memphis
901/682-9065**
Art from around the world and gift items for the experienced traveler are

Oak Court Mall p. 149

available in this dramatic retail environment. A combination travel agency and showplace of exotic decorative arts, the store sells such items as Mexican pottery and hand-painted, lacquered Russian boxes, as well as luggage, airline, and cruise excursions, and gourmet food items from Italy and Provence. (East Memphis)

RIVER RECORDS
822 S. Highland St.
Memphis
901/324-1754
Sports cards, T-shirts, and collectible records, tapes, and CDs are sold at this run-down but personable campus dive. The store also specializes in comic books, posters, and Elvis memorabilia. While it's not on Poplar Avenue, it's just a few blocks south off of Highland, in the University of Memphis campus area. (East Memphis)

OTHER NOTABLE STORES

BURKE'S BOOK STORE
1719 Poplar Ave.

Memphis
901/278-7484
When John Grisham is ready to release his next bestseller, Burke's is among the handful of small mom-and-pop bookstores where he signs books. Located around the corner from Circuit Playhouse, Burke's is known for new, used, and collectible books. The store has tattered rugs, scattered chairs, and a friendly brown dog that wanders the aisles. Specializing in authors of the South, Burke's has a well-read and exceedingly friendly staff. (Midtown/Central)

CHAMPION'S PHARMACY AND HERB STORE
2369 Elvis Presley Blvd.
Memphis
901/948-6622
This old-fashioned apothecary recalls bygone days of the medicine man. An antique medicine wagon is among the many items on display in this full-service pharmacy that also offers herbal and homeopathic remedies and long-forgotten products that haven't seen the shelves of modern-

day drug stores in decades. (South Memphis)

CRUMP–PADGETT ANTIQUE GALLERY AND ESTATE JEWELRY
645 Marshall Ave.
Memphis
901/522-1155 or 800/521-1151
Some of the finest antiques and jewelry in Memphis can be found in this downtown shop two blocks north of Sun Studio at Marshall and Monroe. Georgian antique jewelry dating from the early 1700s, as well as Victorian, Edwardian, Art Nouveau, and art-deco jewelry is for sale, along with Mexican silver dating back to the 1930s. (Downtown Memphis)

FLASHBACK
2304 Central Ave.
Memphis
901/272-2304
Known as Memphis's best vintage furniture store, Flashback specializes in 1950s furniture as well as decorative objects and antiques dating from the 1920s to the 1940s. (Midtown/Central)

HOUSE OF MEWS
944 S. Cooper St.
Memphis
901/272-3777
www.houseofmews.com
Not only is this one-of-a-kind establishment in the Cooper-Young Historic District a nonprofit feline adoption agency, it's also a cat-lover's gift shop. Visitors can "ooh" and "aah" over the array of cute but homeless kittens and cats that find shelter at the shop. They can also cuddle, pet, or admire from afar the more aloof of these creatures. Finding good homes for the cats is the top priority here. Dedicated volunteers both care for the cats and manage the retail side of things in order to fund the feline venture. Cards, mugs, T-shirts, and computer mouse pads are sold here, along with pet supplies including food, combs and brushes, litter, and lots of irresistible kitty toys. Store hours vary according to volunteers'

Want to go antiquing? Call Madaline at Let's Go Antiquing (201 S. Cooper St., 901/722-9080). She organizes tours for groups of 10 to 50 and will lead you through the maze of more than a dozen antiques shops in the Central Avenue and Cooper Street area. Antiques stores of note include:

Abbey Antiques, 2232 Central
Antique Mall, Inc., 2151 Central
Bill Ricks Antiques, 733 Cooper
Consignments, 2300 Central
Crocker Antiques, Gifts and Garden Accents, 2281 Central
Market Central, 2215 Central
Memphis Antique Market, 2265 Central
Midtown Galleries, 2228 Central
Palladio, 2169 Central
Second Hand Rose, 2129 Central
Wellford's Antique Collction, 2288 Central

schedules, so call first if you plan to visit the House of Mews. (Midtown/Central)

MAGGIE'S PHARM
13 S. Florence
Memphis
901/722-8898
Tiny vials of rose oil, lavender flowers, exotic herbs, lotions, and other special products are sold in this Haight-Ashbury-like boutique. It's one of the few second-story businesses in the Overton Square district. Look for the yellow signs and the exterior staircase leading up to the back door. (Midtown/Central)

MANTIA'S INTERNATIONAL FOOD MARKET
4856 Poplar Ave.
Memphis
901/762-8560
Pick up tonight's dinner for the family or a picnic-to-go at this exotic cross between a grocery store and farmer's market. Gourmet pastas, sauces, hard-to-find culinary ingredients, and a mind-boggling selection of cheeses make Mantia's every food-lover's nirvana. (East Memphis)

MIGUELA'S
2055 West Street, No. 12
Germantown

Largest Black-owned Businesses in Memphis (Selected)

Allied Electrical Contractors, Inc., 1190 Walker, 901/942-7725

City-Wide Cab Co., 2240 Deadrick, 901/324-4202

Days Inn—Downtown, 164 Union Ave., 901/527-4100

Dollar Rent-A-Car Worldwide, 2780 Airways, 901/360-8787

Ewing Moving Service, Inc., 827 S. Main St., 901/884-2197

Gilliam Communications, Inc., 363 S. Second St., 901/527-9565

Jackson Person & Associates, Inc., 66 Monroe Ave., Ste. 104, 901/526-8386

Johnson Bryce, Inc., 3861 Delp, 901/369-7500

Ken-Kel Management, Inc., 3120 S. Third St., 901/398-4672

Lawrence Johnson Realtors, 5222 Millbranch, 901/344-9664

Loyal Featherstone Enterprises, Inc., 3319 Kirby Pkwy., 901/360-0201

Olympic Staffing, Inc., 1231 Southbrook Mall, 901/344-9664

Shelby Dodge, 2691 Mt. Moriah Rd., 901/363-0006

Tri-State Bank of Memphis, 180 S. Main St., 901/525-0384

Universal Life Insurance Co., 480 Linden, 901/525-3641

Café inside Davis-Kidd Booksellers, p. 141

901/737-0311

Trippy, trendy, and designer duds collide in one of Memphis's most recent fashion magnets. Name brands draw attention from the area's upscale clientele, but the store has also gained a reputation as one of the few women's apparel shops in Germantown offering such an array of chic but bohemian clothing and accessories, including artsy jewelry. (Bartlett, Cordova, Germantown)

OUTDOORS, INC.
5245 Poplar Ave.
Memphis
901/767-6790
www.outdoorsinc.com

Offering a variety of ski and wilderness equipment since 1974, Outdoors, Inc. sells skis, skiwear, mountain bikes, canoes, climbing equipment, hiking boots, clothing, and backpacks. In addition to the East Memphis location, there are stores at 1710 Union Avenue in midtown (901/722-8988) and at 833 Germantown Parkway in Cordova (901/755-2271). (East Memphis)

PRISCILLA'S PLUS-SIZE CONSIGNMENT AND RESALE
301 E. McLemore
Memphis
901/774-4001

When Priscilla Collins was laid off from a government job a few years ago, she used the opportunity to open her own business—selling plus-size clothing. A proud African American woman and a statuesque size 24, Collins offers shoppers an array of items, from windbreakers and blazers to pantsuits and evening gowns. Many items are used but in good condition, and new merchandise is offered as well. Accessories such as shoes, handbags, and hats are also available at this homey shop. (South Memphis)

RHOLEDIA'S BOUTIQUE OF GERMANTOWN
2115 Merchants Row, Ste. 1
Germantown
901/755-9661

Located on Market Square off West Street, Rholedia's Boutique features unique women's clothing and accessories. Items are moderately priced. (Bartlett, Cordova, Germantown)

SHANGRI-LA RECORDS
1916 Madison Ave.
Memphis
901/274-1916
www.shangri.com

Buy a brick from the old Stax recording studio in South Memphis. Ten dollars will get you not only a nondescript redbrick block, but also a "certificate of authenticity." How do we know they're really from Stax? "I guess you'll have to take our word for it," the salesclerk often responds. Step into Shangri-La and you enter another world: The pungent aroma of patchouli oil arrests the senses;

throbbing hip-hop music blares from the sound system; and the tiny rooms instill claustrophobia with their wallpapering of concert posters, fliers, brochures, and other advertisements. The shop also carries an extensive collection of vinyl records, CDs, and cassettes, as well as reading matter ranging from underground literary journals to alternative comics. (Midtown/Central)

SIDEWALK UNIVERSITY INTERNATIONAL BOOKSELLERS
2287 Union Ave.
Memphis
901/722-2110
African American art, books, and gift items are among the eclectic mix at this unusual bookstore on Poplar Avenue near the Parkway interchange. (Midtown/Central)

THE 7th INNING
3040 Walnut Grove Rd.
Memphis
901/324-0012
A ball and baseball bat signed by Babe Ruth, along with assorted baseball cards and other sports memorabilia are on sale at this one-of-a-kind shop between midtown and East Memphis. One area of the store includes celebrity merchandise, such

as letters and autographs from a broad swatch of the famous—from Sophia Loren and Sandra Day O'Connor to Mickey Rooney and Judy Garland. (East Memphis)

TOBACCO BOWL
152 Madison Ave.
Memphis
901/2310
Tobacco accessories and gifts are the mainstay of this longstanding business, located downtown between Second and Third Streets. Imported cigars for sale include those by Arturo Fuente, Partagas, Macanudo, Royal Jamaican, and Punch. The pipes are made by Comoy, Dunhill, Sasien, and Meerschaum. Decorative cigar cutters, humidors, and tobacco pouches round out the merchandise in this smoker's paradise. (Downtown)

MAJOR SHOPPING MALLS

CARREFOUR AT KIRBY WOODS
6685 Poplar Pike
Memphis
901/759-0448
Anchored by the popular Borders Books and Music store and coffee shop, this compact suburban center

also offers furniture stores; restaurants like Mister B's, Romano's Macaroni Grill, and Schlotsky's deli; and clothing stores Little Lambs & Ivy, Paul Harris Casual Corner, and Jos. A. Bank. On the cusp between Germantown and East Memphis, the Carrefour has an ideal location. Parking is convenient, and while all of the mall's retailers appear to do a brisk business, the mall is usually far less crowded than the larger malls in the metro area. (Bartlett, Cordova, Germantown)

CHICKASAW OAKS PLAZA
3092 Poplar Ave.
Memphis
901/767-0100
More than 20 shops are featured in this small, enclosed mall designed to resemble an eighteenth-century town. Clothes, gifts, antiques, stationery, jewelry, and toys are among the goods for sale. There's also a fine bakery. The centrally located mall should benefit from the construction of the new Shelby County Public Library and Information Center, which is going up next door. (East Memphis)

HICKORY RIDGE MALL
Winchester Rd. at Hickory Hill Rd.
Memphis
901/367-8045
Kids and adults alike love the ornate carousel at this large and well-maintained suburban mall. Anchor tenants include department stores such as Dillard's, Goldsmiths, Sears, and M. M. Cohn. A sunny food court and kiosk shopping are also part of the mix. (South Memphis)

MALL OF MEMPHIS
I-240 at Perkins Rd.
Memphis
901/362-9315
The largest enclosed shopping center in the region boasts the usual blend of department stores and specialty shops, as well as a cinema and a food court. The mall also contains the city's only public ice-skating rink. (South Memphis)

OAK COURT MALL
Poplar Ave. at Perkins Rd.
Memphis
901/682-8928
The region's largest Goldsmith's

Can You Say Spare Change?

What shopper doesn't love cashing in on a bargain? At several area supermarket parking lots throughout Memphis, customers may convert their recyclable aluminum cans into money. Check out the huge bins at the following stores:

Piggly Wiggly *(888 S. White Station, 3040 Austin Peay, 1620 Madison, 5898 U.S. 70, and Sycamore View Rd.)*

Supervalue *(1779 Prescott)*

Kroger *(2680 Frayer Blvd.)*

In 1994 then-newlyweds Michael Jackson and Lisa Marie Presley made the rounds in her hometown in the weeks and months following their quickie Dominican wedding. While in town to attend a gala Elvis Tribute Concert at the Pyramid, the pair were photographed visiting St. Jude Children's Research Hospital, buying up arts and humanities books at Burke's in midtown, and going on an after-midnight shopping spree at a music store in the Hickory Hill area of southeast Shelby County.

Incidentally, the televised tribute concert at the Pyramid, emceed by Priscilla Presley, Marlo Thomas, and others, was a fundraiser for St. Jude, the hospital founded by Thomas's late father, Danny. Performing covers of some of the King's songs were Tony Bennett, Melissa Etheridge, the Velvet Underground's John Cale, Aaron Neville, Billy Ray Cyrus, Chet Atkins, Wet Wet Wet, Bryan Adams, Dwight Yoakam, Iggy Pop, the Mavericks, and Ann Wilson of Heart.

department store, and specialty boutiques selling everything from Godiva chocolates to Disney merchandise, are at home in this swank mall in the heart of the metropolitan area. There's a covered parking garage as well as plenty of surface parking space. Pathways meander around graceful oak trees in the parklike landscaping on the Poplar Avenue entrance to the mall. (East Memphis)

THE REGALIA
Poplar Ave. at Ridgeway Rd.
Memphis
901/767-0100
Although several major tenants have vacated in recent months, the Regalia retains its appealing mix of specialty shops and fine restaurants, such as Owen Brennan's, Mikasa Japan, Salsa Cocina Mexicana, and others. Clothing stores include Elizabeth Edwards and Oak Hall. Among the other businesses located here are Cooker Bar and Grill, the Bayberry Co., Cora-

dini Fine Jewelers, Reverie Fine Linens and Down, a Northwest Airlines ticketing office, and A Pea in the Pod, which specializes in maternity wear. (East Memphis)

SHOPS OF SADDLE CREEK
Poplar Ave. at Farmington/
West St.
Germantown
901/761-2571
Banana Republic, Sharper Image, Brooks Brothers, Ann Taylor, GapKids, Eddie Bauer, and other shops and restaurants are standouts in this upscale shopping center. Also look for Laura Ashley, Victoria's Secret, Williams Sonoma, and Gloria Jean Gourmet Coffee. The Tennessee-based chain Ruby Tuesday operates one of the more popular restaurants in this center. (Bartlett, Cordova, Germantown)

WOLFCHASE GALLERIA
8359 Hwy. 64

Memphis
901/373-4514
The area's newest regional mall, opened in 1997, includes a carousel and miles of specialty stores. The anchors are Dillard's, Goldsmith's, Sears, and JC Penney. The usual array of fast- and full-service restaurants lines the food court area and dots the perimeter of the property. The cinema in the mall offers stadium-style, movie-theater seating. Near the theater entrance is a children's carousel and a whimsical art display featuring a wall of colorful tiles made by patients and children of Le Bonheur Children's Medical Center in Memphis. (Bartlett, Cordova, Germantown)

FACTORY OUTLET CENTERS

BELZ FACTORY OUTLET MALL
3536 Canada Rd.
Lakeland
901/386-3180
Clothing, housewares, toys, books, perfume, and CDs are sold from the dozens of specialty shops that offer savings of up to 75 percent off regular retail. Stores carrying brand names like Bass, Van Heusen, and Bugle Boy will make the drive worthwhile for bargain-hungry shoppers. To reach the mall, take Interstate 40 east toward Nashville. The Canada Road exit and clearly marked signs are about 30 miles from downtown Memphis. (Bartlett, Cordova, Germantown)

TUESDAY MORNING
8104 Club Center Dr.
Cordova
901/752-4458
www.tuesdaymorning.com
This nationally known chain offers discounts of 60- to 80-percent off regular prices on such gift items as framed wall mirrors, art reproductions, and other decorative home furnishings. Other treasures include intricately detailed cast-iron doorstops, full lead crystal eggs, and hand-painted Limnge porcelaln eggs. Store hours vary by season. There are other Tuesday Morning locations at 2876 Poplar Ave., in the Chickasaw Crossing Shopping Center (901/458-5825); and at 6635 Quince Rd., in the Willow Grove Shopping Center (901/752-8971). (Bartlett, Cordova, Germantown)

WILLIAMS-SONOMA
CLEARANCE OUTLET
4708 Spottswood Ave.
Memphis
901/794-7977
The nationally renowned Williams-Sonoma mail-order company operates a distribution center in Memphis. This East Memphis store carries their discontinued items and other merchandise. (East Memphis)

10

SPORTS AND RECREATION

Sports are a sore spot with many Memphis residents simply because the city has fought so hard for so long—without much success—to bring high-profile NBA and NFL teams to the area. The tide may be turning, however, with the arrival of a new Triple-A baseball team. The Memphis Redbirds began play in 1998, and their new downtown baseball stadium, AutoZone Park, will open in the spring of 2000. Leading annual sports events include the FedEx St. Jude Golf Classic at Southwind and the Liberty Bowl football game every December.

Hunting, fishing, golfing, and hiking rank among the area's favorite recreational activities. Hiking trails can be found at the Lichterman Nature Center, Meeman-Shelby State Park, Overton Park, Shelby Farms Plough Recreational Area, and T. O. Fuller State Park.

SPECTATOR SPORTS

Auto Racing

MEMPHIS INTERNATIONAL MOTORSPORTS PARK
5500 Taylor Forge Rd.
Millington
901/358-7223
memphismotorsports.com
The park's biggest event of the year is the National Hot Rod Association Drag Race, usually held during the first week of October. Other seasonal events include the Fast-Forward Mustang Series in May and the Federal Mogul Drag Series in June. Admission prices vary, but regularly scheduled Friday-night races start at $8 per person. (Downtown)

Baseball

Baseball lovers can catch ballpark action north of Memphis in the community of Millington, former training site for the USA Baseball National Team. The facility now hosts a school for umpires, offers a training academy for grounds-keepers, and hosts special amateur and military athletic events. For more information call 901/872-8326.

MEMPHIS REDBIRDS
800 Home Run Ln.
Memphis
901/721-6050
www.memphisredbirds.com
The Memphis Redbirds, a new Triple A baseball team (one notch below the majors), were formed a few years ago after the Double A Memphis Chicks pulled out of town and moved to Jackson, Tennessee. Memphis loves its new team: Attendance was a record-breaking 395,592 during the Redbirds' first full season, April through September of 1998. Sports fans have also warmed to "Nostalgia Man," the team's nostalgic logo—the silhouette of a player from days of old swinging the bat—which can be seen on T-shirts, hats, and bumper stickers around town. The owners of the team founded the Redbirds as a nonprofit entity, and with the expressed aim of returning honor and pride to the game of baseball. They've vowed to keep prices low ($5–$8),

and to place fans first. Community outreach is another goal of the group. (Downtown)

Basketball

UNIVERSITY OF MEMPHIS TIGERS
The Pyramid
1 Auction Ave.
Memphis
901/678-2337
Basketball is Memphis's sport of choice. The University of Memphis Tigers, past NCAA Championship finalists, play home games at the Pyramid. Anfernee Hardaway of the Orlando Magic, a former U of M basketball star, returns each year to host a youth basketball clinic at the Pyramid. For more information on Tigers games, call the teams offices. (East Memphis)

Football

Despite repeated attempts to attract an NFL team, the city remains without a professional football team. Among the short-lived efforts of the 1990s were the Memphis Mad Dogs, a Canadian Football League team that played at the Liberty Bowl Memorial Stadium; and the Memphis Pharaohs, an Arena Football League

TRIVIA

Tim McCarver Stadium, temporary home of the Memphis Redbirds baseball team until construction is complete on their new downtown stadium, is named for one of the city's most famous sports stars. Best known today as an Emmy-winning TV sports broadcaster and analyst, McCarver rose to fame as a catcher with the St. Louis Cardinals, which beat the New York Yankees in the 1964 World Series. McCarver is currently doing commentary for the New York Mets.

team that played a few summer seasons at the Pyramid.

Before relocating to their new stadium in Nashville in 1999, the Tennessee Titans played a season at the Liberty Bowl in Memphis. Alas, Memphians, snubbed by their failure to land a team of their very own, stayed away from the Titans' games in droves. An all-time low-attendance record was set, and the team bailed to the Music City after only one dismal season.

UNIVERSITY OF TENNESSEE VOLUNTEERS
951 Court
901/448-4000
Memphis was awash in orange when the University of Tennessee Vols football team won the 1999 collegiate trophy. It's no surprise that the Knoxville-based team has its share of fans in Memphis—UT houses its prestigious medical school here.

The team's moniker, derived from "Volunteer State," originated during the 1840s and the war with Mexico. When the government requested that

Memphis Riverkings

2,800 men serve in the army during that conflict, more than 30,000 patriotic souls enlisted.

Greyhound Racing

SOUTHLAND GREYHOUND PARK
1550 N. Ingraham Blvd.
West Memphis, AR
501/735-3670 or 800/467-6182
www.southlandgreyhound.com
Live greyhound races include matinees at one and evening races at seven. Shuttles to the track are available from some downtown hotels. Southland offers pari-mutuel betting on greyhounds and horses. (Downtown)

Hockey

MEMPHIS RIVERKINGS
Mid-South Coliseum
996 Early Maxwell Blvd.
Memphis
901/527-5700
www.riverkings.com
The Memphis Riverkings of the Central Hockey League, a team that for years has played at the Mid-South Coliseum from November to mid-March, are heading south, presumably for greener pastures. The team is scheduled to move across the state line to the $30 million DeSoto County Civic Center being built for them in the nearby Mississippi Convention Center. For ticket information call Ticketmaster at 901/527-5700. (Midtown/Central)

RECREATION

Biking

While cycling within the Memphis city limits isn't practical, the athletically inclined can test their pedal mettle along the trails at Meeman–Shelby

Horse Shows

The prestigious Germantown Charity Horse Show, staged by the American Horse Show Association, is held annually over four or five days in early June. The multibreed show includes hunters, jumpers, Tennessee-walking, and American saddlebred horses. It is also the largest horse show in the area, drawing up to 800 horses each year from as many as 25 states. Participants compete for more than $100,000 in prize money and trophies, including the $25,000 Grand Prix. Spectator admission: Outside ring shows during the day are free. Nightly evening performances are $150 for an eight-seat box. The show is held at the Germantown Horse Show Arena, 7745 Poplar Pike, Germantown, 901/754-0009.

State Park, just north of the city. Overton Park in midtown has some gorgeous vistas and meandering trails, but bikers must share the turf with noncyclists and even the occasional golfer who has strayed off the park's course. Smooth trails also await bikers at Shelby Farms in the eastern suburbs of Memphis. The Tour de Wolf is a five-mile trail that begins and ends near Patriot Lake.

Construction is in progress on the Mississippi River Trail, which ultimately will stretch from Chicago to New Orleans. Only one section of this trail is complete, but the good news for local biking enthusiasts is that it's the Memphis portion. This marked trail along existing streets begins near the Pyramid and the Memphis Welcome Center before unfurling northward toward Reelfoot Lake. From Mud Island to Shelby Forest and back is a 50-mile ride. If you'll be making the trip all the way to Reelfoot Lake, plan on pedaling 170 miles each way.

If bikers have their way, the Harahan Bridge will become the first bike and pedestrian trail in the area to span the Mississippi River. Of the three local bridges connecting Tennessee and Arkansas, none are open to bicyclists. The Harahan, built of steel in 1916, was originally intended for trains.

For more information on bicycling in the city, travelers may want to contact one or two of the city's clubs devoted to the sport. The High Tailers Bike Club, nearing its 40th year in Memphis, organizes leisurely group rides on Saturday mornings, and faster, more challenging rides on Sunday mornings. Another group, the Explorers, organizes family-oriented group rides for adults and children on Tuesday nights. A good resource for more information is the Bike Peddler (901/327-4833).

Boating

MEEMAN–SHELBY STATE PARK
Rte. 3
Millington
901/876-5215
Private boats can be launched on the
Mississippi River from Meeman–
Shelby State Park, located 13 miles
north of downtown Memphis off U.S.
Highway 51. (Downtown)

RIVERSIDE PARK MARINA
1874 McKellar Lake Dr.
Memphis
901/946-2000
Boating on McKellar Lake, just south
of downtown, is accessible from
Riverside Park. There are public
docking facilities and access to a
recreational channel, the Mississippi
River, and the Wolf River. No rental
craft are available, however. Marina
office open daily 10–5:30. $3 launch
fee. (South Memphis)

Bowling

BILLY HARDWICK'S
ALL STAR LANES
1576 White Station Rd.
Memphis
901/683-2695
On Wednesday, bowl for three hours
for three dollars, with automatic scoring and discounted soda, draught beer,
and hot dogs. Mon–Thu 10–12, Fri–Sat
10–3, Sun 12–12. $1.07 per game, addi-
tional $1.75 for shoes. (East Memphis)

BRUNSWICK BARTLETT LANES
6276 Stage Rd.
Bartlett
901/386-7701
Automatic scoring is a plus here, as
are the discounts for seniors: Those
55 and older bowl for 99¢ per game,
and rent shoes for free. Sun–Thu
9–12, Fri–Sat 9–3:30 a.m. $3.95 per
game, additional $2.40 for shoes.
(Bartlett, Cordova, Germantown)

BRUNSWICK WINCHESTER BOWL
3707 S. Mendenhall Rd.
Memphis
901/362-1620
The Brunswick lanes in south Memphis also feature automatic scoring.
Sat–Sun and Wed–Thu 9 a.m.–12
a.m., Mon–Tue 2 p.m.–12 a.m., Fri 2
p.m.–2 a.m. $3.15 per game Fri–Sat,
$1.29 per game Sun–Thu, additional
$2.35 for shoes. (South Memphis)

Fishing

*Memphis's year-round fishing season
offers bass, crappie, trout, bream,
and catfish in area lakes and rivers.
Fishing licenses may be purchased at
most retail sporting goods stores.
Children 12 and under do not need a
license. Call Tennessee Wildlife Re-
sources Agency at 800/372-3928.*

MEEMAN–SHELBY STATE PARK
Rte. 3
Millington
901/876-5215

The Memphis Runners Track Club has several groups up and
running. Some of the city's best-known races include the Race
for the Cure 5K, Oak Hall Run for St. Jude, Elvis Presley International 5K, and the Jingle Bell 5K Run for Arthritis. The club's hotline is 901/534-6782.

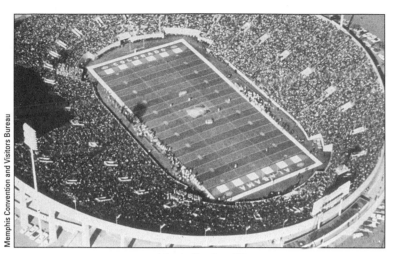

Liberty Bowl, p. 152

Year-round fishing is available on the 125-acre Poplar Tree Lake. Rental johnboats are available at the park boat dock, but fishing may be enjoyed from the pier or bank. Personal boats with electric motors are allowed on the lake for a small launch fee, but no gasoline motors are permitted. A free launch ramp is also available on the Mississippi River. (Downtown)

Fitness Clubs

FRENCH RIVIERA SPA
2005 Exeter 4
Germantown
901/756-1010
This chain of health clubs offers non-members use of their facilities for a $10 fee. This Germantown location is for women only. (Bartlett, Cordova, Germantown)

GOLD'S GYM AEROBICS & FITNESS CENTER
426 S. Grove Park Rd.
Memphis
901/684-1300

A $10 guest fee is charged to non-members who use the club. (East Memphis)

HEALTHPLEX FITNESS CENTER
1003 Monroe Ave.
Memphis
901/227-7054
Travelers may use the facility for eight dollars with a room key from participating local hotels. (Midtown/Central)

INSIDEOUT
2258 Young Ave.
Memphis
901/278-5433
Billed as "the health club for the body, mind, and soul," Insideout is midtown's only health club. The small, independently owned gym offers classes in tae bo, spinning, kick-boxing, self-defense, tai chi, and yoga. All classes are free to gym members. There are also free weights, stair climbers, treadmills, and bikes, and occasional classes on physical health and all-around metaphysical well-being. (Midtown/Central)

Memphis Redbirds, p. 153

Q THE SPORTS CLUB
1285 Ridgeway Rd.
Memphis
901/763-3265
Out-of-town guests may use the facility for $10 per week, for a maximum of two weeks. (East Memphis)

YMCA
245 Madison Ave.
Memphis
901/527-9622
Out-of-town guests may use this state-of-the-art fitness center for eight dollars per visit. Located downtown, the four-story facility includes a wide range of Nautilus, free-weights, and other exercise equipment. The YMCA includes a heated indoor swimming pool, basketball and racquetball courts, and scores of treadmills, stair climbers, stationary bicycles, and rowing machines. Daily aerobics and water aerobics classes also are available. Another YMCA is located at 5885 Quince at Lynnfield, Memphis. There are also several YWCA branches thoughout the area, including a women's-only location at 7553 Old Poplar Pike, Germantown. Mon–Thu 6–10, Fri 6–9, Sat 8–5, Sun 12–5. (Downtown)

Golf

Memphis has many public and private golf courses. Professionals and amateurs are eligible to qualify for the FedEx St. Jude Classic, an annual PGA charity tournament held at the Southwind Tournament Players Club in July. Proceeds benefit St. Jude Children's Research Hospital in Memphis. For more information on the event, call 901/388-5370.

The following 9- and 18-hole courses are operated by the Memphis Park Commission.

AUDUBON PARK
4160 Park Ave.

A Horse by Any Other Name

Memphis may have more horses per capita than anywhere else in the country, but did you know that the city was also once the mule capital of the world? Because of the city's importance to the cotton and timber industries, Memphis served as the world's largest mule-market auction place through the 1940s.

Top Ten Rejected Names for a Memphis Pro-Football Team

1. The Pork Bellies
2. Great Balls A'fire
3. The Fighting Elvi
4. Hound Dogs
5. Slow-cooked Pig Meats
6. Bluff City Blues
7. W. C. Handy's Dandies
8. The Muddy Waters
9. Beale Street Bubbas
10. The Distributors: Home Team of America's Distribution Center

Memphis
901/683-6941
Gently rolling hills cover this par-71 course suitable for riding or walking. Audubon Park's greens average 5,000 square feet and demand accuracy. (East Memphis)

DAVY CROCKETT PARK
4380 Range Line Rd.
Memphis
901/358-3375
This par-72 course is set in a heavily wooded, hilly area. (Midtown/Central)

FOX MEADOWS
3064 Clark Rd.
Memphis
901/362-0232
With its wide-open fairways designed for big hitters, this par-71 course also has water holes on front and back. (South Memphis)

GALLOWAY PARK
3815 Walnut Grove Rd.

Memphis
901/685-7805
Located in the center of East Memphis, this course is marked by wooded, rolling hills. (East Memphis)

OVERTON PARK
1934 Poplar Ave.
Memphis
901/725-9905
A short, nine-hole, par-34 course, Overton Park is used primarily by beginners and seniors. (Midtown/Central)

PINE HILL PARK
1005 Alice Ave.
Memphis
901/775-9434
Rolling hills and lateral hazards are presented in this par-70 course. (South Memphis)

RIVERSIDE
435 S. Parkway W.
Memphis
901/774-4340

This wooded, nine-hole course requires precise shot placement. (South Memphis)

STONEBRIDE GOLF COURSE
3049 Davies Plantation Rd. S.
Memphis
901/382-1886
This public, daily-fee golf course includes a practice range, putting green with practice bunkers, and a snack bar. Open every day except Christmas, 6:30 a.m. to dark. Call for tee times five days in advance. (Bartlett, Cordova, Germantown)

TOURNAMENT PLAYERS CLUB AT SOUTHWIND
3325 Club Dr.
Memphis
901/748-4004
This private club features a range, chipping green, and practice putting green with sand, as well as a pool, tennis courts, banquet hall, and a bar. Tee times must be reserved 30 days in advance. (Bartlett, Cordova, Germantown)

WEDGEWOOD GOLF CLUB
5206 Tournament Dr.
Olive Branch, Mississippi
601/521-8275
A par-72 course with a restaurant and pro shop, semiprivate Wedgewood offers tee times seven days in advance. Facilities include an eight-acre practice range with target flags. (South Memphis)

Horseback Riding

SHELBY FARMS STABLES
7171 Mullins Station Rd.
Memphis
901/382-4250
At this 70-horse stable, guests may roam 450 acres of trails, ranging from beginning-level to advanced. Guides are available, if needed. Guided pony rides are available for kiddies ages three to eight. Rates

For Those Who Prefer Games to Sports

The Memphis Chess Club meets Friday evenings at seven at the Holy Trinity Episcopal Church, 3749 Kimball. For details call 901/366-7642 or 901/358-1731.

Memphis is also the North American headquarters of the American Contract Bridge League (ACBL), a membership organization for people who enjoy playing duplicate and social bridge. Tours of the building are available. For information call 800/467-1623.

The M. A. Lightman Bridge Club is open to all—and novices are welcome. The group's games are all nonsmoking, though smoking breaks are scheduled. For more information call 901/324-3889.

Shelby Farms Stables

are $15 per hour. Open 7–6 in summer, 8–5 rest of year. (Bartlett, Cordova, Germantown)

Soccer

Shelby County Mayor Jim Rout is responsible for southeast Shelby County's new 258-acre recreational park in Shelby County. The $5.7 million tournament-quality soccer complex has 16 regulation fields and a 5,000-seat tournament stadium on 137 acres. The new complex serves local and regional associations.

Swimming

In addition to the swimming pools and other water recreation offered at area attractions such as Mud Island (see Chapter 7: Kids' Stuff), the Memphis Park Commission operates dozens of outdoor swimming pools from June through August. Hours may vary by site. Call 901/325-5759 for details.

Tennis

The Memphis Park Commission offers lessons, tournaments, and leagues at 72 tennis courts in the area. Among the free public tennis courts are those in Audubon Park on Park Avenue at Goodlett, at McKellar Park on Airways Boulevard south of Wilson Road, and at Southside at 736 Getwell Road. For more information call 901/325-5766.

LEFTWICH
4145 Southern Ave.
Memphis
901/685-7907
Call ahead for availability and pricing at this tennis center, located in Audubon Park. Eight outdoor and four indoor courts are available. Indoor courts must be reserved in advance. (East Memphis)

WOLBRICHT TENNIS
CENTER/RIDGEWAY
1645 Ridgeway Rd.
Memphis
901/767-2889
Six outdoor and two indoor courts draw tennis enthusiasts to this centrally located teaching facility in East Memphis. (East Memphis)

11

PERFORMING ARTS

For a city its size, Memphis has an impressive array of first-rate performing arts organizations. Residents support a semiprofessional symphony orchestra, a rising international ballet company, and several theatrical troupes, as well as a variety of choral and instrumental chamber music ensembles. Although Memphis audiences tend to be conservative, many arts patrons in the city are both tolerant and enthusiastic about progressive programming. National and international acts, from dance companies to touring Broadway shows, stop in Memphis to perform at the historic Orpheum Theatre downtown or the state-of-the-art Germantown Performing Arts Centre in the eastern suburbs.

THEATER

Widely regarded as a strong theater town with a diverse and active stage scene, Memphis's ambitious, locally produced offerings encompass all areas of the spectrum. At almost any time of year, audiences may choose from lavish musicals with live orchestras and fully choreographed dance sequences, offbeat and experimental works staged on shoestring budgets, and everything between those two extremes. One of the city's most exciting efforts is the Memphis Black Repertory Theatre, begun in 1997.

CIRCUIT PLAYHOUSE
1705 Poplar Ave.
Memphis
901/726-4656
Off-Broadway works and new plays are repertoire staples of this small and funky theater in midtown Memphis. Circuit Playhouse is a sister house to the larger Playhouse on the Square, the only professional theater company in town. As such, Circuit productions feature top-notch talent. The C. S. Lewis children's classic, *The Lion, the Witch and the Wardrobe*, is usually presented each Christmas, in repertory

with other seasonal favorites. & (Midtown/Central)

FIREHOUSE COMMUNITY ARTS CENTER
985 S. Bellevue
Memphis
901/948-9522
Amateur singers, poets, rappers, dancers, filmmakers and other budding artists have a public forum for expression through Voices Afire and the Memphis Black Arts Alliance. The city's first and only community-based arts center hosts family-oriented "open mike" nights for artists of all ages in search of an audience. & (Midtown/Central)

GERMANTOWN COMMUNITY THEATER
3037 Forest Hill Irene Rd.
Germantown
901/754-2680
Seemingly undaunted by the encroaching urban sprawl and commercial retail development surrounding it, the Germantown Community Theater continues to stage classic productions

in a quaint, historic schoolhouse. & (Bartlett, Cordova, Germantown)

LITTLE THEATER
630 Perkins Ext.
Memphis
901/682-8323
This 100-seat, black-box theater is the more daring of the two stages at Theater Memphis, a vibrant community company run largely by volunteers. Works by such well-known playwrights as Terrence McNally and Sam Shepard have found enthusiastic audiences in the Little Theater, which also stages award-winning new plays each season. & (East Memphis)

PLAYHOUSE ON THE SQUARE
51 S. Cooper St.
Memphis
901/726-4656
Fortunately for audiences, Memphis is overflowing with talented actors and actresses who ensure that most productions staged at Playhouse on the Square will be, at the very least, good—and more often than not, outstanding. The city's only professional

---

Hometown Diva

Memphis is home to one of the opera world's most acclaimed young artists. A beautiful brunette with extraordinary vocal talent, soprano Kallen Esperian regularly stars opposite Placido Domingo, Jose Carreras, and her mentor, Luciano Pavarotti. She has performed in La Scala, Covent Garden, and many of the world's other great opera houses. Esperian's guest appearances guarantee sellouts for Opera Memphis and another local chamber ensemble close to her heart, the Memphis Vocal Arts Ensemble, which is led by her husband, Thomas Machen.

Local Favorites on the Memphis Club Scene

- *Big Ass Truck*
- *Daddy Mack Blues Band*
- *DDT*
- *El-Vez (Mexican Elvis impersonator)*
- *Elvis Herselvis (lesbian Elvis impersonator)*
- *Garrison Starr*
- *Gutbucket*
- *Impala*
- *Jo Jo Jefferies*
- *John Kilzer*
- *Last Chance Jug Band*
- *Lorette Velvette*
- *Neighborhood Texture Jam*
- *Riverbluff Clan*
- *Ruby Wilson*
- *The Grifters*
- *The Marilyns*

Equity theater, Playhouse on the Square presents comedies, classics, musicals, and dramas. *Peter Pan* is a perennial holiday favorite, as is *A Tuna Christmas*. ♿ (Midtown/Central)

RHODES COLLEGE
2100 N. Parkway
Memphis
901/726-3875
Why did this private Presbyterian college launch an annual Tennessee Williams Festival in 1996? The great American playwright wrote his first play, *Cairo! Shanghai! Bombay!*, in 1934 and 1935, while visiting his grandparents, who lived near the Rhodes College campus. The college continues to stage noteworthy student productions throughout the year. The Tennessee Williams Festival is a performance-oriented event held each July, often with noted guests such as the writer's brother, Dakin Williams. ♿ (Midtown/Central)

THEATER MEMPHIS
630 Perkins Ext.
Memphis
901/682-8323
With its spacious Main Stage auditorium seating more than four hundred people, not to mention its black-box Little Theater, Theater Memphis

boasts the finest stage facility in the city. This renowned community theater, now approaching its eighth decade, has a long-standing track record with musicals, romantic comedies, farces, and mysteries. Although TM's ambitious productions predominantly feature amateur actors, the company's robust budget and strong community support result in sets and costumes that are characteristically superior to those presented elsewhere around town. An annual production of *A Christmas Carol* has become a Memphis tradition. ♿ (East Memphis)

THEATER WORKS
2085 Monroe Ave.
Memphis
901/274-7139

An intimate black-box theater near Overton Square serves as a shared home base to some of the city's emerging performing arts groups, as well as a venue for their performances. Among the various residents are Playwrights' Forum, which stages the works of new and undiscovered writers; and Voices of the South, a female duo that adapts short stories by writers such as Eudora Welty for dramatic interpretation onstage. Performance schedules, show times, and ticket prices vary, although most productions staged at Theater Works are very inexpensive. ♿ (Midtown/Central)

CLASSICAL MUSIC AND OPERA

CALVARY AND THE ARTS
Calvary Episcopal Church
102 N. Second St. at Adams Ave.
Memphis
901/525-6602

Calvary Episcopal Church draws downtown working professionals and tourists alike to its two seasonal free concert series, presented in November and December and again in the weeks during Lent. Eclectic local acts ranging from brass ensembles and string quartets to Southern gospel choirs and jazz trios routinely draw standing room–only crowds. The midweek, 30-minute concerts begin at 12:05 p.m. Friends of Calvary and the Arts serve a hot lunch in the church basement following the concerts, at a bargain price of around four dollars. From time to time, Calvary also brings in renowned national acts, such as Chanticleer and Anonymous 4, to perform special concerts. ♿ (Downtown)

CONCERTS INTERNATIONAL
Locations vary
901/527-3067

Noted chamber ensembles and orchestral groups from throughout the United States and overseas are the focus of this annual concert series. Past performers have included the London Chamber Orchestra and the Swiss ensemble Camerata Bern, which featured oboist Heinz Holliger.

Memphis Symphony, p. 167

Bodacious Dames

Cordell Jackson, better known as "Guitar Granny," has lived in Memphis since 1943. With her teased beehive, horn-rimmed glasses, and blistering blues guitar licks, Jackson has appeared on virtually all the popular late-night television talk shows as well as in a series of high-profile beer commercials with former Stray Cat Brian Setzer. In addition, Jackson has had cameo roles in many feature films and continues to run her own Memphis company, Moon Records.

Dixie Carter has patented her strong-and-sexy steel magnolia image throughout such career peaks as playing Julia Sugarbaker on TV's long-running sitcom, Designing Women. But the honey-tongued Southern belle got her start right here in Memphis, starring in such musicals as Carousel at the old Front Street Theatre in the early 1960s. These days, the west Tennessee native, along with her hubby actor Hal Holbrooke, maintains her loyal local fan base by returning to town for occasional stage and cabaret performances. She even tried on Blanche DuBois' formidable slip for a star turn in the Tennessee Williams classic A Streetcar Named Desire a few years ago at the University of Memphis.

Cybill Shepherd is perhaps Memphis's best-known actress. The

Four programs are usually presented in the Harris Auditorium at the University of Memphis, or in area churches and synagogues. Season subscriptions and single tickets are available. (East Memphis)

EVERGREEN PRESBYTERIAN CHURCH
613 University Dr.
Memphis
901/264-3740
The Rhodes College music faculty presents a variety of sacred and sec-

ular classical music programs in the church adjacent to campus. Most events are free and open to the public. ⅄ (Midtown/Central)

MEMPHIS CHAMBER MUSIC SOCIETY
Locations vary
901/758-0150
Local and regional musicians with a love of chamber music gather in some of Memphis's loveliest private homes for three concert series that run from September through May. The concerts

former cover girl shot to stardom when she turned to acting in films like Peter Bogdanovich's The Last Picture Show *(1971)*. The 1980s marked her comeback in the hit TV show Moonlighting, *in which she costarred with Bruce Willis. Shepherd has continued to make occasional films, including the 1950s-era* Memphis, *which was shot locally, and has earned Emmy nominations for her sitcom* Cybill. *The curvaceous blonde, a mother of three, owns a beautiful home on a bluff overlooking the Mississippi River in downtown Memphis. She is currently at work on her memoirs.*

Nobody plays the gutsy broad better than Memphis's own **Kathy Bates**. *The talented Emmy- and Oscar-winning actress won her first Academy Award for her role as a sadistic fan in the film version of Stephen King's* Misery. *Other memorable roles include those in* Fried Green Tomatoes, A Home of Their Own, Titanic, *and* Primary Colors, *for which she was also nominated for an Oscar. She honored her former drama teacher by coming back to town a few years ago for a standing room—only performance of* Love Letters *that costarred her real-life husband. The benefit, held at Germantown High School, raised money for a local playwrights' organization in which her former teacher is active.*

usually sell out far in advance, although individual tickets sometimes become available due to last-minute cancellations. A gala concert at the Memphis Botanic Garden, featuring the noted Chamber Music Society of Lincoln Center, marked the organization's 10th anniversary in April 1999. ♿

MEMPHIS SYMPHONY ORCHESTRA
Locations vary
901/324-3627
The 80-piece Memphis Symphony Or-chestra performs at locations throughout the city from September through May. In January the orchestra's birthday tribute to Elvis Presley is usually a sellout, as are seasonal pops concerts at such outdoor sites as the Dixon Gallery and Gardens. In addition, the orchestra performs masterworks programs as well as children's and family programs. Until the city builds its new downtown performing arts center, the orchestra is without a permanent home. In the meantime, concerts are held in various downtown venues,

at Eudora Baptist Church at Poplar and Perkins in East Memphis, and at the Germantown Performing Arts Centre. &

MEMPHIS VOCAL ARTS ENSEMBLE

**Locations vary
901/683-6774**
Since its debut in 1991, the Memphis Vocal Arts Ensemble has established itself as one of the city's finest performance groups. Each year the chorus presents a series of four to six

Top Memphis Jazz Stars
As ranked by Irwin Sheft, founder of the Jazz Foundation of Memphis, Inc.

Living

1. George Coleman, saxophone
2. Harold Mabern, piano
3. Mulgrew Miller, piano
4. Hank Crawford, saxophone, piano
5. Frank Strozier, saxophone
6. James Williams, piano
7. Donald Brown, piano
8. Bill Easley, saxophone, clarinet
9. Jamil Nasser, bass
10. Tony Reedus, drums
11. Calvin Newborn, guitar
12. Charles Lloyd, saxophone
13. Dee Dee Bridgewater, vocals
14. Charles Thomas, piano

Deceased

1. Phineas Newborn, the genius, piano
2. Alberta Hunter, vocals
3. Buster Bailey, clarinet
4. W. C. Handy (yes, a jazz composer)
5. Jimmie Lunceford and His Band
6. Lil Hardin, piano (Louis Armstrong's wife)
7. Booker Little, trumpet
8. Bill Mobley, trumpet

Ballet Memphis, p. 170

concerts in churches throughout the metropolitan Memphis area. Whether singing fifteenth-century mass settings, Bach cantatas, American folk songs from the Civil War era, or arias and choruses from Italian grand opera, the ensemble is revered for its expressive musicianship and high level of artistic integrity. Though the ensemble performs at various locations throughout the city, they are primarily in residence at St. Mary's Episcopal School's Buckman Arts Center, 60 Perkins Extended. ♿

OPERA MEMPHIS
University of Memphis
South Campus
Campus Box 526331
Memphis
901/678-2706
Opera Memphis, now entering its 42nd season, is the largest opera company in Tennessee. National and international singers are featured in four fully staged productions each year downtown at the Orpheum. Members of the Memphis Symphony Orchestra accompany the productions, which are most often sung in their original languages with English supertitles. While beloved operas by Mozart, Verdi, and Puccini get their due, the company is also gaining a reputation for premiering new American works.

Memphis audiences have been avid opera supporters as far back as 1851, when songbird soprano Jenny Lind performed at the Grand Opera House. In more recent years, Met artists such as Sherrill Milnes and mezzo-soprano Mignon Dunn, a native of Memphis, have returned to perform with Opera Memphis.

Since its formation in 1988, Opera Memphis's National Center for the Development of American Opera has commissioned a variety of new and exciting American operas. Partially funded by the National Endowment for the Arts and other agencies, the company has staged such innovative works as *Different Fields*, an opera about football written by New York librettist Sara Reid and former Cincinnati Bengals player Michael Reid. Other past commissions include

The Bill Black Combo, a Memphis group featuring some of Elvis's backup musicians, was the Beatles' warm-up band of choice for their first American tour. The Fab Four played the Mid-South Coliseum in August 1966. Joining Paul McCartney on one of his mid-1990s U.S. tours was a drummer from Memphis's Orange Mound neighborhood, Blair Cunningham. The drummer's late, older brother, a former member of the Stax house band, the Mar-Keys, died on the same 1968 plane crash that killed Otis Redding.

Riversongs, a blues/folk opera about the great floods of 1927. It was composed by local blues singer and songwriter Sid Selvidge, best known by alternative-rock fans as the independent record maverick who produced Big Star musician Alex Chilton's 1979 solo album, *Like Flies on Sherbert*. Opera Memphis has also premiered an opera based on William Faulkner's *Light in August*, which was later presented at the annual Faulkner and Yoknapatawpha Conference in Oxford, Mississippi. (Downtown)

DANCE

BALLET MEMPHIS
P.O. Box 3675
Memphis
901/737-7322
National and international dancers, choreographers, and guest artists comprise this professional regional ballet company that is regarded as one of Memphis's rising cultural stars. The company's four annual productions at the dowtown Orpheum Theatre are, without exception, breathtakingly performed and beautifully staged. Among the full-length ballets in the company's

repertoire are such classics as *Sleeping Beauty*, *Swan Lake*, and *Romeo and Juliet*. In addition, Ballet Memphis presents a memorable holiday *Nutcracker* each December. (Downtown)

CONCERT VENUES

CORDOVA CELLARS WINERY
9050 Macon Rd.
901/754-3442
Classical music concerts held at Cordova Cellars Winery should come as

Rhodes College, p. 164

Memphis Convention and Visitors Bureau

In Memoriam: O'Landa Draper

Grammy-winning O'Landa Draper (1964–1998) was one of the city's brightest musical stars, revered not only as a recording artist but also as a passionate minister and a tireless servant of the poor. At 21, he founded O'Landa Draper and the Associates, an exuberant black gospel choir that released a series of award-winning CDs throughout the 1990s. With his electrifying smile, shaved head, flashy stage clothes, and irreverent sense of humor, the charismatic minister and his equally spirited choir drew standing room–only crowds at concerts across the United States. Before people such as Kirk Franklin became top crossover artists, Draper energized the genre of gospel by blending southern church music with elements of rhythm-and-blues, hip-hop, rap, soul, and funk.

The Associates, along with the Wallflowers and other rock acts, inaugurated the Hard Rock Café's opening on Beale Street in November 1997. They performed at countless local benefits, ministered to four local homeless shelters, and sang on such programs as Good Morning America. *They also appeared live with Billy Joel on a* Grammy *Awards television broadcast. On the 30th anniversary of Dr. Martin Luther King's assassination in Memphis, Draper assembled an interracial, citywide choir of more than four hundred youths. They sang at a commemorative service in Mason Temple, where Dr. King gave his "mountaintop" speech the night before he died.*

The choir's most recent album, the Grammy-winning Reflections *(Warner/Alliance), debuted near the top of Billboard's gospel charts in early 1998, prompting an invitation to perform at Madison Square Garden in New York City. The choir seemed to be just reaching its stride when Draper died unexpectedly of kidney failure in July 1998. He was 34.*

More than 4,000 people attended his funeral at Central Church in southeast Shelby County. Gospel great Shirley Caesar, politicians, and preachers of all denominations were among those who offered moving testimonials. Draper may be gone, but the choir lives on. Now known as O'Landa Draper's Associates, the ensemble is led by his former fiancée, Patrina Smith, and his mother, Marie Draper.

no surprise to anyone well-versed in the repertoire. Joan Jeanrenaud, former cellist with the acclaimed Kronos Quartet, is the daughter of the winery's owners. The Kronos is an internationally acclaimed, Grammy-winning ensemble noted for its daring performances of avant-garde and contemporary American and world music. They also do a mean rendition of Jimi Hendrix's "Purple Haze." & (Bartlett, Cordova, Germantown)

GERMANTOWN PERFORMING ARTS CENTRE
1801 Exeter Rd.
Germantown
901/757-7256
Since its inaugural season in 1994 and 1995, this modern, 800-seat theater has been hailed by performers from Itzhak Perlman and Ray Charles to Mikhail Baryshnikov for its outstanding acoustics. Internationally renowned chamber music ensembles, nationally known theater troupes, top-name illusionists, dance companies, children's entertainment, and popular recording artists are booked each year at GPAC. In addition to excellent acoustics and spacious seats, this suburban auditorium also offers free parking to its patrons. & (Bartlett, Cordova, Germantown)

MID-SOUTH COLISEUM
996 Early Maxwell Blvd.
Memphis
901/274-3982
Located at the fairgrounds near the Liberty Bowl and Libertyland amusement park in midtown, the Mid-South Coliseum is an aging concert and sports arena that has hosted some of the biggest names in the business, from the Beatles and the Rolling Stones to George Strait. Although in recent years most major concert promoters have begun booking shows at larger, more modern venues such as the downtown Pyramid, the Mid-South Coliseum still manages to attract a fair number of shows. (Midtown/Central)

MUD ISLAND AMPHITHEATER
125 N. Front St.
Memphis
901/576-7241
With the skyline of Memphis and the Mississippi River as its backdrops, this 5,000-seat outdoor amphitheater on Mud Island attracts the top names in popular music. Performances are held here from early spring through late fall. The venue is accessible via a monorail along Front Street in downtown Memphis. & (Downtown)

NEW DAISY THEATER
330 Beale St.
Memphis
901/525-8979
Rock, alternative-music, jazz, and blues musicians take the stage year-round at the New Daisy Theater on Beale Street. Concertgoers who are particular about their surroundings might find this functional but rundown venue a bit on the grungy side. That hasn't stopped performers such as Lucinda Williams, Dread Zeppelin, Jon Faddis, and local favorites such as Big Ass Truck from booking engagements at the New Daisy.

Bob Dylan recorded a video for his 1998 Grammy-winning CD, *Time Out of Mind*, at the New Daisy Theater. Dylan returned there on February 5, 1999, for a concert at the endearingly rundown venue. The $40 tickets sold out in a matter of minutes. (The night of the show, scalpers were getting as much as $200 apiece for them.) Veteran Bob-o-philes said that

The Road to Memphis

Actor Harvey Keitel plays the lead in Finding Graceland, *one of the most recent film projects to be shot in the Memphis area. Keitel stars as an eccentric drifter who claims to be Elvis Presley—still alive all these years after faking his death. Bridget Fonda and Johnathon Schaech costar in the movie, for which Priscilla Presley served as executive producer. Scenes were filmed in Graceland as well as at the Hollywood Casino and RV Park in nearby Tunica, Mississippi. The film never made it to theaters and is now available on video.*

night's electrifying concert, in which Dylan smiled, danced, and even duckwalked across the stage to such hits as "Gotta Serve Somebody," "Make You Feel My Love," and "Tangled Up in Blue," was the best they'd ever heard from the snarling bard. Wheelchair access on the lower level only. (Downtown)

ORPHEUM THEATRE
203 S. Main St.
Memphis
901/525-3000
Undisputedly the most beautifully ornate performing arts venue in Memphis, the grand Orpheum Theatre is a downtown jewel located at the corner of Main and Beale Streets. Crystal chandeliers, gilded plasterwork, and rich tapestries cloak this former vaudeville palace in splendor. Built in 1928 and recently restored, the Orpheum imports touring Broadway musicals such as *Phantom of the Opera* and *Les Miserables*, as well as other acts as diverse as Garrison Keillor's *A Prairie Home Companion*, the percussive dance troupe STOMP!, and musi-

cal concerts by Lyle Lovett and others. Ballet Memphis and Opera Memphis also perform at the beloved venue. In the summertime the Orpheum transforms itself into an old-fashioned movie house for its Friday-night series of such film classics as *Casablanca*, *Gone With the Wind*, and *The Wizard of Oz*. Two recent renovations (1983 and 1997) added more than $15 million in improvements to a building that originally cost less than $2 million to construct. ⓬ (Downtown)

THE PYRAMID
1 Auction Ave.
Memphis
901/526-5177
Soaring 32 stories above the Mississippi River and positioned near the distinctive, M-shaped bridge connecting Memphis with Arkansas, the gleaming steel Pyramid is the city's most recognizable architectural landmark and its premier concert venue and sports arena. Country, rock, and pop performers such as Eric Clapton, Elton John, and Alanis Morissette are among the scores of acts that have played the

Notable Rock Albums Recorded in Memphis

- *III* by Led Zeppelin
- *Eliminator* by ZZ Top
- *Green* by R.E.M.
- *New Miserable Experience* by Gin Blossoms
- *Open All Nite* by Big Tent Revival
- *Pleased to Meet Me* by The Replacements
- *The Sky is Crying* by Stevie Ray Vaughan

22,000-seat arena. The stadium is also home to the University of Memphis Tigers basketball team. & (Downtown)

BUYING TICKETS

Ticketmaster, the primary ticketing agency in the Memphis area, sells tickets for major sporting, music, and theater events. To charge by phone, call 901/525-1515. Ticketmaster outlets include those at area Blockbuster Music stores; Cat's CDs and Cassettes stores; the Mid-South Coliseum box office; the Mud Island concert box office; the Pyramid box office; the Orpheum Theatre box office and the Orpheum Store in Oak Court Mall; Piggly Wiggly supermarkets throughout Shelby County; the Pop Tunes record shop in Collierville; and Video Magic in West Memphis, Arkansas.

12

NIGHTLIFE

Memphis and its suburbs are full of bars and respectable hotel lounges, but for tourists looking to sample the definitive Memphis musical experience, Beale Street is the logical place to begin.

It's been almost a century since W. C. Handy stood here and first trumpeted the notes that gave birth to the blues. In the 1960s and '70s, the street succumbed to neglect and became a classic example of urban blight. The district was essentially rebuilt and reopened in 1993. Critics complain that this major overhaul, while proving financially profitable, has transformed Beale Street into nothing more than a tacky tourist trap and alcohol mall—at best a poor imitation of the thriving black music, entertainment, and economic hub it had been in the 1920s, '30s, and '40s. Yet tourists continue to pack the brick-lined blocks between Main Street and Fourth to take in the sights and sounds of the place where American popular music took root.

The midtown entertainment district known as Overton Square, located east of downtown, simply isn't what it used to be. Once a magnet for trendy nightclubs, stand-up comedy acts, and boisterous restaurants, the block today seems to have almost as many vacant storefronts as it does tenants. Several fine eateries, such as Paulette's, and live theater spaces, including Playhouse on the Square, are among the viable options that remain.

Parties seem to be happening everywhere in Memphis. In warm weather, the Peabody's outdoor rooftop is the setting for Sunset Serenades—casual cocktail parties that provide picture-perfect views of the Mississippi River— plus a sumptuous happy-hour buffet and the best in live rhythm-and-blues, soul, jazz, and rock concerts.

Another popular pastime among downtown's working professionals (and the white-collar types from the Far Eastern hinterlands who hightail it downtown at five) are the famous Alley Parties hosted by the Center City Commission. These festive parties are held regularly on Friday nights throughout the summer.

To find out what's happening on the local club scene, check out the Playbook, *an information-packed, pullout tabloid stuffed inside each Friday's edition of the daily* Commercial Appeal. *Another good source is the free alternative weekly newspaper* The Memphis Flyer. *For blues, the last word belongs to* BlueSpeak, *a feisty newsprint freebie that offers witty, authoritative recommendations on all things related to the blues and other live music around the region. Pick it up.*

DANCE CLUBS

AMNESIA
2866 Poplar Ave.
Memphis
901/454-1366
Among the most prominent of Memphis's gay bars is the jazzy Amnesia, where videos, dancing, and female impersonators draw large crowds. (Midtown/Central)

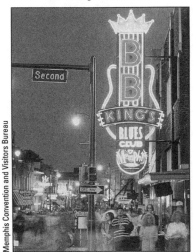

B.B. King's Blues Club

Memphis Convention and Visitors Bureau

DENIM AND DIAMONDS
5353 S. Mendenhall Rd.
Memphis
901/365-3633
Country line dancing on a boot-scootin', 3,000-square-foot dance floor lures Western enthusiasts to this East Memphis club. (South Memphis)

FANTASIA
1819 Madison Ave.
Memphis
901/725-1668
Hip-hop, acid jazz, disco, and reggae are among the many musical backdrops offered at this youthful dance club. (Midtown/Central)

MUSIC CLUBS

Blues

B. B. KING'S BLUES CLUB
143 Beale St.
Memphis
901/524-5464
This premier blues address at Second and Beale opened with much fanfare in 1991, and King still performs here. All-star concerts such as those by Booker T. and the MGs, Sam Moore, Etta James, and countless others make B. B. King's the place to go for the biggest names in blues music. (Downtown)

BLUES CITY CAFÉ
138–140 Beale St.
Memphis
901/526-3637
Smoke curling from his trademark pipe, the great Albert King helped inaugurate this Beale Street club several years ago when half the town (or so it seemed) turned out for a birthday bash in his honor. The blues guitar great died shortly thereafter, in 1992, but the club lives on. Blues City Café

Selected Songs Written or Recorded in Memphis

"Angel of the Morning"—Merrilee Rush

"Blue Suede Shoes"—Carl Perkins

"Dock of the Bay," "Try a Little Tenderness"—Otis Redding

"Great Balls of Fire"—Jerry Lee Lewis

"Green Onions"—Booker T. and the MGs

"Hound Dog," "Love Me Tender," "Heartbreak Hotel"—
   Elvis Presley

"I Walk the Line"—Johnny Cash

"In the Midnight Hour," "Mustang Sally"—Wilson Pickett

"Let's Stay Together," "Tired of Being Alone"—Al Green

"Shaft"—Isaac Hayes

"The Letter"—The Boxtops

"Think"—Aretha Franklin

"When Something Is Wrong with My Baby," "Soul Man,"
   "Hold On, I'm Comin'"—Sam & Dave

"You're My Baby," "One More Time"—Roy Orbison

---

serves the best shrimp, steak, and tamales in the historic district, as well as scorching live blues. (Downtown)

EARNESTINE & HAZEL'S
531 S. Main St.
Memphis
901/523-9754
A former brothel that looks as tired and used up as its past suggests, Earnestine & Hazel's has in recent years become one of downtown's most happening night spots. Several blocks away from the touristy flash of Beale Street, this proud dive offers weekend happy hours, hot rhythm and blues, extended late-night jam sessions, and Sunday-afternoon live music. (Downtown)

KING'S PALACE CAFÉ
162 Beale St.
Memphis
901/521-1851
Nightly blues and jazz, along with re-spectable New Orleans–style food, are served up at King's Palace Café. (Downtown)

LEGENDS
326 Beale St.
Memphis
901/523-7444
The thin cotton curtains may sag in the

Memphis has one of the country's most active chapters of the National Academy of Recording Arts and Sciences (NARAS), the group responsible for the Grammy Awards. From its headquarters on Beale Street, the NARAS office oversees a range of programs aimed at everything from educating school children in the arts to supporting local musicians. They are also advocates for the music industry at large. Of the recording industry's $12 billion in annual sales, about 20 percent comes from independent record labels. Memphis has more than one hundred of them, including Loverly, Ardent, Upstart, Shangri-la, Frankenstein, and Fat Chance. It is estimated that independent record labels in Memphis have an economic impact of $12 to $15 million in annual retail sales alone. Factoring in income from recording studios, publishing, and touring, the total soars to $20 million.

front windows of this small, yellow-brick building just east of Handy Park on Beale Street, but this is *the* place to absorb some genuine Memphis-music history. Willie Mitchell, the trumpeter and bandleader who produced Al Green's early hits at Hi Records back in the early 1970s, owned this night-club in the mid-1990s. (In the old days, one longtime tenant of this squat structure was the One Minute Dairy Lunch, a sort of forerunner of today's fast-food restaurants and convenience stores. The café was in business from 1921 to 1953, and reportedly served as many as 3,600 hot dogs per day!) (Downtown)

NEWBY'S LOUNGE
539 S. Highland St.
Memphis
901/452-8408
This spacious student hangout shares space with an endearingly bleak strip of beer joints, pawn shops, tattoo parlors, and the obligatory blood bank—your usual college-campus collection—near the Univer-

sity of Memphis. Live music on two stages can be expected nightly. Folkie singer/songwriter Todd Snider (*Songs from the Daily Planet*) got his start here, and he has returned peri-odically since hitting the pop charts two years ago. (East Memphis)

RUM BOOGIE CAFÉ
182 Beale St.
Memphis
901/528-0150
Guitar gods such as Stevie Ray Vaughan, Albert Collins, ZZ Top's Billy Gibbons, and others have auto-graphed musical instruments on dis-play at this beloved Beale Street watering hole. The nightly live music can be smokin', as can the kitchen, which cooks up a mean pot of Cajun-style red beans and rice. (Downtown)

Rock/Rhythm and Blues

ALFRED'S
197 Beale St.
Memphis
901/525-3711

An ace house band covers the golden oldies every Sunday night at this Beale Street club facing W. C. Handy Park. Live rock music is featured on other nights of the week, and in warm weather the bar's outdoor corner patio makes for some interesting people-watching. Alfred's is currently undergoing a major renovation that its owners promise will make the place "bigger and better." (Downtown)

BARRISTER'S
147 Jefferson Ave.
Memphis
901/527-8662

Avant-garde Klezmer saxophonist John Zorn, alternative Dixieland band the Squirrel Nut Zippers, and Mud Boy and the Neutrons are among the cutting-edge acts that have packed the hip and aspiring-hip into this midtown bar and live-music club tucked inside an alley near the Med Center. The club's ownership has shifted in recent years, but Barrister's continues its sporadic booking of bands you're unlikely to hear anywhere else in the region. (Downtown)

ELVIS PRESLEY'S MEMPHIS
126 Beale St.
Memphis
901/527-6900

Opened in June 1997 by the operators of Graceland and the Presley estate, this swank theme club and restaurant offers live rockabilly music, gospel brunches, and occasional jazz concerts. While the elaborately designed menus tout the obligatory Presley weaknesses such as fried peanut butter-and-banana sandwiches and meatloaf, the food quality at this slick tourist magnet can be inconsistent. The merchandise in the showcase seems to be given more priority than the meals served. However, the place is high on atmosphere: Blue velvet drapes adorn the stage, and the club offers an upstairs, outdoor terrace as well as a wine cellar in the basement. (Downtown)

HARD ROCK CAFÉ
315 Beale St.
Memphis
901/529-0007

Jakob Dylan and the Wallflowers were among the national headliners who opened up Memphis's First Hard Rock Café back in November of 1997. Since then, live music, including rock, blues, and heavenly gospel brunches, has augmented the renowned establishment's extensive music memorabilia collection, gift shop, and . . . oh yes, food and drink offerings. Of the 4.2 million visitors estimated to visit Beale Street annually, it seems all of them stop here. Incidentally, the Hard Rock Café chain was founded in London in 1971 by native Memphian Isaac Tigrett, who went on to start the House of Blues chain and who is still active in the local and national music scene. (Downtown)

TRIVIA

Three 6 Mafia is Memphis's most successful urban act since the Bar-Kays. The hard-core rap group had a hit 1998 single in "Tear Da Club Up," and a gold album to boot.

The *Beale Street Caravan*, a locally created and nationally distributed radio show produced by the Memphis-based Blues Foundation, airs weekly on WKNO FM 91.1. The popular new show, produced by Sid Selvidge and hosted by famed Memphis Horns trumpeter Wayne Jackson and saxophonist Andrew Love, is now heard on more than 220 stations. The program features live music from blues festivals and other events throughout the United States and beyond.

Country and Western/Folk

HERNANDO'S HIDEAWAY
3210 Old Hernando Rd.
Memphis
901/398-7496

Hernando's Hideaway looks more like a haunted house that's seen better days, but those well-versed in the history of this legendary honky-tonk may be willing to risk venturing into this rundown South Memphis area. Jerry Lee Lewis and his equally talented but underappreciated sister, Linda Gail Lewis, have been known to take the stage for some barrelhouse, rockabilly piano pounding. (South Memphis)

LUCY OPRY
2984 Harvester Ln.
Frayser
901/358-3486

Nationally known bluegrass acts and down-home jam sessions are staged on Friday nights in this former United Auto Workers union hall in Frayser. Bring the family because the focus here is on wholesome, all-ages entertainment. Admission varies but is usually inexpensive. No alcohol or tobacco products are allowed. (Downtown)

JAVA CABANA
2170 Young St.
Memphis
901/272-7210

Poetry readings, acoustic music, and some of the funkiest atmosphere on the planet await at this retro-beatnik coffeehouse in the Cooper–Young Historic District. Be sure to bring some loose change for the kinetic, coin-operated Elvis Impersonators' Shrine in the front window. Although the café's Viva Memphis! Wedding Chapel has moved into the Center for Southern Folklore on Beale Street, Java Cabana has retained its quirky charm. (Midtown/Central)

SILKY O'SULLIVAN'S
183 Beale St.
Memphis
901/522-9596

Acoustic folk and rock musicians occasionally perform at this no-frills Beale Street bar, whose greatest asset is the historic brick facade fronting its outdoor patio. This carefully preserved structure is all that remains of the famous Gallina building, an ornate saloon and hotel dating from 1891 and once known as "The Pride of Beale Street." Be sure to check out the live, beer-drinking billy goats in the adjacent courtyard. (Downtown)

PUBS AND BARS

ALEX'S TAVERN
1445 Jackson
Memphis
901/278-9086
Alex's boasts the distinction of being the city's oldest bar, but the joint's got other things going for it. Various big-screen TV sets, ubiquitous beer and spirits, late-night dining, and a pool table and decent jukebox round out its myriad charms. (Midtown/Central)

BELMONT GRILL
4970 Poplar Ave.
Memphis
901/767-0305
This dark, cozy bar sits along the congested Poplar Avenue corridor near the intersection of White Station. In a small, green-brick building with an orange, neon sign, the Belmont Grill makes for an agreeable compromise when you're craving another beer and

a late-night cheeseburger, but your significant other is adamant about going somewhere with a halfway decent wine list. (East Memphis)

BOTTOM LINE
1817 Kirby Pkwy.
Memphis
901/755-2481
Out in the 'burbs beyond East Memphis, near the Germantown border, the Bottom Line serves up superior pub grub in a relatively large, softly lit, and comfortable setting that seems to attract a healthy share of businessmen in search of a little downtime. (Bartlett, Cordova, Germantown)

HIGH POINT PINCH
111 Jackson
Memphis
901/525-4444
This cavernous bar and restaurant in the Pinch District, in the northern end of downtown, has an extensive menu full of sandwiches, salads, munchies, and beer. Live entertainment is also offered at the High Point, but the place is best loved by locals as a favored

Borders Books and Music Café, p. 185

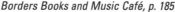

Alan Howell/Memphis Business Journal

Top Ten Nightspots in Memphis
by Tim Sampson, former editor of *Memphis Magazine*
and a humor columnist for the *Memphis Flyer*

1. **Wild Bill's** (1580 Vollintine), the closest thing Memphis has to a real blues bar, offers live blues on the weekends, beer in quart bottles, and plenty of dancing. While it has been discovered by the college crowd and most celebrities who come through town, it's still worth the trip.

2. A bit more sterile and geared toward tourists is **B. B. King's Blues Club** (143 Beale St.), which offers live music seven nights a week by local, regional, and national acts. This Beale Street anchor is one of the hottest spots in town.

3. The biggest and most popular gay bar in Memphis is **Amnesia** (2866 Poplar), with a jazz bar, video bar, and warehouse-sized dance floor that's packed on weekend nights.

4. Memphis's premier martini bar, **Side Street Grill** (35 S. Florence), comes complete with black-and-white movie stills on the aged walls, jazz floating through the room, and one wild clientele and staff. It's a nonstop party until three in the morning. While you're there, try one of their steaks.

5. The **P&H Café** (1532 Madison) is exactly what it claims to be: "The Beer Joint of Your Dreams." A gathering spot for both blue-collar and intelligentsia alike, P&H is a good place to play pool and shuffleboard, drink cold beer, and eat a truck stop–worthy burger. Make sure you ask to meet the owner, Wanda.

---

after-work gathering place or late-night party spot. (Midtown/Central)

JUSTIN'S GRILLE
7020 E. Shelby Dr.
Memphis
901/758-2432
Whether you're weary from a workout at the fitness center next door, or pooped from scoping bargains at the Wal-Mart that anchors this suburban shopping center, you'll find respite at Justin's Grille, where you can kick back with a cold one or grab a bite to

eat. Sultry pop-rock vocalist Jo Jo Jefferies has established a huge following at Justin's, where she does covers of everyone from Sarah McLachlan and Shawn Colvin to Paula Cole. (South Memphis)

KUDZU'S
603 Monroe Ave.
Memphis
901/525-4924
This green and blue building sits on a somewhat desolate street around the corner from Sun Studio and the Delta

6. **In the Grove** (2865 Walnut Grove) is the kind of place you have to see to believe. Every wall, table, chair, and ceiling is hand-painted in various styles, making each room seem alive. The dining areas are comfy, but the best place to have a drink is on one of the overstuffed sofas. Live music is offered on occasion.

7. Join the very eclectic crowd at **Young Avenue Deli** (2119 Young Ave.) for good eats and a full bar (including one of the city's biggest beer selections). This cavernous restaurant/bar/pool hall/live-music club is very relaxed, and is located in the heart of the historic Cooper-Young, with shops, art galleries, coffee houses, and other restaurants huddled together like one big party. Monday nights alternate with salsa and swing music.

8. There are no frills, no ferns, and no fancy drinks at **Old Zinnies** (1688 Madison). This is the place for friendly service, friendly clientele, great cheeseburgers, cold beer, and the best shooter you'll ever have. Make way for the college crowds after ten.

9. **Le Chardonnay** (2105 Overton Square) is one of the best spots to sample the grape. This bistro's wine list is extensive, the place is cozy and dark, and the wood-fired gourmet pizzas are great.

10. One of Memphis's newest and best live-music venues, the **Hi-Tone Café** (1913 Poplar) is a blend of 1950s kitsch (wait 'till you see the sign) and great neighborhood atmosphere. There's local and national live music every night, from swing to rockabilly to good ol' rock 'n' roll.

Axis Contemporary Arts Center. Kudzu's charms, apart from the fact that it takes its name from the thriving southern green vine, include the Wednesday-night Trivia Quiz and a tree- shaded deck out back. (Midtown/Central)

NEIL'S BAR
1827 Madison Ave.
Memphis
901/278-6345
The kitchen's always open at Neil's, a popular neighborhood bar in mid-town. Among the more popular items on its four-page menu are hot wings, chicken quesadillas, steaks, and chili-cheeseburger-in-a-bowl. (Midtown/Central)

NORTH END
346 N. Main St.
Memphis
901/526-0319
Imported beer, a vast menu, and consistent live music attracted diners and late-night revelers to the North End long before the historic Pinch

Songs with Memphis in the Title

"Big Train From Memphis"—John Fogerty
"I've Been to Memphis"—Lyle Lovett
"Letter to Memphis"—The Pixies
"Maybe It Was Memphis"—Pam Tillis
"Memphis Hip Shake"—The Cult
"Memphis in the Meantime"—John Hiatt
"Memphis Pearl"—Lucinda Williams
"Memphis Psychosis"—Mick Farren and Tijuana Bible
"Memphis Rhythm"—Bob Marley
"Memphis to Nixon"—Beat Farmers
"Memphis Underground"—Herbie Hancock
"Memphis Yodel"—Jimmie Rodgers
"Memphis, Tennessee"—Chuck Berry
"Music Makin' Momma (From Memphis, Tennessee)"—
   Hank Snow
"Night Train to Memphis"—Roy Acuff
"Retreat from Memphis"—Mekons
"Rose of Memphis"—Rodney Crowell
"Stuck Inside of Mobile with the Memphis Blues Again"—
   Bob Dylan
"Walking in Memphis"—Marc Cohn

District became a popular nightspot in the early 1990s. This is one of the favored hangouts for people spilling out of the Pyramid after sporting events or concerts. (Downtown)

P&H CAFÉ
1532 Madison Ave.
Memphis
901/726-0906
Chain-smoke all you like in this funky midtown nook. P&H is best known for its flamboyant owner, Wanda Wilson.

With her mane of frosted curls, outrageous outfits, and rakish, wide-brimmed hats, she's a standout in any crowd—and a staunch supporter of smokers' rights. (Midtown/Central)

SLEEP OUT LOUIE'S
88 Union Ave.
Memphis
901/527-5337
Quite possibly the last of the Yuppie holdouts, this popular downtown bar and restaurant attracts more than its

share of the city's young and beautiful, as well as some of the rest of us. The stylish but casual restaurant serves up tasty chicken sandwiches and pasta dishes, and the bartenders will do their best to remember your favorite drinks. (Downtown)

ZINNIE'S
1688 Madison Ave.
Memphis
901/726-5004
Known by locals as *the* midtown gathering place, this friendly bar—within an endearingly imperfect, rose-colored, Victorianesque building—has a big-screen TV, seating on two floors, and a private room upstairs. There's also a patio overlooking nothing in particular, but that doesn't seem to deter the die-hard fans who return time and again to this homey establishment. (East Memphis)

MOVIE HOUSES OF NOTE

CINEMA SHOWCASE 12
5117 Old Summer Rd.
Memphis
901/763-3456
Tucked beneath a freeway overpass and beyond the pink and purple neon of an X-rated entertainment complex lies this 12-screen cineplex that's worth visiting if you take your movies seriously. If it's an acclaimed documentary, the latest Ingmar Bergman film, or another alternative, art-house favorite, chances are Cinema Showcase will be the only place in town showing it. The theater's owner/operator has endeared himself to fans who rely on this comfortable, if off-the-beaten-path, theater for cinematic offerings other than the latest Hollywood blockbusters—although these can be viewed here, too. Dis-

counted tickets, priced at $3.50, come with a small popcorn and Pepsi during the theater's weekday bargain hour. (Bartlett, Cordova, Germantown)

MALCO'S RIDGEWAY FOUR
5851 Ridgeway Parkway Dr.
Memphis
901/681-2020
www.malco.com
The nicest, most centrally located movie theater in the city is this four-screen complex at Poplar and Ridgeway, just inside the I-240 loop. Comfortable seating; consistently clean lobby, theater, and restrooms; and tasty popcorn draw film buffs to this cineplex. First-run films as well as the occasional art film can usually be found here. The Malco chain, which operates 12 other theaters throughout the city, offers discounted admission before six o'clock. (East Memphis)

COFFEEHOUSES OF NOTE

BORDERS BOOKS & MUSIC
Carrefour at Kirby Woods Mall
Poplar Ave. at Kirby Pkwy.
Memphis
901/754-0770
Friday and Saturday nights at Borders usually include live music. A "spoken word" night is held about once a month, usually on Wednesday. After browsing, get your caffeine fix at the café. (Bartlett, Cordova, Germantown)

DAVIS–KIDD BOOKSELLERS AND CAFÉ
Poplar Ave. at Perkins Rd. Ext.
Memphis
901/374-0881
Davis-Kidd features live music from all genres on weekends, not to mention a lodge-like fireplace pit. (East Memphis)

DELIBERATE LITERATE
1997 Union Ave.
Memphis
901/276-0174
This place offers no regular entertainment, but a conference room is available for those who want to stage their own events. (Midtown/Central)

JAVA CABANA
2170 Young Ave.
Memphis
901/272-7210
Java Cabana features live blues and jazz entertainment on Saturday night only. (Midtown/Central)

OTHERLANDS
641 S. Cooper St.
Memphis
901/278-4994
Along with coffee, Otherlands offers live world-beat music most Saturday nights. (Midtown/Central)

PRECIOUS CARGO
COFFEE STATION

381 N. Main St.
Memphis
901/323-9332
A diverse blend of jazz, reggae, blues, and comedy nights, in addition to plenty of open-mike nights, add an air of uncertainty and spontaneity to this coffeehouse in the Pinch District. Call for hours. (Downtown)

STARBUCKS AT BOOKSTAR
Poplar Plaza
Poplar Ave. at Highland St.
Memphis
901/323-9332
Starbucks features occasional live music and poetry readings, along with all the caffeine you can handle. (East Memphis)

CASINOS

All of the following casinos are located in northwest Mississippi, about 12 miles south of the state line, off Highway 61.

Don't Forget to Duck

Ducks Unlimited, a wildlife conservation organization, has its headquarters in Memphis. But not everyone is thrilled by the group's presence. Bumper stickers reading "Ducks Eliminated" imply that the organization's goals are geared more toward ensuring hunters' bounties than toward perpetuating an infinite supply of nature's quackers.

Ducks Unlimited aside, Memphis's most notorious claim to duck fame has to be the novelty tune that was recorded here in the late 1970s. It was here that the Donald Duck–like DJ Rick Dees recorded the inexplicable (or in Daffy's case, "de-thspicable") hit tune, "Disco Duck."

Alan Howell/Memphis Business Journal

Elvis Shrine at the Java Cabana, p. 186

asts. An 18-hole golf course and a retail complex opened in 1997. (South Memphis)

HARRAH'S TUNICA CASINO
1600 Harrah's Dr.
Robinsonville, Mississippi
800/HARRAHS

As one of the first casinos to open in the northern Delta area, Harrah's runs a sophisticated establishment that includes separate nonsmoking gaming areas. Throughout the facility there are slots and table games including Caribbean stud poker, blackjack, craps, and roulette, along with above-average restaurants and lounges. (South Memphis)

BALLY'S SALOON & GAMBLING HALL
1450 Bally's Blvd.
Robinsonville, Mississippi
800/38-BALLY

Western decor is the theme around which this 40,000-square-foot casino and old-time saloon was built. Live entertainment is featured in the casino's 1,000-seat theater. Gaming options include 65 tables and more than 1,200 slot machines. (South Memphis)

GRAND CASINO
13615 Old Hwy. 61 N.
Robinsonville, Misssissippi
601/363-2788 or 800/WIN-4-WIN

Grand Casino is the closest casino to Memphis. The complex sprawls across more than 400,000 square feet, 140,000 square feet of which is devoted to gaming at slots and tables. Grand offers patrons six restaurants, a hotel, an RV park, and an 800-seat theater where live shows are performed. Kids Quest is an all-ages childcare center. The casino also has a Teen Arcade geared toward the next generation of gaming enthusi-

HOLLYWOOD CASINO, HOTEL, & RV PARK
Casino Strip
Tunica, Mississippi
800/871-0711

Casablanca on the Mississippi? That's the theme of this 54,000-square-foot casino with slots, gaming tables, Hollywoodish restaurants, and a working soundstage. Adjoining the casino is a hotel and an RV park. (South Memphis)

HORSESHOE CASINO & HOTEL
1021 Casino Center Dr.
Robinsonville, Mississippi
800-363-ROOM

The Diamond Sunday Champagne Brunch is one of the draws for gaming enthusiasts and nongamblers alike at Horseshoe Casino and Hotel. Shrimp, steaks, Napa Valley wines, and other specialties are served in elegant surroundings by the casino that prides itself on "superior" service. The Horseshoe offers live entertainment, more than 1,000 slots, and nearly 50 gaming tables spread over 30,000 square feet.

The casino was the top-rated tourist attraction in Memphis in 1998, in terms of attendance. It attracted an estimated 4.9 million visitors. The center also features the Bluesville Showcase Nightclub and a Blues and Legends Hall of Fame Museum. (South Memphis)

SAM'S TOWN HOTEL AND GAMBLING HALL
**1477 Commerce Landing/
Casino Strip
Robinsonville, Mississippi
www.vegas.com/hotels/
samstown/tunica
800/456-0711**
Corky's, with its famous ribs and barbecue, is just one of the five restaurants located within the Sam's Town Hotel and Gambling Hall, a casino voted the best in the area for the past two years. The top-name entertainment, including country acts ranging from George Jones and Wynonna to Leeann Rimes and Lorrie Morgan, is among the best offered in the Memphis area. The hotel also offers free covered parking. (South Memphis)

SHERATON CASINO
**Casino Center
1107 Casino Center Dr.
Robinsonville, Mississippi
800/391-3777**
Its distinctive Tudor architectural style distinguishes the Sheraton from other casinos on the strip south of Memphis. The 92,000-square-foot mansion houses more than 1,000 slots and 50 gaming tables, as well as restaurants and a comedy club. (South Memphis)

Memphis Convention and Visitors Bureau

13

DAY TRIPS FROM MEMPHIS

Day Trip: Alex Haley Home, Henning, Tennessee

Driving time from Memphis: 60 minutes

Located about an hour's drive north of Memphis in Henning, Tennessee, the Alex Haley House and Museum is a significant tourist destination that should appeal to anyone interested in African American history.

Artifacts from Haley's distinguished writing career and mementos of the extensive genealogical research that took him back to his family's African heritage are displayed in the small house. Family portraits and antiques original to his parents' home are among the other objects awaiting visitors inside this charming home in rural Tennessee.

Haley is buried at a gravesite here, as is "Chicken George," the chief character in Haley's literary masterpiece, *Roots*. A filmed version of the epic in the late 1970s became one of the most critically acclaimed television miniseries in the history of the medium.

Fred Montgomery, the mayor of the small community of Henning, was a lifelong friend of Haley's and now periodically leads personally guided tours of the late, Pulitzer Prize–winning author's home.

The museum is open Tuesday through Saturday from 10 a.m. to 5 p.m., and Sunday afternoons from 1 to 5. Admission is $2.50 for adults and $1.00 for students. For more information, call the museum at 901/738-2240.

Other points of interest in the Henning area include the old **CME Church**, and the remains of an earthen fort and Confederate breastworks at nearby **Fort Pillow State Historic Area**. Fort Pillow also features camping, picnicking, and boating facilities, as well as 15 miles of scenic wildlife trails. For more information about the Alex Haley House and Museum or

MEMPHIS REGION

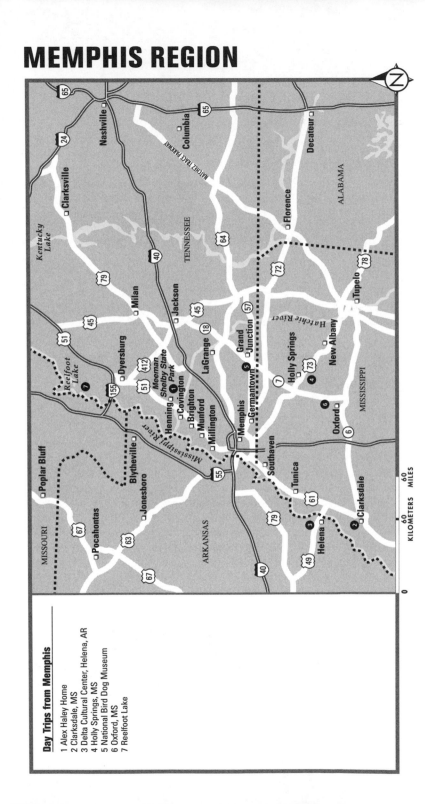

Day Trips from Memphis

1 Alex Haley Home
2 Clarksdale, MS
3 Delta Cultural Center, Helena, AR
4 Holly Springs, MS
5 National Bird Dog Museum
6 Oxford, MS
7 Reelfoot Lake

Henning, contact the Lauderdale County/Ripley Chamber of Commerce at 901/635-9541.

Getting there from Memphis: From downtown, take Highway 51 north through Millington and other towns such as Munford, Brighton, and Covington. Henning is about nine miles north of Covington. Entering Lauderdale County, you'll drive across the Hatchie River. The museum is about three miles beyond the bridge. Take a right at the Alex Haley rest area, and follow the signs to Henning and the Haley home.

Day Trip: Delta Cultural Center, Helena, Arkansas

Driving time from Memphis: 75 minutes

In the fall of 1990, a gem of a museum opened in a restored 1912 Missouri Pacific train depot in the small Mississippi River town of Helena, Arkansas. Since then, the Delta Cultural Center has continued the ambitious task of tracing the roots and legacies of the people who have called the Delta their home.

Helena's distinction as one of the oldest Mississippi River settlements is well documented, as is the transformation of the vast hardwood forests that once covered the flat, fertile Delta lands to the present-day cotton fields. Blues and Delta folk music is another major focus of the center.

Outside, quaint diners, shops, and antiques and record stores dot the old downtown Main Street where the depot is located. A leisurely stroll through the area is like a trip back in time.

Music lovers, take note: It's well worth planning a visit to Memphis to coincide with the **King Biscuit Blues Festival**, held annually the second weekend in October in Helena, Arkansas. One of the premier blues events in the country, it's named for harmonica great Sonny Boy Williamson, a Helena native who, in the 1930s, began advertising a popular brand of flour (King Biscuit) during broadcasts of the local *King Biscuit Blues Radio Hour.*

Laid-back, down-to-earth, and wonderfully unsophisticated, the King Biscuit Blues Festival is a four-day party with live blues and Southern gospel music at its best. Acts such as Koko Taylor, Buddy Guy, Anson Funderburgh and Sam Myers, and Pinetop Perkins routinely play to enthusiastic crowds lounging on the grassy levee along the Mississippi River. People sip beer or snooze in the sun, watch children rolling down the hill, and gear up for music stretching late into the night. Although Helena is doable as a day trip from Memphis, if you plan to make the King Biscuit trek overnight, plan ahead: The few hotels and bed-and-breakfasts in the area are usually booked a year in advance of "King Biscuit" time. For more information call 501/338-9144.

Getting there from Memphis: Drive south on Highway 61 past Tunica and on to Lula. Turn right onto Highway 49, take the bridge across the Mississippi River and into Arkansas, and follow the signs to the Helena business district.

Day Trip: Reelfoot Lake, Tennessee

Driving time from Memphis: 90 minutes
About 100 miles north of Memphis, Reelfoot Lake lies in the northwest corner of Tennessee, near the borders of Kentucky and Missouri and in the counties of Lake and Obion. The lake and adjoining wildlife management area, **Reelfoot National Wildlife Refuge** and **Reelfoot Lake State Park**, cover approximately 25,000 acres, 15,000 acres of which include still waters and wetlands teeming with plant and animal life.

Formed by a series of violent earthquakes during the winter of 1811 to 1812, today Reelfoot Lake is the world's largest natural fish hatchery. Among the 54 species of fish to be found in its waters are bream, crappie, largemouth bass, and catfish. Bluegill and bass attract anglers to the area, which is open year-round.

But fish aren't the only spectacle: Two of the area's most beloved natural attractions are the majestic bald cypress trees and the American bald eagles that draw thousands of bird-watchers each winter. Located along the Mississippi Flyway, Reelfoot Lake also attracts thousands of ducks, geese, and other migratory birds. The lake has an average winter population of 125,000 geese and 215,000 ducks, the most common being the Canadian goose and the mallard.

Families may enjoy picnicking, bicycling, canoeing, or cruising the lake in pontoon boats. Public ramps, fishing piers, and scenic boardwalks are scattered around the lake. Other attractions include local crafts shops, a children's park operated by the Kiwanis Club, and a wildlife interpretive center and museum.

A Fourth of July fireworks display, arts and crafts festivals, and duck-calling contests are among the seasonal events staged at Reelfoot. For more information, call the Reelfoot Lake Tourist Council at 901/538-2666.

Getting there from Memphis: Drive north on U.S. Highway 51 just beyond Dyersburg.

Day Trip: National Bird Dog Museum, Grand Junction, Tennessee

Driving time from Memphis: 45 minutes
Just when you're saying to yourself in utter amazement, "You know, Memphis has it all!" there's something else out there awaiting your surprise and approval. About 50 miles east of the city, along a peaceful, two-lane highway, is the world's only museum devoted to bird dogs. The National Bird Dog Museum in Grand Junction, Tennessee, was founded in 1991 by the Bird Dog Foundation "to preserve and extol the joys of bird hunting on the North American continent," and to highlight the "talents of 36 distinct breeds of dogs."

Why a museum? If the magnificence of a poised beagle and the regal stance of a retriever aren't reasons enough, it may help to know that the community has been hosting the National Bird Dog Championship and Field Trials since shortly after the turn of the century.

A bronze sculpture before the museum entrance and under the American and Tennessee state flags depicts a hunter, pointer, and setter "on point," with 22 quail on the rise. It's billed as the nation's largest bronze sculpture of an outdoor sports scene. Inside, paintings, photographic displays, trophies, and other artifacts document the history of the best-known bird dogs, and videos demonstrate the strengths and talents of different breeds.

Closed Mondays, the museum is free (donations are accepted) and open to the public Tuesday through Saturday from 10 a.m. to 2 p.m., and Sunday afternoon from 1 to 4. For more information call 901/764-2058 or 901/878-1168.

Other points of interest in Grand Junction include the historic **Ames Plantation**, 4275 Buford Ellington Road, which hosts the **National Bird Dog Field Trials** each February. The beautiful, nineteenth-century farmstead includes many restored and furnished log structures, and is open the fourth Thursday afternoon of each month from March through October, or by appointment.

Fayette County is an architectural treasure trove of more than 100 antebellum homes, churches, and buildings dating from 1829 to the early 1900s. One of the more interesting accommodations in this western part of the state is the **One Pleasant Retreat Bed-and-Breakfast**. Located about 40 miles east of Memphis and 30 miles from Germantown, at 420 Hotel Street in Williston, the inn is a restored antebellum home complete with gardens and stables and furnished with fine antiques and equestrian engravings from England and Ireland.

National Bird Dog Museum

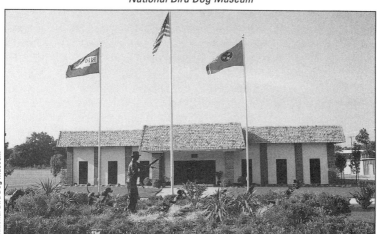

National Bird Dog Museum

Amenities include use of the stables, jumping facilities, trails, and thousands of acres for riding. Special weekend packages include a trip to see English fox hunting at the **Longreen Hunt Club**, followed by breakfast. Also available are gourmet luncheons, candlelit dinners, and tours to Ames Plantation, the **Field Trial Museum**, a sheep farm, and a wool museum.

Getting there from Memphis: Drive west on Highway 57 for about 50 miles to the small town of La Grange.

Day Trip: Holly Springs, Mississippi

Driving time from Memphis: About 90 minutes

Holly Springs was named by the Chickasaw Indians, early inhabitants who regularly bathed there in the supposedly medicinal waters within a grove of holly trees. But visitors today seek two things: its wealth of historical architecture, and gutbucket blues in a beloved rural shack.

Many of the more than three hundred structures listed on the National Register of Historic Places are open only during the annual spring pilgrimage. (In the South, the term "pilgrimage" is used to describe seasonal openings of antebellum and Victorian homes.) More than 20 Mississippi cities and towns host pilgrimages each year. The **Holly Springs pilgrimage celebration**, held each April since 1938, includes Civil War reenactments, candlelit dinners, musical entertainment, and concerts in historic churches.

If your visit doesn't coincide with the pilgrimage, there is still history to be seen. Open by appointment only, **Montrose**, 307 E. Salem St., 601/252-2943, is an elegant antebellum mansion with a spiral staircase and elaborate plasterwork interiors that today is headquarters of Holly Springs' **Garden Club**. Admission to Montrose is three dollars for adults, free for children under 12.

Also on East Salem Street are **Oakleigh**, a stately mansion whose splendid past is still visible on its weathered exterior; and **Cedarhurst** and **Airliewood**, two Gothic brick homes dating from the 1850s. Other historic points of interest in Holly Springs include **Rust College**, on North Memphis Street. Its most famous graduate is Leontyne Price, legendary soprano of the Metropolitan Opera, and a native of Laurel, Mississippi. Founded in 1868, the college is home to one of the oldest existing buildings in the state.

If pre–Civil War grandeur isn't your cup of tea, look no further than a tiny wooden shack on the outskirts of town. Blues lovers in search of an authentic, old-time juke joint make weekly pilgrimages of another sort to **Junior Kimbrough's Juke Joint** place, about 11 miles west of Holly Springs and just east of Chulahoma, Mississippi. The vacant storefront is situated on Highway 4, and, while there's no more Junior Kimbrough (he passed away in 1998), his sons are said to be keeping the tradition alive. Music usually begins around nine on Saturday night, and often as early as four or five on Sunday afternoon.

Getting there from Memphis: Take U.S. Highway 72, accessible from Poplar Avenue in Collierville, southwest of Memphis, passing through such cities as New Albany. Highway 78 leads directly into Holly Springs. Or, travel south on Interstate 55, go east at the Senatobia exit, and follow Highway 4 through Chulahoma and into Holly Springs.

Day Trip: Clarksdale, Mississippi

Driving time from Memphis: About 60 minutes
McKinley Morganfield, better known as Muddy Waters, was raised on a plantation on the outskirts of Clarksdale. The tiny cyprus-log shack where

Goodness, Gracious, This Ain't Graceland!

In what may seem an attempt to emulate his one-time Sun Records label mate, Elvis Presley, 1950s rockabilly sensation Jerry Lewis has opened up his Mississippi Ranch to the public. While a far cry from the King's Graceland, "the Killer's" home boasts a piano-shaped swimming pool among its decorative idiosyncrasies.

*Still, the **Jerry Lee Lewis Ranch** has not become a huge Memphis-area tourist attraction, perhaps in part due to its limited hours of operation. Currently, tours are available weekdays and Saturdays, or by appointment. To reach the "Great Balls of Fire" singer's spread, drive south from Memphis on Interstate 55 and take the Nesbit Road exit. The ranch is at 1595 Malone in Nesbit, Mississippi. Tickets are $15 for adults, $7 for children. Call 601/429-2141 for more information.*

he grew up is in the process of being preserved. A museum in Clarksdale commissioned by members of the Texas rock and blues band ZZ Top houses a replica of a wood guitar taken from Waters' childhood home.

Waters is among the dozens of Delta musicians memorialized in the **Delta Blues Museum** in Clarksdale. Established in 1979 through the Carnegie Public Library, the museum collects and preserves artifacts pertinent to the history of the blues. A visit to the Clarksdale museum is a worthwhile excursion for blues lovers, who will find thousands of books, recordings, tapes, CDs, photographs, and other souvenirs associated with the world's great blues players.

The museum, at 114 Delta Avenue, attracts about 1,000 visitors monthly from around the world. It's in the process of relocating to a renovated train depot in downtown Clarksdale. For more information call 601/624-4461.

The **Clarksville–Montgomery County Museum** has recently opened a $3-million, three-story, 31,000-square-foot addition, which includes gallery space, classrooms, an auditorium, museum store, and a concessions area. A sculpture garden is located between the new building and the original structure, a former post office built in 1898.

In addition to its annual **Robert Johnson Day** in May, and the **Sunflower River Blues and Gospel Education Program** in August, every October Clarksdale stages an annual conference dedicated to another favorite son—playwright **Tennessee Williams**.

Getting there from Memphis: Follow Highway 61 south past Tunica and the casinos. The highway runs directly through Clarksdale.

Day Trip: Oxford, Mississippi

Driving time from Memphis: 75 minutes
The University of Mississippi ("Ole Miss") campus happens to be located here, but it's the downtown **Courthouse Square** that's the real lifeblood of this artsy, literary-minded community.

The grand, pillared white Courthouse, rebuilt in 1873 after being burned by Federal troops in 1864, is a national historic landmark. Surrounded by an elegant black wrought-iron fence, the courthouse makes a striking anchor for the idyllic, small-town city center that's perfect for strolling at an unhurried pace.

Also located in this area of shops is the renowned **Square Books**, one of the all-time great bookstores of the South. It's informal and friendly—the kind of place where a bookworm could browse for hours. Square Books had an upstairs coffeehouse long before it was in vogue to do so, and all sorts of famed writers do book signings here—both before and after they become famous.

No visit to Oxford's square would be complete without stops at three business establishments. First, head out early in the morning for the unpretentious **Bottle Tree Bakery**, where you'll find big, doughy bagels and

King Biscuit Blues Festival, p. 191

Leslie Chin

one of the most potent cups of coffee you've ever tasted. **Southside Gallery**, just across the street, has some great contemporary photography, decorative art, and folk art by a variety of Southern artists, including such "outsiders" as Howard Finster. The occasional show of photographic images by the great Mississippi writer Eudora Welty also entices art lovers on a consistent basis. Finally, the best restaurant in Oxford is, without question, **City Grocery**. It's gourmet food without all the fuss, served in sophisticated yet surprisingly down-home surroundings. Salads are California-fresh, but the gumbo is New Orleans–spicy. Local art works adorn the exposed brick walls, and Delta blues pours from the sound system.

Best-selling author John Grisham, a former resident who now lives in Virginia, is publisher of the ***Oxford American***, an erudite Southern magazine that has its small editorial offices here. William Faulkner still reigns

T i P

Want to ooze down historic Highway 61 in style? Those who'd rather forgo the tour-bus route should check out American Dream Safari. An enterprising local blues lover recently launched this highly personalized tour service, which offers three- to seven-day pilgrimages of blues haunts throughout Memphis and the Delta region in a fully restored, 1955 pink Cadillac (Bruce Springsteen and Aretha Franklin not included). For more information call 901/382-6848.

supreme. The Nobel Prize–winning author lived and wrote in Oxford. His home, **Rowan Oak**, Old Taylor Rd., 601/234-3284, is a modest, pre–Civil War structure through which tourists may pass. The outline of Faulkner's novel *A Fable* is just as he left it—scribbled on a wall in the study. Call ahead for hours and tour information.

Two of the most interesting sites at the University of Mississippi, which was founded in 1848, are the **Center for the Study of Southern Culture** (601/232-5993) and **the University of Mississippi Blues Archives** (601/232-7753). The Center, a unique research institution focusing on Southern music, history, lifestyles, and folklore, sponsors a variety of symposia, conferences, and special programs each year. The blues collection contains a wide array of blues recordings and other materials, including a personal record collection donated by guitar great B. B. King.

The university campus is a green sea of rolling hills dotted with august buildings shaded by huge magnolia trees. During the Civil War battles of Shiloh and Corinth in December of 1862, General Grant and his troops occupied Oxford. Only a few of the original university buildings survived the 1864 burning of the area.

Thanks in part to the university's strongly supported athletics program, not to mention international highbrow conferences devoted to Faulkner, Oxford has seen an explosion in the number of hotels and other lodging facilities offered here. A variety of chain motels and inns can be found on the interstates leading in and out of the city, and within the downtown center are a few good bets as well. The basic but clean **Holiday Inn** on Lamar is only a few short blocks from Courthouse Square. The **Oliver–Britt House Bed-and-Breakfast**, located between the square and the university campus, offers a bit more atmosphere. It's at 512 Van Buren Avenue, 901/234-8043.

Getting there from Memphis: There are a couple of ways to reach Oxford. The easiest is usually via Interstate 55. Take the interstate south to the Batesville exit 234A, then go east on Highway 6 to Oxford. An alternate route is southeast on Highway 78 to Holly Springs, then south on Highway 7 to Oxford.

EMERGENCY PHONE NUMBERS

Emergency
911

Ambulance
901/458-3311

Fire Department
901/458-3311

Poison Control Center
901/528-6048

Police Department
901/528-2222

Sexual Assault Resource Center
901/528-2161

Shelby County Assistance
901/576-2161

Shelby County Sheriff
901/577-5555

Suicide and Crisis Intervention
901/274-7444

U.S. Coast Guard, Group Lower Mississippi
601/544-3912

MAJOR HOSPITALS AND EMERGENCY MEDICAL CENTERS

Baptist Memorial Hospital–East
6019 Walnut Grove Rd.
901/226-5000

Baptist Memorial Hospital–Medical Center
899 Madison Ave.
901/227-2727

Le Bonheur Children's Medical Center
50 N. Dunlap
901/572-3000

Methodist Hospital–Central
1265 Union Ave.
901/726-7000

Methodist Hospital–Germantown
7691 Poplar Ave.
Germantown
901/754-6418

Methodist Hospital–North
3960 New Covington Pike
901/384-5200

Regional Medical Center at Memphis
877 Jefferson Ave.
901/545-7100

St. Francis Hospital
5959 Park Ave.
901/765-1000

St. Jude Children's Research Hospital
332 N. Lauderdale
901/495-3300

UT Bowld Hospital/University of Tennessee Medical Center
951 N. Court Ave.
901/448-4000

RECORDED INFORMATION

Library and Information Center
901/725-8895

Memphis Hotline
901/57-ELVIS

Safety Tips for Tourists
901/543-5333

Time
901/526-5261

Weather
901/522-8888

POST OFFICES

Airport Mail Center
(Open 24 hours)
4233 Louis Carruthers Dr.
901/345-1500

Main Branch
555 S. Third St.
901/521-2186

161 E. Calhoun
901/521-2144

1 N. Front St.
901/576-2013

VISITOR INFORMATION

Collierville Chamber of Commerce
901/853-1949

DeSoto County Economic
Development
601/429-4414

Germantown Chamber of
Commerce
901/755-1200
www.germantownchamber.com

Memphis Chamber of Commerce
901/543-3500

Memphis Convention and Visitors
Bureau
901/543-5300

Memphis Visitors and Trolley Maps
901/751-0158

Memphis Visitors Information Center
901/543-5333
TDD: 901/521-6833 (local)
TDD: 800/410-1TDD

Millington Chamber of Commerce
901/862-1486

West Memphis Convention and
Visitors Bureau
870/732-7640

CITY TOURS

Blues City Tours
901/522-9229

Carriage Tours of Memphis, Inc.
901/527-7542
888/267-9100

Coach USA (Memphis)
901/382-6366

Friends of German Heritage and
Culture: Germania Travel Consultant
901/794-0347

Gray Line USA Tours of Memphis
901/346-8687

Heritage Tours
901/527-3427

Kirby Charters and Tours
901/332-9388
800/748-1659

Memphis Queen Line Riverboats
901/527-5694
800/221-6197

Sekisui International Travel
901/747-0009

CAR RENTAL

Alamo Rent-A-Car
901/332-8412

Avis Rent-A-Car
901/345-3514
800/331-1212

Budget Car and Truck Rental
901/398-8888
800/TRY-1-CAR

Dollar Rent-A-Car
901/345-3890

Enterprise Rent-A-Car
901/525-8588
800/RENTACAR
www.ERAC.com

Hertz
901/345-5680

National Car Rental
901/345-0070

Tom Bell Leasing
901/366-1685

Vans to Go, Inc.
901/382-7676

DISABLED ACCESS INFORMATION

Alliance for the Blind and Visually Impaired
901/766-0600

Center for Independent Living
901/726-6404

St. Joseph's Hospital Interpreting Service (Deaf Interpreting)
901/577-3783 (Voice)
901/577-3784 (TTY)

Tennessee Relay Center
800/848-0299 (Voice)
800/848-0298 (TTY)

COMMUNITY RESOURCES

Black Business Association
901/527-2222

Friends for Life (AIDS Support Group)
901/272-0855

Memphis Gay and Lesbian Community Center
901/324-4297

Vegetarian Awareness Network
800/872-8343

BABYSITTING AND CHILD CARE

Annie's Nannies, Inc.
901/523-8307

Around the Clock Learning Center
901/529-0374

Bartlett Child Care Center, Inc.
901/388-3020

Children's World Learning Centers
(Hourly)
901/365-0411

Cooper Cottage Child School
(Drop-ins)
901/278-9624

NEWSPAPERS

BlueSpeak
901/527-6163

Commercial Appeal
901/529-2211

Daily News
901/523-1561

Downtowner
901/523-7118

Memphis Business Journal
901/523-1000

Memphis Parent
901/529-4520

Mid-South Christian Banner
901/372-1205

Shelby Sun Times
901/755-7386

Tri-State Defender
901/523-1818

MAGAZINES

Agenda
901/251-7000

Memphis Magazine
901/521-9000

BOOKSTORES

B. Dalton Bookseller
4522 Mall of Memphis
901/794-1566

Barnes & Noble
6385 Winchester Rd.
  901/794-9394
2774 N. Germantown Pkwy.
  901/386-2468

Bookstar
Plaza Theatre
  3412 Poplar Ave.
  901/323-9332
Germantown Village Square
  7680 Poplar Ave.
  Germantown
  901/757-7858

Borders
6685 Poplar Ave.
Germantown
901/754-0770

Brentanos
Oak Court Mall
4465 Poplar Ave.
901/763-1945

Burke's Bookstore
1719 Poplar Ave.
901/278-7484 or 800/581-5156

Davis–Kidd Booksellers
387 Perkins Rd.
901/683-9801

Waldenbooks
3359 Raleigh Springs Mall
  Austin Peay Hwy.
  901/388-6012
Wolfchase Galleria
  2760 N. Germantown Pkwy.
  901/373-5301

Waldenbooks Waldenkids
6025 Hickory Ridge Mall
901/360-8023

Xanadu Bookstore
7235 Winchester Rd.
901/757-9885

RADIO STATIONS

KJMS 101.1 FM, urban
   contemporary
KSUD 730 AM, contemporary
   Christian
KWAM 990 AM, gospel
KXHT 107.1 FM, hip hop
WAVN 1240 AM, gospel
WBBP 1480 AM, gospel
WCRV 640 AM, Christian
   family radio
WDIA 1070 AM, black adult con-
   temporary/rhythm and blues
WEGR 102.7 FM, album-oriented
   classic rock
WEVL 89.9 FM, eclectic,
   listener-supported
WGKX 105.9 FM, country
WGSF 1210 AM, Spanish
WHBQ 560 AM, sports talk
WHRK 97.1 FM, urban
   contemporary
WJCE 680 AM, soul
WKNA 88.9 FM, news/talk/National
   Public Radio
WKNO 91.1 FM, classical and
   National Public Radio
WKSL 107.5 FM, top 40
WLOK 1340 AM, gospel
WMC 790 AM, talk radio
WMC 99.7 FM, adult contemporary
WMFS 92.9 FM, rock
WOGY 94.1 FM, country
WOOM 1380 AM, praise and
   worship
WOWW 1430 AM, self-help
WPLX 1170 AM, easy listening
WQOX 88.5 FM, adult contemporary

WRBQ 103.5 FM, rhythm and
   blues/soul
WREC 600 AM, talk radio, live
   sports broadcasts
WRVR 104.5 FM, adult
   contemporary
WRXQ 95.7 FM, new rock, soul,
   oldies
WSRR 98.1 FM, oldies
WUMR 91.7 FM, jazz
WVIM 95.3 FM, contemporary
   Christian
WYPL 89.3 FM, radio reading
   service for the blind (Memphis
   Public Library)

TELEVISION STATIONS

WREG 3, CBS
WMC 5, NBC
WHBQ 13, Fox
WKNO 10, Public Broadcasting
WLMT/UPN 30, Independent
WPTY 24, ABC
WPXX 50, PAX

INDEX

ABOUT THE AUTHOR

Originally from Indiana, **Linda Romine** has lived in Memphis for nearly a decade. As a journalist and critic, she has written for a variety of newspapers, magazines, and travel publications. Travel assignments have taken her to Europe, Russia, South America, the Caribbean, and throughout North America.

Alan Howell, Memphis Business Journal

JOHN MUIR PUBLICATIONS and its City•Smart Guidebook authors are dedicated to building community awareness within City•Smart cities. We are proud to work with the Memphis Literacy Council as we publish this guide to Memphis.

Founded in 1974, the **Memphis Literacy Council** has helped more than 10,000 adults improve their reading and writing skills. In 1994, MLC received the Laubach Award for Excellence as the "Outstanding Volunteer Literacy Program" in the United States, beating out 940 other programs for the honor.

For more information, please contact:
Memphis Literacy Council
902 South Cooper
Memphis, TN 38104
901/327-6000
mlc@mem.net

Memphis Literacy Council